CLIMATE PORN

KEVIN J. MOONEY

BOMBARDIER
BOOKS

Published by Bombardier Books
An Imprint of Post Hill Press
ISBN: 979-8-89565-064-6
ISBN (eBook): 979-8-89565-065-3

Climate Porn:
How and Why Anti-Population Zealots Fabricate Science, while Targeting
American Capitalism, Freedom, and Independence
© 2026 by Kevin J. Mooney
All Rights Reserved

Cover Design by Jim Villaflores

BOMBARDIER BOOKS

Post Hill PRESS

Post Hill Press
New York • Nashville
posthillpress.com

Published in the United States of America
1 2 3 4 5 6 7 8 9 10

In memory of Kathleen Marie Mooney, the backbone of our family and an endlessly devoted mother who put us all on the right path. RIP, Mom.

TABLE OF CONTENTS

FOREWORD

by John Berlau
Senior Fellow & Director of Finance Policy
Competitive Enterprise Institute
Washington, DC

K evin Mooney is a journalist's journalist. He has broken story
after story that have exposed illogic and shady dealings of
established political and policy elites and have shown how
their misguided policies cause tremendous harm for Americans
in building their lives. His stories have resulted in Congressional
hearings, federal investigations, and—though not as often as they
should—positive changes in policy and media reporting culture.

I was honored when Kevin asked me to write the foreword
to this great book, *Climate Porn*. In the book, Kevin calls me "a
long-time friend and ally," and I reciprocate the compliment.
Being a great friend is one of Kevin's many fine traits.

In his reporting, Kevin has revealed that the Association of
Community Organizations for Reform Now (ACORN)—despite
numerous convictions of the group's members for voter registration fraud and other crimes—received $53 million over the years
in grants from the US government. Reporting from Kevin and

others on the group led to Congress banning federal funding for ACORN in 2009, and the group's dissolution a year later.

Over the years, Kevin began to specialize in reporting on the established environmental movement, and how its results—and sometimes its intentions—do not lead to a bettering of the situation of humans or even wildlife. In fact, as I note in my book *Eco-Freaks: Environmentalism Is Hazardous to Your Health*, their situations are frequently worsened with life-threatening consequences due to policies pursued in the name of the environment.

Kevin's reporting revealed how Putin's Russia colluded with the US environmentalists— though not all activists were aware— to fund propaganda against fracking in the US that would threaten Russia's international energy sales. And as Kevin recalls in this book, when Al Gore was on the verge of winning an Oscar for his documentary *An Inconvenient Truth*, Kevin—quoting experts including myself and an Oscar nominated documentarian— showed that Gore fell far short of the Academy's traditional standards for truthfulness in the animated sequence about polar bears dying. Kevin's reporting showed that the study that was the basis of that sequence showed that far from the "significant numbers" of polar bears drowning due to climate change that Gore claimed, there had been only four documented drownings. Furthermore, those drownings were due to a sudden windstorm, not to a lack of ice due to global warming, as the sequence claimed. Gore's documentary still won, but Kevin's story awakened thousands of policymakers and member of the public to the truth.

In *Climate Porn*, Kevin's skills and talents as a journalist are fully on display, but so is his vast knowledge of history and his constructive thinking on practical policy solutions to set things right. He centers his book on the area of the US he knows best: his home state of New Jersey. He describes vividly the

Revolutionary War battles of the Second Battle of Trenton and Battle of Princeton that took place in the Garden State, and explains why those battles were so important to securing victory over Great Britain.

Kevin then fast forwards to today to show how the very liberties secured 250 years ago are in peril because of the collusion of socialists, progressives, and the Green movement. In particular, he shows how New Jerseyans—including the practical conservationists who love nature and watching whales—are harmed by government subsidies to Big Wind. Kevin demonstrates that not only do enormous wind turbines—more than three times the height of the Statue of Liberty and some of them are only about eight miles from the beach— obstruct the beautiful views of whales that Garden State residents have enjoyed for decades on the Jersey Shore, the noise that they generate—according to credible statistical evidence—may be responsible for a recent uptick in whale deaths in the area.

In *Climate Porn*, Kevin doesn't just present problems—he advocates many constructive solutions. To use a metaphor from nature, Kevin gets in the weeds of how to uproot destructive regulations in describing how courts and Congress can utilize the Supreme Court decision, ending broad "Chevron deference" courts have shown to regulatory agencies and the Congressional Review Act to overturn regulations. And on the eve of this nation's 250th anniversary, Kevin calls for adults and children to acquaint themselves with the principles of liberty our Founding Fathers laid out in the Declaration of Independence and other founding documents.

My friend Kevin triumphs in *Climate Porn* with a full satisfying read that hopefully will spur positive action by patriots and true conservationists.

INTRODUCTION

Dead whales have a story to tell and it's not one the climate activists will like. That's because they are largely complicit in what has happened in the past few years. While they bend and twist themselves into all sorts of contortions to deny responsibility, the evidence points to a strong correlation between the wind initiatives climate activists favor and the rising number of carcasses washing up on the beaches. Beginning sometime in December 2022, New York and New Jersey became the scene of a particularly acute rise in whale deaths. We are talking mostly about humpback whales, called "humpies" by beach residents. In *Moby Dick*, Herman Melville offers up a searing comparison between the majesty of living whales in the ocean and the lack of any animating qualities in the dead whales when they wash ashore. The cadavers that beach dwellers have encountered here in the twenty-first century serve as a symbol of corruption and waste in much the same way as they did for Melville. But with a few modern caveats.

Along the way toward launching new conservation efforts aimed at saving the whales, citizen activists soon discovered that the larger, more well-established self-described environmental organizations were not on their side. As we shall see, that's partly because many of them are bought and paid for by the wind industry. The money trail is deserving of exposure as it points to a larger trend that should concern anyone devoted to conservation and environmentalism as they are defined in the dictionary. The outfits pushing wind farms, which are every bit as ecologically damaging as they are economically damaging, are now part of the climate movement. That co-option began sometime in the early 1970s when a command-and-control approach to environmentalism out of Washington, DC, displaced local, parochial efforts. This transformation set the stage for contemporary climate activism that has nothing to do with preserving the environment, saving endangered species, or improving human health. Instead, climate movement has everything to do with collapsing constitutional government, ending national sovereignty, and attacking American-style capitalism. Once that is understood, the motivations and behavior of what some have aptly labeled "Big Green" come into focus. The United Nations remains a major incubator for climate schemes detached from sound science and economics, as does the European Union. But with the upcoming 250th anniversary of America's Declaration of Independence, there's an opportunity here to reassert national sovereignty at least here in the US. But we are faced with an either-or choice. Either we will become an independent, free country again, or we will succumb to the globalist machinations of unaccountable international bodies. The good news is that under the reloaded Trump administration there have been some incremental movements back in the right direction. But what's needed is more than just a speed bump. To secure enduring and lasting changes, the administration and its allies will need to completely dismantle the "Climate Industrial Complex" through a determined deregulatory effort. The final chapter seizes on a

formal legislative proposal that deserves greater support and amplification that would translate into a lasting victory for the cause
of American freedom. By restoring constitutional structures, the
climate movement can be brought to heel. By awakening the
public to the dangers of a movement that resists debate and open
inquiry, its practitioners can be exposed.

But before we can get to this point, we need to tell the story
about everyday Americans who have been victimized by the collapse of constitutional government. Because we've been told there
is a climate emergency, due process has been suspended, elected
officials neutered, and unaccountable bureaucrats empowered.
There is no time for democratic debate and deliberation. Only
emergency government action will suffice as it lays waste to livelihoods, careers, and reputations. Who are these victims?

They include your friends, neighbors, relatives, and fellow
countrymen in varied professions and trades. There are also people in the academia in government positions, and in business
who have lost their careers after speaking out against the climate
agenda. Property owners have also lost their livelihoods. But a
countermovement is underway. Updated scientific research that
points to natural variability as opposed to human activity as the
primary drivers of climate change is also finding expression.
There's also a broad cross section of American citizens who have
come to recognize that the policy changes climate activists seek
to implement are in fact quite bad for the environment. We can
also call on climate activists as their own worst witnesses since
there is now some tacit admission on their part that their climate
schemes do not work as advertised.

Suddenly free-market environmentalism that reaches back
to earlier and prouder American traditions is finding renewed
expression. But the hour is late, and proponents of centralized

planning operating under the climate moniker currently have the upper hand. Why is that? There's the natural ebb and flow of history Thomas Jefferson nicely encapsulated: "The natural progress of things is for liberty to yield and government to gain ground." But there are also sources for American renewal that are not available in Europe and other parts of the world. As we shall see, this means restoring the natural law to its proper station in our constitutional order.

Another problem concerns a cultural unwillingness to tackle pornography for misguided libertarian reasons. The harmful effects pornography has on the psyche, senses, and overall human health is a well-established reality. But the deleterious impact climate pornography has had on the scientific method is a relatively new phenomenon. There's fallout here not just for the scientists themselves but also for young students who are being told they have no future. Because climate porn is running rampant in the media and academia, the prevailing view among future generations is that the American way is the wrong way and that it is catastrophic to the climate and unjust to third world communities. This is a lie, and it's one that can be uprooted. But it requires something in the way of willpower. There are pockets of citizen activists, genuine scientists, alterative media outlets, and even politicians who have this in spades. They are willing to be vilified, to risk becoming deplatformed, and to suffer professional setbacks. The prospects for American freedom and independence depend greatly on their success.

CHAPTER 1

Saving the Whales, Taking on Big Wind, and Debunking the Climate Narrative

Somewhere between placid Long Beach Island and gaudy Atlantic City, there's a place where fortuitous beachgoers can become whale watchers. The bottlenose dolphins are everywhere off the coast, and you can see them humping up and down in their pods in contrast to sharks that cut straight across the water. The whales are not exactly rare, either, and that spout shooting straight up out of the water just a few miles offshore is not a boat. The largest sea creatures are quite the sight for summertime visitors and year-round residents.

Unfortunately, both the whales and the dolphins appear to be endangered by offshore wind turbines.

I say "appear" because government officials leading the climate movement deny that wind initiatives harm marine life.

At the federal level, former President Joe Biden's National Oceanographic and Atmospheric Administration and Bureau of

Ocean Energy Management repeatedly denied any connection between whale deaths and wind power.[1] At the state level, former New Jersey Governor Phil Murphy, a two-term Democrat, and his administration were every bit as adamantine in denying any link between the dead whales washing up on the shore and the wind energy schemes they supported.[2]

Yet Jersey Shore residents working to preserve their beach views have accumulated considerable evidence that debunks the drivel government agencies pass along to pliable, passive media organs. The problem, beach dwellers say, is not just the wind farms themselves but also the wind energy vessel surveys that are set in motion prior to each new project.

It's on the Jersey Shore that we find the disconnect that exposes what the climate movement is all about—its true motivations and its desired policy outcomes. Political figures who ran on a platform of promoting environmentalism, preserving open spaces, and protecting endangered species advocated projects up and down the East Coast that did quite the opposite. The climate movement's anti-scientific, anti-economic, and anti-American impulses were all on full display during the push for offshore wind power.

The disconnect doesn't end there. The largest, most well-funded environmental advocacy groups—such as the Natural Resources Defense Council (NRDC), the Sierra Club, the National Wildlife Federation (NWF), and the League of Conservation Voters (LCV), to name just a few—have not exactly been going to bat for the whales or for pristine beaches.

Instead, they are either running silent or advocating some version of "responsible wind power" that theoretically gives marine life ample room to maneuver.[3] In their public statements, groups like the NRDC argue that "climate change is the major environmental challenge of our time."[4] Other traditional green causes like "Save the Whales" therefore must be subservient to any efforts aimed at heading off what we are told is a pending climate catastrophe.

So, what gives? Jersey Shore residents devoted to environmentalism find themselves in the surreal position of squaring off against politicians who campaigned as environmentalists and conservationists. Even worse, they are up against self-described environmental activists who invest heavily into the political class.

Defining and Understanding Climate Porn

Welcome to the world of what I and others aptly described as "climate porn."

Actual pornography can come in many forms. There are videos, audio, social media, and pictures. All involve indulging in fantasy and distortions of reality. Studies show that excessive exposure to porn can lead to decreased sexual satisfaction, an increased likelihood of divorce, and mental health problems.[5] In similar fashion, excessive exposure to propaganda passed along as climate science can lead to decreased faith in human possibilities, a reduction in the quality of life, and harmful public policy choices. The incessant utilization of worst-case scenarios in climate literature subtracts time and attention away from more reality-based scenarios that can be met through human ingenuity. By deliberating inflating and exaggerating future climate impacts, climate activists make it more difficult for contemporary government figures to pivot and adjust toward more probable climate events that could be managed with proper planning. Put another way, human society will be better equipped to handle climate impacts if they are richer and wealthier. It is the most economically destitute and least industrialized societies that are the most vulnerable. Climate activists seem hell-bent on keeping them that way.

Unfortunately, the field of "climate science" continuously indulges in pornographic-type fantasies tied in with deliberate distortions of reality that ultimately do great harm to human health and well-being. Climate porn is built on an edifice of anti-scientific pursuits designed to impose the advocates' desired policy outcomes. But there is a cure gaining steam, and it comes to us from independent-minded scientists willing to push back against the vast network arrayed against them.

For example, multiple studies suggest that wind farms lead to rising energy costs and ecological damage. Yet they're dismissed by climate activists who, addicted to climate porn, insist everything must take a back seat to the impending "climate crisis." Manmade contributions to global warming are such a dire emergency, these activists argue, that wind power is needed to transition away from fossil fuels. Otherwise, human emissions will cause a climate catastrophe replete with unnatural warming and rising sea levels that will doom the planet.

This isn't what the scientific research shows. But—as this book documents—the climate movement is not about science any more than it is about climate. Ultimately, it's about a quest for political power and a desire on the part of neo-Marxists and economic central planners to target and dismantle American-style capitalism.

Point to any initiative launched in the name of climate change and it's a sure bet it seeks to circumvent American constitutional government, impose a global regulatory scheme, and undercut the free market. Notice, for instance, that any climate agreement forged internationally or nationally invariably bypasses elected chambers. In addition, climate and environmental laws impose a top-down regulatory approach that torpedoes America's federalist system.

In this book, we are not going to distinguish too much between climate and the environment as such, since the climate movement has hijacked any remaining remnants of environmentalism as it's defined in the dictionary. Moreover, as we shall see, climate policies are not exactly good for the environment or conservation. It's time to blow the lid off a campaign that is rooted in anti-Americanism, antagonistic to human freedom, diametrically opposed to sound science, and hell-bent on globalism.

For decades, climate activists have had the upper hand thanks to friends in high places. Internationally, the bureaucracies of the United Nations and European Union remain fully committed to climate activism. In the United States, former President Joe Biden adopted a "whole-of-government approach to climate" that prioritized wind and solar power. Blue-state governors like New Jersey's Phil Murphy followed in lockstep, using the "climate emergency" as a rationale for bilking taxpayers.

Biden's Interior Department approved the Atlantic Shores South offshore wind energy project in July 2024.[6] The effort originated as a fifty-fifty joint venture between Atlantic Shores Offshore Wind, LLC (Atlantic Shores), Shell New Energies US LLC, and EDF-RE Offshore Development, LLC (a subsidiary of EDF Renewables North America). Commonly referred to as Atlantic Shores, the company proposed up to two hundred total wind turbine generators and up to ten offshore substations with subsea transmission cables. Just a few years ago, the proposed wind project off the Jersey Shore looked on track to become a reality.

But Donald Trump had pledged during his 2024 presidential campaign to put an end to government-funded wind power initiatives, and the ground began to shift very quickly once he took office. As the Biden White House receded into history in January 2025, opponents of offshore wind farms suddenly found that they had the political wind at their backs.

Standing up against such projects, up and down the East Coast, is a broad cross section of citizen activists. A battlefield for their activism is Long Beach Island, or LBI as it is commonly known—a barrier island and popular beach vacation spot that sits along the Atlantic Ocean off Ocean County, New Jersey. The group Save Long Beach Island (Save LBI) draws from property owners, business owners, homeowners, and representatives within the tourism and fishing industries.[7] It is headed by Bob Stern, an engineer who previously worked in the US Department of Energy. He estimates the group has about five thousand members and supporters through social media and email. Allied groups include Protect Our Coast New Jersey and Defend Brigantine Beach, an area sandwiched between LBI and Atlantic City.

Save LBI is not opposed to wind power per se. Individual members hold a range of views on climate and the future challenges to humanity. But they are all united in their belief that the spacing, proximity, and concentration of what the planned project envisions would wreck their beach communities without having any appreciable benefits for the climate. Save LBI's website and literature are replete with visual renditions and photo simulations of what the proposed Atlantic Shores wind turbines would look like off the Jersey Coast.

Save LBI also packed its website with information about the potential economic and environmental fallout from the project.[8] One of the slide presentations shows how large the windmills would be compared to familiar objects. With some reaching a height of 1,046 feet, the windmills would be larger than the Statue of Liberty, the Washington Monument, oceanfront hotels—and they would even approach the size of some skyscrapers. This would completely fence in the Jersey Shore, increase airborne noise, dilute the scenery, and, yes, damage the environment.[9] Beach views would be irreparably harmed, along with natural habitats.

On the economic front, Save LBI made it clear the project would devastate property values and businesses. The group published information showing New Jersey electricity costs would increase 22 percent for residential rates, 27 percent for commercial rates, and 32 percent for industrial rates. That's more than $53 billion above (2024) market prices. Save LBI projects that would mean a 25 percent loss in tourist visits to LBI, more than $450 million in lost revenue, more than 5,300 in lost jobs, and $1.3 billion in lost value for oceanfront properties.[10]

Litigation began in earnest at the state and federal levels in 2023 when Save LBI and its allied groups filed suit against the New Jersey Department of Environmental Protection and the National Marine Fisheries Services, a division of the US Department of Commerce. But the coup de grâce may have come in January 2025. In a carefully calibrated suit filed against a slew of federal agencies, Save LBI upped the ante and cited a wide range of environmental laws.

Thomas Stavola Jr., the attorney representing Save LBI, said in a press release, "This lawsuit serves as the first of its kind, launching a wide-ranging challenge against Atlantic Shores' federal approvals, based on violations of environmental statutes such as the National Environmental Policy Act, the Endangered Species Act, the Marine Mammal Protection Act, the Outer Continental Shelf Lands Act, the Coastal Zone Management Act, and the Clean Air Act.… We believe we have organized a compelling case that will demonstrate that these federal agencies were derelict in their respective duties to take critical information into account, and moreover, made arbitrary assumptions that entirely failed to disclose and consider the injurious impacts of the Atlantic Shores South project."[11]

The timing of the suit could not have been better for wind opponents, as President Trump rolled out an executive order placing a freeze on both leasing federal areas for new offshore wind projects and issuing federal permits for projects that are underway. The one-two punch of the innovative federal lawsuit and Trump's executive actions marked a major turning point.

As Bob Stern explained in a statement on behalf of his group, Trump's order did not outright cancel existing leases or rescind previous project approvals, but it did put into place the legal mechanisms to do so. That's because his order calls for a review of existing leasing and permitting practices, and a report submitted back to the president to identify any legal, environmental, or other bases for rescinding or amending prior approvals. The order also directs Attorney General Pam Bondi and Interior Secretary Doug Burgum to intervene in pending litigation and seek changes in relief consistent with the order.

"This makes Save LBI's recently filed broad federal litigation, along with prior ones, which we believe the administration is aware of, critically important," Stern said in an interview. "They are likely to serve as test cases for how the new Interior Secretary and attorney general implement the results of their leasing and permitting review."[12]

He continued: "The legal arguments and detailed supporting technical analysis in our lawsuits should also provide strong justification for the secretary of the Interior to cancel existing leases and rescind project approvals."

The goal of the Save LBI federal suit is to rescind all federal approvals for offshore wind projects and specifically get the Atlantic Shores South project halted. That goal now appears within reach even before any decisive court action. Just a few weeks after the suit was filed, the New Jersey Board of Public Utilities announced that it would terminate its fourth round of offshore wind solicitations without awarding a bid. Another major blow came when Shell New Energy, the fifty-fifty joint venture partner, announced it was withdrawing.

Whales, property owners, homeowners, business owners, tourists, and anyone with a stake in beach communities got at least a temporary reprieve. The planned construction of two hundred, thousand-foot-plus-high monstrosities about eight miles off Long Beach Island was put on hold.

While this was a major victory for beach community stakeholders, the flawed state and federal processes that enabled the project in the first place still need to be addressed. Save LBI has since rolled out several action items that could find implementation in the Trump administration. This matters because climate activists have not exactly given up on the project.

For starters, Save LBI would like federal legislation designed to eliminate tax credits and other incentives in the Inflation Reduction Act to make certain that green energy companies cannot profit at the expense of taxpayers. They are also asking Trump's Interior Department to cancel the lease area, not just for the purpose of canceling any current projects but also to prevent any future projects from moving forward. Save LBI is also doubling down on its litigation, since it's now possible that the Justice Department lawyers may agree with some or even all of their claims. A court judgment determining the Atlantic Shores approvals were not lawful in the first place would set a strong precedent to prevent similar approval methods from being used.

A year out from the 250th anniversary of America's birthday, the bill Trump signed into law on July 4, 2025, freed taxpayers from at least some green subsidies. But the court cases continue to churn.

Then there are the ongoing efforts to protect the North Atlantic right whale. As Save LBI points out, a safe migration corridor along the East Coast is imperative to protect this creature. There are good reasons to believe wind projects block and impede the whale's migration.

And finally, Save LBI is asking federal officials to allow for greater public input on any upcoming projects. The Trump administration's decision to review the leasing and permitting for East Coast wind projects came as welcome news. But in the future, the public and any opposition groups should not be excluded from voicing their concerns, as they were under the Biden administration.

A search for climate activists who would get behind all or any of these suggestions would be in vain. Instead, the heavy lifting is left to average citizens, the real environmentalists.

Stern regarded the Trump administration's review of the leasing and permitting practices to all offshore wind projects as an opportunity for everyone involved with Atlantic Shores South to "reflect on how a project with virtually no benefit, high cost, and significant environmental damage proceeded so far."[13]

He added: "Our work on this over the last few years showed that the entire process of site selection and project review was fundamentally flawed."

In an interview, Stern commented on how the 2024 US Supreme Court ruling overturning the so-called "Chevron doctrine" could boost Save LBI's case against the feds. The demise of Chevron puts the public on more of an even keel with the unelected administrative agencies that had been running wild since the 1984 ruling in *Chevron v. Natural Resources Defense Council.*[14] Now that the court has reversed itself, agencies are no longer given deference when it comes to the interpretation of controversial regulatory rules.

"Hopefully, this means the courts will give equal weight to both arguments in a case like ours when it comes to making interpretations of the law," Stern said. "From a layman's perspective I don't know why any party should get a deference on anything. You should be on a level playing field and let the arguments decide."[15]

Getting beyond questions of interpretation, Stern is not sure how far the demise of Chevron extends to hard facts and numbers.

"We challenged NOAA's numbers in terms of how far the noise extends and how this noise impacts marine life," Stern said. "We are making the argument that the numbers used by NOAA are not scientifically based and greatly minimize the impact the project would have."

One of the slide presentations posted by Save LBI on its website contrasts the New Jersey proposal with projects in Europe located farther offshore with less of an impact.[16] When a climate initiative in the United States surpasses the green ambitions of Europe, it's time to stop and ask some hard questions. New Jersey Governor Murphy's stated rationale was to wean residents and businesses off conventional fuels for the purpose of reducing global warming. Climate remains the go-to fallback position for such political figures and the wind industry. But an analysis by the Heritage Foundation shows that any temperature changes that might result from the wind project would be so infinitesimal as to be meaningless.[17] Meanwhile, the project would blow a hole in the wallets of state residents.

This battle has significant implications not just for America's coastlines but for its very system of constitutional government and free enterprise.

No Climate Consensus but Plenty of Fraud

Contrary to the climate porn widely reported in media outlets, uncritically taught in K–12 schools and propagandized across college campuses, there is no genuine consensus on what drives climate change. But there are updated studies that now indicate natural variations as opposed to human emissions are largely responsible for warming and cooling trends. That reality is not in line with the political agenda of the climate movement, however, which is highly reliant on deceitful alterations of scientific data.

The UN Intergovernmental Panel on Climate Change, or IPCC, has been the main enabler of government policies putting the screws to American industry and independence. The IPCC released its *First Assessment Report* in 1990. The *Sixth Assessment Report*, the latest in the series, was produced in 2023. The seventh is a work in progress. Up until now, each report has been built around the idea that human emissions are producing dangerous and even catastrophic levels of global warming.

Thankfully, in recent years, there has been something of a course adjustment. It began with the "Climategate" scandal in November 2009, when a still-unidentified whistleblower leaked thousands of emails from the Climate Research Unit at the University of East Anglia in Great Britain that showed IPCC "scientists" were willing to cook the books to get results supposedly demonstrating that climate change was a dire threat.

Now, the countermovement gaining traction under Trump has provided genuine scientists with the opening they need to push back. This matters, because scientists who have produced research that runs counter to the pronouncements of the IPCC and other government bodies can be counted among the climate movement's victims. These individuals and organizations have been deplatformed, silenced, and muzzled because they do not march in lockstep with the climate establishment. This has been done to the great detriment of the scientific process.

For example, Willie Soon, an astrophysicist and geoscientist based in Salem, Massachusetts, who heads up the Center for Environmental Research and Earth Sciences (CERES), has been making waves with fresh research that challenges the popular narrative on climate. In partnership with the Heritage Foundation, CERES published a new study in December 2024 making the case that the United Nations had failed to properly account for total solar irradiance (TSI) when reaching its conclusions. (TSI is the term used to describe the sunlight or energy that arrives at Earth.) The joint Heritage and CERES study also raised questions about the impact of the Urban Heat Island (UHI) effect on weather stations around the world.

The CERES report challenging these assumptions is not exactly an outlier. The Nongovernmental International Panel on Climate Change (NIPCC), as the name implies, is a nongovernmental organization of scientists and scholars who have joined together to present their own assessment of the science and economics of global warming. The obvious advantage is that because it is not a government agency, its members have no politically biased notions about climate change and the role of human greenhouse gas emissions. The NIPCC can thus pursue its research in a dispassionate, objective manner without any coercive influences dictating policy preferences.[18]

On questions of substance involving warming and cooling trends, contrarian climate scientists with expertise in relevant fields have been gaining traction. But the political battle has only now been joined. While it's important to continue the debate—and to show that there *is* a debate, since the climate establishment denies this—it's equally important to call attention to who the real victims and villains are in the realm of public policy. The real threat to humanity comes not from climate change as such, but from the climate change activists and their policies.

How Climate Activism Served as a Dress Rehearsal for COVID Shutdowns

Destructive climate activism has even bled into other areas of policy. For example, COVID policies and climate activism go hand in hand, with the latter giving tactical inspiration to the former. COVID-19 governmental mandates, school closures, business closures—and all-too-successful efforts to silence critics—were pulled straight from the climate activism playbook. Parents who wanted their taxpayer-funded schools reopened were vilified. So were business owners and religious leaders who dissented from shutdown edicts. In retrospect, it was the average citizens who lost the most during the COVID-19 shutdowns. Meanwhile, political figures who championed the shutdowns saw to it that they were largely immune from the policies they implemented.

Likewise, political figures and celebrities leading the charge for climate initiatives, and who attack those who produce and use fossil fuels, have no problem owning beachfront property, flying private jets, or riding in SUVs. It's the rest of us who have to suck it up.

As part of the progressive Left, climate activists have borrowed from the Left's slick, manipulative use of a "victimhood" narrative. They tell us incessantly that the most vulnerable populations are also the most susceptible to the effects of man-made climate change: those living in poverty, low-income households, people with medical disabilities, children, third world nations, and the broadly defined "underprivileged." The movement has identified three main villains in this victimization narrative: the capitalist system, the fossil fuel industry, and constitutional checks and balances that mitigate against sweeping government actions. In reality, it is the most vulnerable populations in the poorest regions that have suffered the most from the anti-energy impulses of the climate movement. The time has long since passed to turn the victimhood narrative back against leftists operating under the false guise of a climate emergency.

That's an achievable goal thanks in no small part to some serious overreaching on their part—and the rise of a counter-movement. The East Coast hosts several of them, in addition to Save LBI.

The "Save the Whales" campaigns on the East Coast provide an overdue opening for free-market environmentalists to have their say. The federal environmental laws Save LBI cites in its litigation have been misused, abused, and misapplied to enrich green activist groups and their attorneys.

Moving from New Jersey farther south to Virginia Beach and into the Carolinas, an agile group known as the Committee for a Constructive Tomorrow, or CFACT, has been asking all the right questions of federal agencies. CFACT fills a much-needed niche in the environmental debate space, since command-and-control efforts having squeezed out free-market solutions to environmental and climate challenges since the early 1970s.

In March 2024, CFACT joined with allied organizations to file suit against the Biden administration over another offshore wind project. This one comes compliments of Dominion Energy, a publicly traded utility company headquartered in Richmond, Virginia. Unlike the Jersey project, Dominion's Coastal Virginia Offshore Wind effort is already well underway. The CFACT coalition argues that the Bureau of Ocean Energy Management, the National Marine Fisheries Service, the Interior Department, and the Commerce Department violated the Endangered Species Act when they approved the Dominion Energy Project. The suit names the agencies and Dominion Energy as defendants.

CFACT has called attention to statistical evidence showing that offshore wind sonar surveys first authorized by the National Oceanic and Atmospheric Administration (NOAA) in 2016 are responsible for whale deaths. After Joe Biden took control of NOAA, they did a 180, releasing an analysis concluding that there are "no known links between large whale deaths and ongoing offshore wind activities."

The "biological opinion" the feds issued is flawed, CFACT president Craig Rucker argues, because it only looked at each wind project individually rather than taking "a more comprehensive approach" that accounted for the whales' migratory pattern.

Like his allies up in Jersey, Rucker has expressed dismay that some of the larger environmental groups such as the Sierra Club and the Natural Resources Defense Council have not come out against offshore wind plans that can damage natural habitats.

"There's no way an environmental group should be in favor of offshore wind," Rucker said. "They are always opposed to offshore oil drilling which involves only speculative harm. But here we actually see dead whales washing up on beaches in Virginia and other places along the East Coast and this is happening in increased numbers. But all we hear from the environmental groups is crickets."

CFACT successfully petitioned the Trump Justice Department to stay the course. This way defendants could adopt a more intensive review of the permits the Biden administration awarded to Dominion.

Rucker is particularly concerned about the North Atlantic right whale population, which is listed as endangered. Only 350 remain—with only about 70 females capable of producing new offspring, according to court records.

"Whales are a migratory species, meaning they are not just staying off the coast of Virginia," Rucker explained. "The population will be impacted by projects up and down the East Coast whether it's in New Jersey, Maryland, Rhode Island, Massachusetts, or other states. That's the problem with how the feds operated under Biden. They needed to look at the cumulative effect on the whale population up and down the coast."

CFACT's goal is to have Dominion cease construction of the Virginia Offshore Wind Project, which would consist of 176 wind turbines located twenty-five miles off the coast of Virginia Beach.

The Dominion project is already well underway. Rucker estimates the company already put half of what they need during the summer of 2024 to get the wind farm up and running. But he finds that his group is uniquely qualified to take down the project.

"I'm not aware of any other conservative think tank that has actually been granted standing on an ESA case for defending a species," Rucker said. "We think of ourselves as kind of a Greenpeace of the Right."

Because Rucker has taken an active role in Save the Whales campaigns, this likely helped him and CFACT to gain standing. Even so, they remain at a disadvantage financially against some of the large, established green groups like the Sierra Club and the NRDC. As Rucker explains, the left-leaning environmental advocacy groups view the offshore wind project as an extension of the Virginia Clean Economy Act, a state-level version of what is now termed the Green New Deal.

That "deal" arose on February 7, 2019, when Representative Alexandria Ocasio-Cortez of New York and her Senate counterpart, Massachusetts Senator Ed Markey, introduced resolutions calling for a "10-year national mobilization effort" to completely end the use of fossil fuels in the United States, and to transition the nation's economy to so-called renewable energy sources. Media outlets began using the term "Green New Deal" to describe the resolutions, which serve as a blueprint for the movement's major goals and its preferred methodology for achieving those goals.

From that moment, anything that might traditionally be viewed as a conservation or environmental cause, including save the whales campaigns, would take a back seat to the Green New Deal's assaults on capitalism and free markets.

Today, a solution may be in order, compliments of Save LBI. The New Jersey group plans to petition NOAA to designate a migration corridor for the right whale, since it involves a critical habitat vital to the survival of the species. If NOAA complies, wind turbines would be prohibited from operating in the area.

Despite all the environmental damage, proponents of offshore wind claim it's still needed to offset the anticipated damage to the climate from CO_2 emissions. Save LBI's Bob Stern would like to see more evidence that is the case.

"Show me the benefit," he said. "Congress goes ahead and passes the Inflation Reduction Act with all these tax credits to offshore wind, but I haven't seen a single piece of paper, much less a report, that shows how offshore wind is going to benefit the climate. I don't think expensive programs should go forward based on just vague statements."

Yet they have, in many instances.

Observations Versus Modeling

Scientific observations, as opposed to computer models, tell us the climate is always changing and natural influences are primarily, if not entirely, the cause. Humanity is not a blight on the planet, as activists claim, and rising levels of CO_2 actually have environmental benefits.

But central planners, big-government schemers, and globalists have seized upon climate change as the rationale for their real agenda.

That agenda has nothing to do with the climate or the environment. This is why, for example, climate activists operate in effective opposition to the Endangered Species Act and other environmental laws. The strategy at work is highly dependent on the willful distortion of scientific data. This fantasy-peddling is an example of climate pornography, one the public has been forced to stare at since the inception of the IPCC. The goal is to arouse the senses, induce excitement, and inspire extreme, unhealthy actions. They've come close to succeeding.

But there are some hopeful indications that the climate movement has passed its high-water mark. A countermovement is now underway that is making some serious headway in the second Trump administration. The American Energy Alliance, a Washington, DC–based nonprofit that favors free-market energy policies, has put together a list of "50 actions" the Trump administration has taken to unleash American energy. The list is focused in part on unwinding the United States from international climate agreements and Biden-era initiatives that lock down domestic energy production under the auspices of climate change. There's a firm understanding that American freedom and American energy independence go hand in hand.

Still, the climate movement maintains structural and financial advantages that can be instantly reactivated by the federal bureaucracy—the unelected fourth branch of government that has taken hold of America. How much success President Trump has in reining in the fourth branch is an open question despite some early success.

Today, in the run-up to the 250th anniversary of American independence, this book will attempt to pull back the veil on the real motivations of the climate movement and its ideology. It will show how the instruments of unaccountable government power have been turned against free-thinking scientists, homeowners, business owners, academics, honorable public servants, and private citizens. They are part of a copious list of genuine victims who have a story to tell, one that turns the climate narrative upside down. The upcoming anniversary of American independence provides an ideal opportunity to explore this subject matter, since it is nothing less than American independence that climate activists continuously target.

CHAPTER 2

From Net Zero Back to "America First" Energy Policies

"Net zero" was all the rage during the Biden administration. Taking inspiration from the UN Paris Climate Agreement of 2015, Biden sought to put the United States on a path to net-zero greenhouse gas emissions, across the entire economy, no later than 2050.

This chapter will explore this forward charge toward radical emissions reductions and more recent efforts by President Donald Trump to reverse Biden's changes and rein in the climate activists—net zero versus America First.

"Net zero" means achieving a balance between the amount of greenhouse gases (mainly carbon dioxide) put into the atmosphere and the amount removed from it, by either natural or artificial methods. The first step in the Biden administration's net-zero process involved reducing net emissions by 61 to 66 percent below 2005 levels by 2035.[19] Blue-state governors pursued their own versions of net zero with California's Gavin Newsom leading the charge. Newsom committed his state to pursuing "the most ambitious climate action of any jurisdiction in the world." He pledged to "build out a 100 percent clean energy grid" and achieve carbon neutrality by 2045.[20]

Circle back to January 2021 when the Biden administration instituted its "whole-of-government approach" to combating the "climate crisis."[21] In its moves toward net zero, the administration essentially took stage direction from outside activist groups that positioned some of their former staff members in high-level positions. There are several examples, but one stands out: Allison Clements.

The Institute for Energy Research (IER)—a Washington-based nonprofit that favors free-market policies—initiated a series of Freedom of Information Act (FOIA) requests beginning in 2022 after the Federal Energy Regulation Commission (FERC) issued new policy directives that would have greatly impeded the construction of new natural gas pipelines. This was noteworthy, because FERC's statutory mandate is to ensure reliable gas supplies at a reasonable cost to consumers. But although Congress established FERC as an "independent agency" in 1977, IER's FOIA actions broke loose emails, Zoom calls, Zoom chats, Microsoft Team chats, text messages, calendar records, and phone bills that provided insight into how FERC had become a tool for climate activists under Biden.[22] Correspondence between Commissioner Allison Clements and her former employers at the Natural Resources Defense Council and the Energy Foundation demonstrated that FERC's independence had fallen by the wayside.

FERC includes five commissioners who are appointed by the president and confirmed by the Senate. There may be no more than three commissioners from one political party serving at any given time. FERC's pipeline-impeding directives were unfurled along party lines while Democrats held a 3–2 majority. Clements was one of those in the majority.

Making Smart Use of FOIA

The tenacity and determination the IER team exhibited in pulling loose communications FERC clearly did not want to release turned out to be a tremendous public service. The FERC policy statements, which were ultimately withdrawn, would have created new openings for green pressure groups to file suits aimed at halting pipeline construction.

How did we arrive at this point?

The vilification of carbon dioxide is an attack on humanity itself. Which makes sense, because the climate movement views humanity as a blight on the planet. Humans generating more CO_2 are anathema to the climate activists who posture as advocates for a pristine Earth. They correctly recognize that a regulatory regime built around CO_2 could control virtually every human activity.

In 2007, the US Supreme Court in *Massachusetts v. EPA* ruled that greenhouse gases qualify as pollutants under the Clean Air Act. Under the act, the EPA must regulate pollutants that in the agency's judgment can "reasonably be anticipated to endanger public health or welfare." The Supreme Court left it up to Obama's EPA to determine whether it wanted to expand its authority by controlling carbon dioxide emissions. Not a good idea. Progressive government figures do not typically give up political power once they're given it.

This is what the Obama administration did when in 2009 it finalized an "Endangerment Finding," enabling the EPA to set limits on CO_2 emissions from power plants, autos, and trucks, while also imposing methane fees on oil and gas companies. The Endangerment Finding simultaneously allowed the Obama and Biden administrations to bypass Congress, all in the name of fighting climate change. By falsely identifying carbon dioxide as a pollutant, the central planners in the Obama administration removed any meaningful limits on regulatory authority.

But in Trump's reloaded presidency, a frontal assault is underway against what some aptly describe as the "climate-industrial complex."

In March 2025, EPA Administrator Lee Zeldin launched what is arguably the most audacious deregulation effort in American history, built around thirty-one initiatives designed to unleash American energy and lower the cost of living for average citizens. How permanent any changes turn out to be, though, depends largely on how much success Zeldin has in pursuing reconsideration of the 2009 Endangerment Finding—the great enabler for some of the most onerous, anti-freedom pieces of legislation in recent history. Environmental advocacy groups predictably went into meltdown when Zeldin moved to potentially strike down this, the holy grail of climate regulations. Litigation will inevitably ensue if the Trump administration does rescind the Endangerment Finding. But it's important to note that Congress never authorized the EPA to regulate CO_2 emissions. Moreover, the composition of the high court has changed to the point that it may be inclined to reverse the ruling in *Massachusetts v. EPA*.

Tom Pyle, the IER president, struck a hopeful tone in an interview about transformative policy changes now underway.

"EPA Administrator Lee Zeldin is taking a hatchet to Obama and Biden's regulatory agenda, looking to revise or rescind thirty-one onerous regulations that add costs to Americans for goods and energy," Pyle said. "The regulations range from regulating emissions from power plants, which could shutter existing coal power plants, to limiting the type of cars available for purchase in favor of electric vehicles."

But the problems, as Pyle explained, are not just economic. There's also a significant national security risk attached to the oversized regulations pushed during the Obama and Biden years. For one thing, the limits to consumer choice that were put in place under both administrations could have been "disastrous" for the US power grid, Pyle said.

By favoring intermittent solar and wind over more reliable forms of energy, the climate activists in the federal government made America more vulnerable to self-imposed blackouts and the actions of hostile foreign actors. Pyle is particularly concerned with what he identifies as "highly aggressive cyberattacks from China" that could damage America's energy infrastructure.

Such national security concerns will hopefully provide added impetus to Trump's "America First" energy agenda. The changes Zeldin has set in motion will be fought in court and argued in Congress. But there is good reason to believe that, on balance, the regulatory load will be lightened in the coming years, and we'll have an opportunity to double down on what Pyle views as "the golden moment for American energy."

But to achieve anything in the way of a permanent, lasting victory will mean tackling the pseudo-scientific edifice of climate alarmism.

The distortions and exaggerations attached to what passes for climate science have translated into heightened levels of anxiety among the public. Called "eco-anxiety" or "climate anxiety," it describes heightened levels of climate concern that can even be debilitating to one's mental health.[23] And it's concentrated among high school and college students, who have been brainwashed in the climate catastrophe for much of their lives.

Unfortunately, much of the literature devoted to "eco-anxiety" accepts the premise of an impending climate catastrophe. Even so, it offers compelling data to show the concept is a genuine problem. That's partly the result of classroom climate porn, designed to advance political and policy agendas.

The other distorting influence making young people anxious is government funding of science that insists on a results-oriented approach to the research. Bluntly stated, scientists working in climate-related fields cannot expect to receive government grants unless they produce the desired results justifying more government regulations.

Fortunately, private outfits are beginning to emerge with well-credentialed researchers willing to challenge government-funded climate hysteria.

In Defense of CO_2

Enter the CO_2 Coalition. This educational foundation, established in 2015, includes hundreds of scientists and researchers from across the globe devoted to informing the public and policymakers about the benefits of CO_2. The coalition's members have invested considerable time and effort into debunking flawed climate models that greatly exaggerate global warming.

Will Happer, a retired Princeton University physicist who founded the coalition, sat down for an interview with the Freedom Institute in February 2025 to discuss the state of climate science, just as the Trump administration was letting loose its deregulatory efforts.

"It's dangerous to make policy on the basis of lies," Happer warned. The incessant demonization of CO_2 does a great disservice to the cause of honest scientific research and the broader public interest, he argued. He traced the origins of climate alarmism to the early 1990s.[24]

"I was in Washington at the time as a government bureaucrat, and I could see it getting started," Happer said. "It was being pushed by Senator Al Gore and his allies. At that time, there were still many honest scientists in academia who didn't go along with all the alarmism, but they gradually died off and were replaced by younger people who have never known anything except pleasing their government sponsors with politically correct research results that they expect."

Earth's climate has always been in a state of flux, subject to gyrations driven by natural influences, Happer explained. The most recent warming period follows on the heels of the Little Ice Age, which ended in the nineteenth century, and our planet will inevitably head into another cooling period, if it hasn't already. Policies that operate under the assumption that only human activity can induce climate change omit this larger geological record, and do so by design. In particular, Happer sees "net zero" policies as misguided, since in his estimation the human influence on climate has been greatly overstated.

The false scientific "consensus" that says mankind is primarily responsible for potentially catastrophic global warming stems from a 2013 research paper formally titled "Quantifying the Consensus on Anthropogenic Global Warming in the Scientific Literature," compliments of researchers Cook et al. The paper appeared in an edition of *Environmental Research*, and it's the source of the oft-cited claim that 97 percent of scientists accept as fact that manmade global warming is real. But let's look at that.

The figure is pulled from an examination of about twelve thousand academic papers on climate change, broadly speaking, and global warming in particular. Out of all those papers, which were published between 1991 and 2001, more than 66 percent expressed no opinion on anthropogenic warming. That should be the major takeaway. But it's also worth noting that about 33 percent were open to the idea of anthropogenic warming, 0.7 percent rejected anthropogenic warming, and 0.3 percent were unsure of the cause.

So where does that 97.1 percent figure come from? Apparently, of the 33.6 percent who did express an opinion on man-made global warming, 97.1 percent agreed that humans are causing global warming.[25]

This sly manipulation of statistics relies on a subset of a subset of a larger study. The Cook paper is also silent on the question of how dangerous global warming might be. Other researchers have argued that the sample Cook collected includes papers that are not entirely relevant or representative of data providing insight into man-made global warming.

But the most damning critique comes from David Legates, a former director of the University of Delaware's Center for Climate Research. Legates joined with three energy policy analysts to take a deeper dive into what Cook produced. After reviewing the same collection of papers from the Cook study, Legates and his team concluded that a "mere 0.3 percent of all papers, or 1 percent of the 4,014 papers expressing an opinion on the matter, claim that the majority of warming since 1950 is man-made."[26] That's what you call a tiny number.

"The 97 percent figure is a false talking point," Kevin Dayaratna, the chief statistician with the Heritage Foundation, said during an interview. "The Cook study misleads as to where there might be any kind of consensus, while glossing over areas of uncertainty and disagreement in the scientific community. There is a debate over how much man-made global warming there might be, certainly no consensus."

Dayaratna describes himself as a "lukewarmist," meaning he sees mostly though not exclusively natural influences at work behind the global warming that began in the mid-twentieth century. Even so, someone like Dayaratna, who rejects alarmist theories, could still be grouped in the fraudulent 97 percent consensus.

That's one of the conclusions the Friends of Science Society, a group based in Calgary, came to after performing a study on the phony 97 percent figure in 2014. The Canadian group points to "significant manipulations and redactions of source data" at work in arriving at the 97 percent figure.[27]

"The purpose of the 97% claim lies in the psychological sciences, not in climate science," the study says. "A 97% consensus claim is merely a 'social proof'—a powerful psychological motivator intended to make the public comply with the herd...."[28] No one wants to be the odd man out. The Friends of Science Society analysis of these surveys further shows that there is no 97 percent consensus on human-caused global warming. In fact, none of these studies indicate any agreement with a catastrophic view of human-caused global warming.[29]

But there is a consensus among the political class, particularly those of a progressive, anti-constitutional bent, on the need for more centralized planning and controlled spheres of influence that do not allow for dissent.

Richard Lindzen, an emeritus professor of meteorology at the Massachusetts Institute of Technology, provides a compelling overview of how climate propaganda is molded and shaped.

"The desperation of political figures often drives them so far as to claim that climate change is an existential threat (associated with alleged 'tipping points')," Lindzen wrote in a paper for the Claremont Institute. "This despite a complete absence of theoretical or observational support, and despite the fact that official documents produced to support climate concerns (for example, the Working Group 1 reports of the United Nations Intergovernmental Panel on Climate Change, or IPCC) never come close to substantiating these worst-case projections."[30]

As Lindzen observes, what's happening is quite the opposite of science. The climate movement is fixated on gaining power rather than pursuing serious inquiries.

"The ability to award trillions of dollars to reorient our energy sector means that there are recipients of these trillions of dollars," Lindzen wrote. "These recipients must share just a few percentage points of these trillions of dollars to support the campaigns of these politicians for many election cycles and guarantee the support of these politicians for the policies associated with the reorientation."[31]

"Follow the money," and then the seemingly illogical shift to inefficient, unworkable energy schemes under Obama and Biden becomes more understandable.

Revisiting the Climategate Scandal

The fatal scientific salvo against the climate movement came early during the Obama years. The entire edifice came crumbling down during the "Climategate" scandal, which erupted in the fall of 2009. Political activists masquerading as scientists got exposed in a series of emails leaked from the Climate Research Unit (CRU) at the University of East Anglia in Great Britain.

Their email exchanges made clear that the primary authors of alarmism were willing to cook the books, manipulate data, violate the scientific method, and muzzle dissenting voices when Mother Nature did not cooperate with their theories linking human activity to dangerous levels of global warming. The email exchanges also made clear that CRU staff had engaged in a cover-up. They'd made a concerted effort to resist open records requests from scientific skeptics who'd pressed for CRU records to be open and available for public scrutiny. By concealing their data, climate activists prevented scientists from outside CRU from replicating their work to see if it withstood rigorous testing.

Put simply, Climategate demonstrated a willingness on the part of climate activists to abuse the scientific method when it did not conform with their political agenda. James Delingpole, a British author and journalist, has driven home this point many times in his extensive coverage of Climategate. As Delingpole explains, the scientific method is set in motion when someone makes a claim and then attempts to substantiate that claim with data. The next and final step is to allow others to replicate their work and to see if it holds up.[32]

Dan Kish, a senior fellow with the Institute for Energy Research, cites the evidence indicating that alarmist positions on climate do not square with sound science.

"Climate alarmists and their allies in the media like to apply the term 'denier' to anyone who does not accept their premise," Kish said in an interview. "But Climategate shows *they* are the real deniers. Every year you see a new set of facts coming out showing that these catastrophic predictions and estimates are wrong, and every year they deny the facts."[33]

Climategate intersected with the Fifteenth Session of the Parties to the United Nations Framework Convention on Climate Change

(UNFCCC), widely known as COP15, which took place in Copenhagen, Denmark. The scandal was likely responsible for delaying UN efforts to implement an international "cap and trade" agreement that would have restricted fossil fuel emissions.

But a few years later, with President Barack Obama in office, the United States succumbed, signing the Paris Agreement during COP21 in December 2015.[34] Under this agreement, participating countries must establish their own "nationally determined contributions" (NDCs) to emissions, to help prevent what the UN views as a coming climate catastrophe. President Donald Trump took executive action to withdraw the United States from the Paris Agreement after he was elected in 2016, but President Joe Biden promptly reinserted the nation back into the agreement. The back-and-forth continued when Trump once again withdrew from Paris in January 2025 without going through the UN's bureaucratic rigmarole, designed to make withdrawing as cumbersome as possible.

Kish sees an opportunity for Trump to dismantle the "climate-industrial complex" in his second term by taking steps to permanently repeal the Paris Agreement.

"We have the anniversary of Climategate to help give momentum to the Trump agenda," Kish observed. "But we also have the anniversary of COP29, which tells us the UN is still pressing ahead with its climate agenda."[35] COP29 took place in Baku, Azerbaijan, in November 2024, when the UN reiterated its commitments to NDCs.

Kish credits Paul Tice, a senior fellow with the National Center for Energy Analytics, for seizing on the right strategy in a piece for the *Wall Street Journal*. Tice proposes that Trump submit the Paris Agreement to the US Senate as a treaty, instead of falling back on another executive order. Treaties require a two-thirds majority in the Senate for approval.

"This move would effectively put an end to the Paris Agreement, which was always a treaty and should have been called one," Kish said. "But there's another step here involving CO_2 regulations that should be tackled, and I think Trump has the courage to do this."[36]

Tice proposed that the incoming Trump administration revoke the 2009 Endangerment Finding that declared CO_2 a pollutant, on the basis of highly specious findings. As discussed, the Supreme Court's ruling in *Massachusetts v. EPA* empowered Obama's EPA to decide whether greenhouse gases should be regulated under the Clean Air Act.

"This decision flew in the face of everything we learned from Climategate," Kish said. "The Clean Air Act was never crafted to cover CO_2 emissions. The court basically allowed the EPA to expand its power over the economy through all kinds of regulations."[37]

Save LBI Finds a Receptive Federal Audience

The one-two punch Team Trump has directed against the Paris Agreement and the Endangerment Finding speaks to a willingness to spend political capital and implement lasting changes. For stakeholders in the East Coast beach culture, Trump's 2024 election victory was not merely fortuitous; it was a near miss from what could have been irrevocable damage. A Kamala Harris victory would have had Jersey residents staring at two hundred wind turbines, each at least one thousand feet tall, just eight miles or so off the coast of LBI, Brigantine, and Atlantic City.

However, the election's positive reverberations came quickly for the residents of South Jersey.

In March 2025, Trump's EPA sent the Clean Air Act permit for Atlantic Shores South's proposed offshore wind project back to the regional EPA office that had issued it, for reevaluation. Save LBI can take a bow, since this action came in response to their petition challenging the merits of permit approval while seeking further review.

"This is a significant event because to my knowledge it is the first time that a federal approval for any offshore wind project has been overturned, and it highlights the lack of full disclosure and questionable science and mathematics that has characterized other applications and approvals," Stern, the Save LBI president, said in a press release. For the moment, this means Atlantic Shores does not have all the federal approvals it needs to install wind turbines off the Jersey coast.[38]

"We are hopeful that other federal agencies, particularly the Interior Department and NOAA, will take note of the EPA's action and reconsider their prior approvals, especially those dealing with marine mammal impact," Stern continued. "We have written to both asking for that."

The proposed offshore wind project is an example of how the climate movement, in its lust for political power and money, has generated a whole new class of victims. Delivering long-overdue justice to the legions of individuals who have been victimized by climate policies is no small task. But it's imperative to tell their stories now. If the climate movement becomes ascendant again in a future administration, the victims will not all be spoken of in the past tense.

Dayaratna, the Heritage statistician, joined with Diana Furchtgott-Roth—director of the think tank's Center for Energy,

Climate, and Environment—and other policy analysts to produce a report showing that there is no limit to who can be victimized by anti-energy policies.[39]

The story of human advancement is intertwined with the story of energy, the Heritage scholars explain. By this they mean that in the absence of reliable energy, much of human progress, including improved health care, food systems, and cleaner environments, is not possible. As they put it in their report:

> This relationship between economic development and energy use is so strong that there is not a single nation with a high per capita income and low per capita energy usage. Conversely, there is not a single country with high energy use per capita and low per capita income. Higher energy use allows for higher productivity, increased agricultural yields, and higher household consumption, which eliminates the drudgery of subsistence farming. Either these farmers now have access to innovative farming technologies and techniques, or they have the economic mobility to learn other skills and contribute in other ways to their society. As evident by the numerous examples of medical technology improving with energy access, high-energy-use nations have access to more doctors and safer drinking water, which results in lower maternal and child mortality. Additionally, the rising level of wealth allows for activities such as investing capital in pollution-mitigation measures. If low-energy-use countries are prevented from accessing affordable and reliable energy

resources to improve their economies, their progress will stall and may cause residents to search abroad for other opportunities.

There are plenty of examples of climate activists living on the high while pushing for policies that work to the great disadvantage of the poor. Yet they continuously and shamelessly couch their anti-energy, anti-freedom, anti-population, and, yes, anti-science agenda in virtuous language. Since they've set the table in this manner, it's only fair game to question the motivations lurking behind climate activism. As beach residents living up and down the East Coast quickly learned, the climate rationale for offshore wind was a canard right from outset. Follow the money standing behind the various projects and it leads back to well-endowed, narrow special interests. Even worse, the money trail sometimes leads back to hostile foreign entities. Ethics, honesty, and justice do not figure into the equation. That's not difficult to discern when climate proposals are subjected to vigorous debate and open inquiry, which is why every effort is made to ensure that neither is permitted.

CHAPTER 3

Climate Activism as a Threat to Scientific Inquiry and Discovery

M orality plays on the part of climate activists come fast and furious whenever the science underpinning their theories of human-caused global warming is called into question. Skeptics are dismissed as being too few in number to be taken seriously. Even worse, they are labeled as "deniers," implying they are on par with Holocaust deniers.

Since climate activists have been caught red-handed manipulating scientific data, it's not difficult to turn the "denier" label back in their direction. In at least some instances, they are knowingly cooking the books and undermining the scientific method to strong-arm policies that harm the poorest populations. But there's more than just dishonesty at work here. Besides being anti-science, the climate movement at its basest level is not just immoral but also explicitly anti-life, anti-human, anti-energy, and anti-American.

The leading figures promoting global warming hysteria are also adept at practicing "projection," which in psychology refers someone attributing their own unacceptable urges and inclinations to someone else. For instance, in an interview with *60 Minutes* in 2008, former Vice President Al Gore repeated the canard that "the science is settled" and equated skeptics to "flat-earthers" and moon-landing deniers. But who is really "anti-science"? The problem for people like Gore is that icons of science—such as current and former astronauts, including those who took part in the Apollo program—are among the most prominent skeptics of climate alarmism. They include Buzz Aldrin, an MIT engineer and the second man to walk on the moon, along with Harrison Schmitt, a Harvard geologist, former U.S. senator for New Mexico, and second to last man to walk on the moon. Both point to natural influences rather than human emissions as the major cause of recent global warming.[40]

They are hardly alone. Aldrin and Schmitt are part of a larger group called The Right Climate Stuff, which includes retired astronauts, engineers, and scientists urging NASA to adopt a more perspicacious view of scientific findings as they relate to climate. The group has expressed concerns that unfounded alarmist predictions will damage NASA's reputation and undermine objective research.

The retired NASA crew took particular aim at the political activism within the UN that had interjected itself into the IPCC. They warned that proposed "carbon-tax wealth-transfer" payments would lower living standards in developed countries while making it more difficult for underdeveloped countries to emerge from poverty.

In April 2013, The Right Climate Stuff released its first report asking its team, "To what extent can human-related releases of CO_2 into the atmosphere cause earth surface temperature increases that would have harmful effects?"[41] Here are some of their major findings:

- *Carbon-based anthropogenic global warming (AGW) science is not settled.* This refers only to the carbon or CO_2 role in induced warming.
- *Natural processes dominate climate change (although many are poorly understood).*
- *Non-carbon-based AGW anthropogenic forcings are significant.* These include land use change, Urban Heat Island (UHI) effect, black carbon, and aerosols.
- *Carbon-based AGW impact appears to be muted.* Other sources are not necessarily muted; the impacts of changing solar activity, El Nino/La Nina—southern oscillation (ENSO), Pacific Decadal Oscillation (PDO), Atlantic Multidecadal Oscillation (AMO), black carbon, etc., are observable.
- *Empirical evidence for carbon-based AGW does not support catastrophe.*
- *The threat of net harmful total global warming, if any, is not immediate and thus does not require swift corrective action.*
- *The US government is overreacting to concerns about anthropogenic global warming.*[42]

As discussed, climate policies can have severe fallout for the most vulnerable populations. They can also do serious damage to the scientific process, since climate activists place a premium on desired outcomes at the expense of objective research. No branch of science is immune, including the one that might have most to say about climate.

Astronomers Worried About Their Carbon Footprint!

Suddenly, it appears that astronomers have too big of a "carbon footprint"! Apparently, "research infrastructure," including astronomical space missions and ground-based observatories, is the primary culprit. The human emissions surrounding these scientific endeavors are contributing to an earthly situation that is not sustainable, according to climate activists.[43] So, before probing any further into the formation of galaxies, nebulas, and star clusters, they'd better fall in step with the international climate agenda to ensure the survivability of planet Earth.

In Australia, astronomers are told the operation of their observatories, the electricity used for office buildings, and even space flights themselves call out for a radical transformation. That's one of the major takeaways from a study published in *Nature Astronomy* that identifies a range of "environmentally unsustainable" practices that must be discontinued:

> To combat these environmentally unsustainable practices, we suggest that astronomers should strongly preference the use of supercomputers, observatories and office spaces that are predominantly powered by renewable energy sources. Where current facilities do not meet this requirement, their funders should be lobbied to invest in renewables, such as solar or wind farms. Air travel should also be reduced wherever possible, replaced primarily by video conferencing, which should also promote inclusivity.[44]

Astronomers racing ahead with research involving dark matter, black holes, supernovas, gravitational lensing, galaxy formation, and exoplanets, to mention just a few areas of contemporary interest, best not offend the sensibilities of climate activists. Anytime lobbying and funding are mentioned in the same sentence, independent-thinking scientists need to carefully weigh the costs of defiance. Climate activists go to great lengths to defund and deplatform pretty much anyone involved in research that debunks their narratives.

The timing here is particularly unfortunate. Breakthroughs in human knowledge tend to occur when there are technological leaps, as we are seeing today. NASA's James Webb Space Telescope, for instance, is staring back further in space and time than humanity ever has before. Its images have yielded new clues about the formation of galaxies a few hundred million years after the Big Bang (not very long in astronomical terms).

The space telescope has also provided insight into the evolution of supermassive black holes lurking at the centers of galaxies, including our own. Then there are the fresh discoveries involving exoplanets that might possibly harbor the conditions for life. The same is true about the largest moons in our solar system, which likely contain liquid oceans.[45]

These are the kinds of revelations that call out for heightened examination. But climate concerns occupy a privileged position over and above new areas of inquiry. In fact, astrophysicists are calling on their colleagues to hit the brakes before they plunge forward with new initiatives that are a bit too heavy on the emissions.

"We have to slow down," says Jürgen Knödlseder, the research director at the Institut de Recherche en Astrophysique et Planétologic (IRAP) in France. Knödlseder is a proponent of what he calls "slow science." He is the lead author of a new study that analyzed the carbon footprint of forty-six space missions and thirty-nine ground-based observatories. His study estimates that emissions from all active observatories are somewhere in the neighborhood of twenty million tons of carbon dioxide. Knödlseder's team is convinced this is far too much, arguing this level of emissions is comparable to those annually produced by the countries of Estonia, Croatia, and Bulgaria.[46]

The French astrophysicists are not exactly outliers on slowing down scientific research to preserve the planet. In fact, they fit into a broader coalition of astronomers "working to address the climate crisis."

Astronomers for Planet Earth (A4E) boasts 2,100 members from eighty-one countries working in collaboration to address "the climate crisis" from the perspective of what is arguably the oldest of all the sciences. Their website is replete with videos, webinars, blogs, and other media resources devoted to saving the planet.[47] But even as these stargazers inform the public that they proceed from a "unique point of view," they also follow in lockstep with climate narratives that have found favor in legacy media platforms, government agencies, and academic institutions.[48]

The astronomers advocating for measures to save the planet have the obligatory section on their website exploring the carbon footprint of their profession. Here they express concerns about the climate impact of their travel to scientific meetings and the need for initiatives that make their research practices more environmentally sustainable.

Event organizers best be on guard! Otherwise, they might bring too many well-credentialed, cutting-edge scientists together to the detriment of their home planet.

In fact, A4E has released an official "Statement on Conferences and Meetings," aimed at addressing the "immediacy and severity of the climate crisis" and the urgent need to meet emissions reductions in line with UN climate agreements. Among the criteria attached to the statement is a recommendation to "minimize the environmental impact" of any astronomical meetings. Astronomers who want to keep careful track of their own seemingly unfortunate contributions to dangerous emissions even have access to a "flight footprint calculator." A4E also recommends that event organizers go with "food and beverages that are sourced locally, sustainably and ethically and minimize plastic as well as waste by communicating this explicitly to caterers and vendors, if not included as requirements when selecting them." Virtual participation is encouraged while stipulations are attached to in-person interactions where carbon emissions are unavoidable.

But the recommendations A4E has presented to the astronomy community are about more than just climate. They are attached to a larger policy agenda that is tucked away at the end of the statement, crafted to curtail the carbon footprints of international gatherings. For example, A4E does carve out some exceptions for "traditionally underrepresented groups and countries" that stand to benefit from face-to-face meetings. And here is how A4E concludes its listed recommendations: "By following the criteria outlined above, we can strive for more sustainability in our field and contribute to system change, decolonisation, diversity, equity, and inclusion."[49] How DEI initiatives intersect with the primary mission of astronomers is not explained. But it's made clear that DEI is a priority for A4E.

So is "social justice." The astronomers advocating for reduced human emissions see a palpable connection between climate activism and progressive causes folded within the seemingly benign language of civil rights. Right from its inception, A4E coalesced around causes that seem, at best, peripheral to scientific inquiry. The group even acknowledges as much:

> Astronomers for Planet Earth was created to improve the lives of all people by addressing the climate crisis. Communities that have been exploited historically are the ones most affected by climate change. Therefore, a discussion about climate solutions must involve social justice and racial equity. It requires us to think about how black, indigenous, and people of color are bearing the brunt of the crisis, enduring the first consequences of our changing world.[50]

Astronomers for Planet Earth marked its five-year anniversary in January 2025 with an international celebration made possible through Zoom technology. To be sure, A4E's ongoing efforts to popularize astronomical discoveries are worthy of applause. By "revealing the uniqueness, wonder and fragility of the Earth," through astronomical lenses, the group surmises that the public will become sufficiently motivated to "nurture its stewardship and care." That's because "There is no Planet B!" Yes, there may be habitable exoplanets, but none we have the technology to reach just now. So, we'd better take care of our home world.

But does that mean putting the screws to ground-based and spaced-based astronomical endeavors? Presumably, these missions should be either curtailed or radically restructured to avoid additional contributions to dangerous levels of CO_2.

There is no escaping the "fragility" of human existence from an astronomy perspective. The serene night sky belies a violent universe filled with incessant collisions and explosions. But there are occasional reminders. In July 1994, amateur and professional astronomers observed the comet Shoemaker-Levy 9 striking Jupiter and leaving visible scars on the planet's cloud tops that could be observed for months. As the largest planet in the solar system, Jupiter is ideally positioned to pull in asteroids and comets, not just because of its size but also because of its massive gravity.

The 1994 collision is a reminder that Earth could be vulnerable to catastrophic collisions like the one that led to the extinction of the dinosaurs. Remember: T. rex and friends did not have a space program! In some respects, Jupiter operates as a vacuum cleaner, insulating the inner planets, including Earth; but this protection is not indefinite.

There are astronomers who monitor near-Earth asteroids to see if any pose a potential threat. That's time well spent, since American ingenuity can likely alter the trajectory of an asteroid. NASA's first-ever mission to conduct one method of deflection, by shifting an asteroid's movements through a kinetic impact, was highly successful back in September 2022. The space agency's Double Asteroid Redirection Test (DART) team demonstrated their spacecraft's kinetic impact can steer a potentially threatening celestial body away from Earth.[51] That's a worthwhile investment of time, resources, engineering, and, yes, human emissions.

Such technology is leaping ahead at a time when climate activists, including some practicing astronomy, want to put the kibosh on ambitious missions that could improve (and protect) the human condition.

Here, we have to ask whether it's climate change that should most concern policymakers with purview over space missions. Or is it the pretensions of the climate change movement? The astronomers describing themselves as advocates for planet Earth might want to ask what the endgame looks like if their climate policies come to full fruition. Constraints on future missions that build on the success of DART, all in the name of climate activism, could put humanity on the fast track to the kind of cataclysm A4E seeks to avoid. Then again, the group is built around the idea that there is an urgent climate crisis and that there is no real debate about the role of fossil fuels and human CO_2 in producing dangerous levels of global warming.

But astronomy says otherwise.

In fact, fresh research into the role of the sun, the position of the solar system, cosmic rays, and the Milky Way galaxy's spiral arms indicate that natural influences, not human activity, drive climate change. This is precisely the kind of research that predictably comes under attack, as it's disruptive to the political agenda behind the climate movement.

Fortunately, updated research probing astronomical influences on climate is gathering renewed momentum at a time that may be ripe for advancing "America First" policies. The journey back to scientific research that prioritizes observations over modeling is an arduous one. But it remains in motion thanks to a few key individuals inside and outside government.

Senator James Inhofe Blows a Hole in the False Consensus

When results that are politically desirable for climate activists do not materialize, typically an effort is made to deplatform and silence the research in question. Fortunately, former Senator James Inhofe, an Oklahoma Republican, was not cowed when it came time to circulate scientific findings that blew a hole in the idea that there is a scientific consensus on the causes of global warming. More than any other elected official, it was the late Senator Inhofe who allowed contrarian theories to find expression.

In 2007, Inhofe's staff publicized research projects centered on temperature changes on Mars and the impact of cosmic rays.

The findings were not in line with "consensus" thinking on climate change and were largely ignored in the press. But they gave rise to updated studies that link astronomical and other natural influences with warming and cooling periods.[52]

The Red Planet has captured the public's imagination since telescopes first fleshed out its geological detail in the nineteenth century. Mars's red color can be attributed to the large supplies of iron oxide within the dust, rocks, and soil covering the planet.

By astronomical standards, Mars is somewhat tiny, only about half the size of Earth. But for amateur astronomers, Mars is every bit as tantalizing as it is frustrating. Aside from the moon, it is the only object in the solar system whose surface is visible from telescopes on Earth. That's particularly true when Mars reaches opposition, which happens every two years. Opposition means that, as seen from Earth, Mars is positioned directly opposite from the sun. This opens avenues for the best viewing of Mars, because Earth is positioned in a straight line between the sun and Mars, while Mars appears brightest and closest to Earth.

The polar ice caps and other geological features are visible even through amateur telescopes with aperture sizes between six and eight inches. The planet's 25-degree tilt produces ice caps. By comparison, Earth has a 23.5-degree tilt, which would explain why the two planets experience seasons that are somewhat similar. Martian winters and summers are much more severe. The white polar ice caps are typically what stand out the most.[53]

The data that captured Inhofe's attention dates to 2005, when NASA's Global Surveyor and Odyssey missions showed that the ice caps made of carbon dioxide at the Martian south pole had been contracting for three summers in a row. Habibullo Abdussamatov, head of the Pulkovo Astronomical Observatory in Russia at the time, surmised that the data from the Mars missions demonstrate that global warming on Earth is primarily caused by changes on the sun.

"The long-term increase in solar irradiance is heating both Earth and Mars," Abdussamatov told *National Geographic News*, adding that the sun's heat output is largely responsible for the climate change experienced on both planets. "Man-made greenhouse warming has made a small contribution to the warming seen on Earth in recent years, but it cannot compete with the increase in solar irradiance," Abdussamatov said.

This isn't what climate activists want to hear. Unfortunately for them and their agenda, the revelations on Mars are but a subset of a larger field of research that links warming and cooling trends to natural influences.

The same year Inhofe publicized the findings on Mars, he also called attention to research done at the Danish National Space Institute. It was there that Henrik Svensmark, the leader of a solar climate research team, put together findings that showed how cosmic rays emanating from exploding stars drive climate. These rays, Svensmark and his team explain, help to produce cloud cover. Higher levels of cosmic rays translate into increased cloudiness that cools Earth, while fewer cosmic rays mean fewer clouds and more warming.[54]

The sun also gets in on the act, according to Svensmark's research, since its magnetic field fluctuates in its ability to repel cosmic rays coming from the galaxy before they can reach Earth. Whenever the sun is less active, more cosmic rays penetrate to Earth, leading to colder conditions such as the Little Ice Age that climaxed three hundred years ago.[55]

Inhofe passed away at the ripe old age of 89 in 2024, but not before he played an instrumental role in ensuring that well-credentialed climate skeptics found expression. As for Svenmark, his research was hardly the final word where cosmic rays are concerned.

Another key player here is Nir Shaviv, a physicist with the Hebrew University in Jerusalem, who links climate change with the journeys the sun, Earth, and other celestial bodies take through the Milky Way galaxy. Shaviv postulates that cold spells tend to occur when the solar system passes through the spiral arms of the galaxy, where cosmic rays are most intense. His research shows these colder periods occur roughly every thirty-four million years, when the solar system intersects with the midplane of the galaxy. Increased cosmic rays generate more cloud cover, which, as we have seen, tends to cool the planet. Conversely, Shaviv finds that warming periods occur when there are fewer cosmic rays and therefore less cloud cover.[56]

In Shaviv's view, anthropogenic emissions are at the periphery of climate impacts, while cosmological factors are largely responsible for warming and cooling trends. The solar system, including Earth and other planets, takes about 225 to 250 million years to complete its cosmic journey around the Milky Way's center. During this journey, Earth passes through one of the galaxy's four spiral arms about once every 135 million years or so. This being the case, the solar system can be expected to intersect with two of the four spiral arms each cosmic year, but no more than that. (A cosmic year, also described as a galactic year, is the time it takes for the sun to orbit once around the center of the Milky Way galaxy.)

This is where Svensmark's cosmic ray theory comes into play, since there is a higher probability Earth will pass relatively close to a supernova with explosions that produce more cosmic rays. Higher levels of cosmic rays mean more cloud cover, and more cloud cover means global cooling. In 2003, Shaviv joined with

Jan Veizer, a Canadian geochemist, to publish a research paper that found about 75 percent of the variance in global temperatures over the last 545 million years (known as the Phanerozoic geological period) could be attached to cosmic ray fluctuations. Going a step further, the two scientists theorized that cosmic ray flux, and not CO_2, was the dominant factor impacting climate on multimillion-year time scales.

Shaviv and Veizer have predictably come under attack. In 2004, a group of scientists challenged their methodology while reaffirming the view that human CO_2 emissions are driving global warming. Stefan Rahmstorf of the Potsdam Institute for Climate Impact Research, and his colleagues in Canada, France, Germany, Switzerland, and the United States, described the data linking cosmic rays and temperature as "extremely uncertain."[57] They argue, for example, that the reconstruction of past cosmic ray activity is not based on a sufficiently large enough sample of meteorites. Rahmstorf and his team conclude that man-made carbon emissions are in fact responsible for the most recent global warming trend.

But the point is the debate continues to rage despite widespread assertions that the "science is settled." Underscoring that point, Willie Soon and his team of CERES scientists describe the findings of the UN's Intergovernmental Panel on Climate Change (IPCC) as nothing more than "pseudoscientific assertions" that are easily debunked.[58] CERES scientists made waves in July and August 2023 when they coauthored three peer-reviewed papers that challenged the findings of the IPCC. Several key observations greatly unsettled climate activists.

The CERES team concluded that the IPCC "substantially underestimated" how much "urbanization bias" had discombobulated their global surface temperature data. (An urbanization bias, also known as the "urban heat island" effect, occurs when highly localized warming affects thermometer stations across urban regions.) Another problem CERES detected with the IPCC relates back to how the CERES team made use of temperature data outside urban areas that point to a "more nuanced history of temperature changes" going back to the mid-nineteenth century.

Then there's the sun. The CERES scientists take issue with how the IPCC estimated total solar irradiance (TSI) because the samples only amounted to a very small subset utilized by the scientific community.

"Several of the TSI estimates the IPCC had neglected in their analysis suggest that most of the warming since the 19th century could be natural—especially from the non-urbanized data," CERES said in a blog post. "Others suggest that the warming has been a mixture of natural and human-caused factors. Others agree with the IPCC's attribution statements. Given these uncertainties, we have concluded that the scientific community is not yet in a position to say whether the global temperature changes since the mid-19th century have been 'mostly human-caused' (as IPCC AR6 claimed), 'mostly natural' or some combination of factors."[59]

Those who agree with the IPCC's sweeping assertions took aim at CERES. Beginning in September 2023, a website called RealClimate.org began publishing blog posts attempting to discredit their work. CERES characterized the blog posts as "false and misleading" in lengthy rebuttals on its own site.[60] Regardless, and just as CERES concluded, it's becoming more difficult to pretend there is no scientific debate over how much natural versus human influence there is on the climate.

Soon and company continue to make the case that "the IPCC was overly confident and premature in its detection and attribution statements."[61] A paper CERES authored in partnership with the Heritage Foundation landed multiple punches against the climate establishment. They went into great detail describing how "urbanization bias" appeared to be contaminating weather station data. After examining the total solar irradiance datasets going back to 1850, CERES also found several estimates suggesting that the global warming that has occurred since then was "mostly natural."

The Natural Influences Driving Sea Level Rise

Cracks are beginning to emerge in the narrative set up to scare and cajole the public into accepting less freedom and autonomy. The unfounded hysteria over sea-level rise is near the top of that list.

Because many media outlets and academic journals falsely assume that only warming periods and human activity can have significant impacts on sea-level rise, they typically seize on definitions of that concept that are "ambiguous" and "insufficient," observes David Legates, a climatologist and professor emeritus at the University of Delaware and a visiting fellow at Heritage Foundation. Legates presented his major findings in a March 2024 paper for Heritage. He cautions policymakers against halting all man-made emissions of CO_2 and other greenhouse gases in the United States, as climate activists urge, since there is "no evidence" these actions would mitigate whatever processes cause sea levels to rise, whether natural or man-made.[62] For one thing, Legates writes, it's a mistake to presuppose, as many media definitions do, that land is "immovable" when clearly it isn't. Land may rise or descend in response to several factors, he explains:

> Isostatic processes—where the crust [of the Earth] returns to a state of equilibrium due to the addition or removal of surface forces—usually occur over long-time scales, often involving ice sheet formation and removal. But changes in coastal elevation also can be induced by glacial outwash, channelization of rivers, pumping of groundwater, and changes in land use.[63]

The Delaware climatologist argues that sea levels have been rising since the end of the last Ice Age, about 22,000 years ago, and more is at work than CO_2. He regards alarmists' positions on sea-level rise as part of a larger media narrative on "extreme weather" and related issues that, in his view, falsely conflate recent trends with human activity.

"Sea levels were rising at an accelerated rate between 7,000 years and 15,000 years ago, and that change in the rate of global sea level rise was not solely due to atmospheric carbon-dioxide concentrations," Legates writes. "A much better explanation is that most sea level rise is a response to the interglacial period and that equilibrium of the polar ice caps has not yet been attained."[64]

The often-circulated idea that sea levels will rise between fifteen and thirty feet from 2023 to 2100 is "clearly political hype and does not represent the science, even as advocated by climate alarmists," Legates contends. He calls for a deeper grasp and appreciation of the natural processes at work. "Understanding the intricacies of how sea levels rise and fall is considerably more nuanced than simply linking sea levels to changes in temperatures due to carbon dioxide emissions," Legates writes. "Clearly, when news reports highlight locations where coastal inundation has been the greatest (such as in Miami Beach and Virginia Beach), something other than global-warming-driven sea level rise must also be operating. Otherwise, the story would be the same in all coastal areas of the world."[65]

Factors other than CO_2 "play a nontrivial role in sea level fluctuations and variability," he says. This is where the effects of planetary rotation and gravity enter the equation. The sun's activities have an impact on portions of the Pacific and Indian Oceans, while the gravitational pulls of other heavenly bodies can alter how the Earth rotates, according to his paper:

> Variations in the Earth's rotation are induced by interactions within the sun–Earth–moon system (including the effects of Jupiter and nearby planets) and the solar wind that affects the Earth's magnetosphere. As a result, water is redistributed among the tropics and poles due to the increase in the equatorial diameter of the Earth that occurs when the Earth's rotation increases.

> Sea levels, therefore, rise in the equatorial Pacific and Indian oceans during periods of the Grand Solar Minima, while they decrease during the Grand Solar Maxima. Observed variability in sea levels of 20 years to 26 years in duration can be attributed to the Earth's rotation. The Earth's gravitational attraction also is an important component in global and regional changes in sea levels.

Overall, where gravitational forces are stronger, sea levels will be higher, which is counterintuitive. In fact, as an ice sheet melts, sea levels decrease near the melting ice sheet but rise at a considerable distance from the melting ice sheet due to changes in gravitational forces. Since gravity is not constant over the entire planet, local and regional variations exist in sea level resulting from differences in the gravitational force.[66]

Legates also addresses concerns related to rising sea levels, such as the potential for storm surges and flooding in coastal areas. He concludes that coastal warning systems are far more efficient in protecting life and property than any efforts to reduce the amount of CO_2 in the atmosphere. That's because sea levels are rising from natural causes that have nothing to do with anything mankind has produced or emitted.

Beginning in April 2020, during the COVID pandemic, Governor Murphy of New Jersey ordered all his state's parks closed, effectively shutting amateur astronomers out of locations that were relatively free from the effects of light pollution in comparison to the suburbs.[67] That was a raw deal for committed amateurs trying to catch a glimpse of Martian features that are typically within range only every few years.

But the mentality behind the COVID-19 lockdowns and its restrictive policies intersects with the mentality motivating contemporary climate activism and policies. During the pandemic, we lived in the kind of world that climate activists had wanted us to live in for decades. That's a world that restricts human movement and human freedom while suspending constitutional government.

"Now more than ever, New Jersey's commitment to combating and adapting to climate change is unwavering," Murphy said during a press conference after the 2024 election. "Regardless of which administration is in power at the federal level, our state is not going to back down. We're going to do everything we can to reduce emissions, protect our precious environment and build a more sustainable future."[68]

Get in the way of that agenda with sound science or economics or, God forbid, reassert the freedoms the US Constitution was designed to secure, and you can put your career and livelihood in jeopardy—as many climate scientists have discovered.

What largely guides and motivates climate activism and environmental regulations today is a concept known as the "precautionary principle"—an idea that is diametrically opposed to the philosophy behind the American founding. There are various definitions, but the Wingspread Declaration (named for the conference center where environmental activists gathered in 1998) produced a definition that has gained favor among the green groups, NGOs, and UN agencies that comprise the international environmental establishment:

> When an activity raises threats of harm to the environment or human health, precautionary measures should be taken even if some cause-and-effect relationships are not fully established.[69]

Think carefully about what this means. Forget about needing any hard evidence to establish a real risk from some proposed human activity. If it's possible to simply *imagine* a purely *hypothetical* risk from that activity—even if it rests on nothing but hysteria, fear, and misinformation—then by all means we should shut down or preemptively ban that activity, as a "precaution."

Since all human actions entail *some* degree of risk, think of how this "zero-risk" principle might inhibit *any* human activity. By the logic of the "precautionary principle," George Washington would have been prevented by regulators of his day from crossing the Delaware River on Christmas night 1776, since it involved an unacceptable level of risk and there were too many uncertainties. There would have been no Apollo moon missions because, well, that might not work and there were inherent risks. Alan Shepard's famous "fix your little problems, and let's light this candle" comment back to Mission Control before his own flight would not have found a receptive audience.

A more recent and relevant example of the "precautionary principle" involves the PennEast Pipeline, which would have delivered abundant supplies of natural gas from the Marcellus Shale in Pennsylvania to New Jersey. Thanks to innovative drilling techniques made possible through American ingenuity, natural resources that were previously beyond reach are now accessible. Yet because well-funded climate activists convinced the public the pipeline project *might* result in ecological damage, it was ultimately canceled.

But what degree of hypothetical damage? The portion of the pipeline that would have made use of existing infrastructure to cross the Delaware (yes, close to where Washington crossed) had a small "carbon footprint," contrary to what the public was told. And it seems that projects preferred by progressives aren't subject to the same "precautionary" concerns. The proposed 120-mile-long, 36-inch-diameter underground pipeline is small stuff in comparison to the "affordable housing" eyesores that have laid waste to once-bucolic regions in and around Washington

Crossing Park. The pipeline would have been much preferable, for both economic and environmental reasons.

Heading into the final months of 2025, an energy crisis took hold in New Jersey in the form of exorbitant utility bills. Electricity prices rose as much as 20 percent in some parts of the state. In retrospect, it is worth asking how the PennEast Pipeline might have alleviated those energy costs. It's also worth exposing the relationship between green energy mandates and rising energy costs. Variations of those same questions can be asked in reference to similar projects across the country. Even more relevant is the fact that First Amendment freedoms, including free speech and freedom of association, don't square with the precautionary principle. After all, open, unfettered debate can unsettle "scientific consensus" talking points.

The mentality among climate activists is that there should not even be a *risk* of a risk. That's not the American way. As more ratepayers and taxpayers are added to the list of Americans victimized by climate policies, the appetite for a return to constitutional self-government will only grow.

But the hour is late, and the central planners and globalists have a big head start.

CHAPTER 4

Deplatforming, Silencing, and Muzzling Climate Realists

U pdated scientific research does not support the idea that man-made climate change is a catastrophic threat to the health of the planet. In fact, a growing body of evidence shows natural influences are at least partially if not largely responsible for the most recent warming trends.

So why haven't more scientists been willing to speak out and challenge the UN "consensus" linking human emissions with dangerous levels of global warming?

Marc Morano, founder and editor of the website *Climate Depot*, has the answer. "Anyone who questions the climate change scare is attacked and threatened," Morano told me in an interview. "As more and more scientists speak out, dissenting from the climate change orthodoxy, the attacks against them have increased. Climate campaigners seem to think that if you can't counter the message, silence the messenger."

Climate campaigners have several poisoned arrows in their quiver, according to Morano. These include smears, intimidation, lawsuits, and threats of criminal prosecution. In several instances, well-credentialed scientists have been either forced out of their positions or pressured to abandon their research.

Roger Pielke Jr., a professor in the Environmental Studies Program at the University of Colorado, falls into the latter category. "The incessant attacks and smears are effective, no doubt, I have already shifted all of my academic work away from climate issues," Pielke wrote in 2015. "I am simply not initiating any new research or papers on the topic and I have ring-fenced my slowly diminishing blogging on the subject."[70]

In a piece for the *Wall Street Journal*, Pielke detailed how his research was "attacked by thought police in journalism, activist groups funded by billionaires and even the [Obama] White House."[71]

"My research led me to a conclusion that many climate campaigners find unacceptable: There is scant evidence to indicate that hurricanes, floods, tornadoes or drought have become more frequent," he wrote.[72]

That's not what the late Congressman Raúl Grijalva, Democrat from Arizona, wanted to hear back in 2015 when he was ranking member of the House Committee on Environment and Natural Resources. Grijalva launched an investigation into seven academics, including Pielke, who were not in line with his own views on climate.

"Congressman Grijalva doesn't have any evidence of any wrongdoing on my part, either ethical or legal, because there is none," Pielke declared in a written commentary. Grijalva "simply disagrees with the substance of my testimony."[73] In his blog, Pielke talked about the toll the investigation took on him and his family.

"My 11-year-old asked me if I was going to jail. Really nasty stuff," he wrote. "My older kids in high school had teachers pull them aside to ask about their father's 'investigation.' Smear campaigns are about collateral damage. A lot of this is about eliminating unwelcomed voices in the debate."[74]

Unfortunately, Pielke was just one of many free-thinking scientists and researchers asking inconvenient questions at a time when the climate movement was at the apex of its power.

Morano tells the story of hurricane-forecasting pioneer and atmospheric scientist Bill Gray, who had his federal funding cut off once it became clear to government figures that he did not accept the premise of man-made global warming theories.

Gray's story begins when Al Gore was vice president and one of Gore's colleagues called Gray and invited him to lunch. Here is how Gray described the back and forth:

> I said, "Fine I'll be glad to come—and what is the purpose of this?" And they said, "Well, uh, climate change." I asked, "Who else are you having in?" And he mentioned Tom Karl and a lot of these warming people. And I said, "Well, I'll be honest with you. I'll be glad to come in and have lunch with you, that's fine. Yes, I'll have respect for the...vice president of the U.S. But I will tell you that I'm not a believer in global warming—human-induced global warming— there's natural global warming." And I told him, "I'll be honest, if you still want me to come in, fine." "Well," he said, "they'll get back to you." And then I never heard from them.[75]

Gray did not hear from Gore's people directly, but he received their message loud and clear. Shortly after this exchange, the National Science Foundation cut off Gray from the federal grants he had been receiving from NOAA to study hurricanes. Government funding, you see, only goes to those who toe the line.

There's someone else who found this out the hard way. Patrick Michaels, who served as Virginia's state climatologist for almost thirty years, was another free-thinking, independent-minded scientist who ran into the buzzsaw of the climate police. Michaels, who died in 2022, made his mark as a self-described "lukewarmist" who believed there was some human contribution to global warming. But he did not believe human emissions would translate into a climate catastrophe.

Michaels was also an indefatigable critic of climate models that did not comport with scientific observations. He was forced out of his job in 2007 after clashing with then–Virginia Governor Tim Kaine.

The trouble for Michaels began when Kaine reportedly told him not to use his official title in discussions about climate change.[76] Comments from sources familiar with what went down indicated there was no room for dissenting voices on climate.

"Nobody dislikes [Michaels] because of his day job," *The Washington Post* reported, but because he "moonlights as one of the country's most aggressive and, in some circles, most reviled skeptics about the scientific consensus on climate change." Critics of Michaels lamented that he "creates the false impression of another side to a closed debate."[77]

Michaels had his own take on Kaine's maneuverings. "I resigned as Virginia state climatologist because I was told that I could not speak in public on my area of expertise, global warming, as state climatologist," Michaels said in 2007. "It was impossible to maintain academic freedom with this speech restriction."[78]

This problem is hardly limited to Virginia. Other states have found ways to deplatform and remove inconveniently skeptical state climatologists.

David Legates, now a retired University of Delaware professor, also once served as his state's climatologist. But he was asked in 2007 by then–Governor Ruth Ann Minner to stop using his title in any public comments on climate change.

"Your views on climate change, as I understand them, are not aligned with those of my administration," Minner said. "In light of my position and due to the confusion surrounding your role with the state, I am directing you to offer any future statements on this or other public policy matters only on behalf of yourself or the University of Delaware, and not as state climatologist."[79]

Legates described the intolerant atmosphere for climate skeptics: "I've had several friends who have essentially been told if you speak out as climate—on climate change, you will essentially be fired."[80] In 2011, Legates was formally asked to step down from his position.[81]

The playbook doesn't vary much, and the Left Coast certainly does not want to be outdone. Oregon State Climatologist George Taylor, previously the president of the American Association of State Climatologists, also discovered that his skeptical views about climate alarmism had no place in government.

In 2005, the Oregon governor's office declared, "George Taylor doesn't represent the governor's office, and he doesn't represent the state of Oregon."[82] Apparently, there is no room in government for free-thinking scientists. If they become too attached to the evidence, and less enthused with propaganda, they will find themselves out of a job.

The termination of state climatologists skeptical of alarmist theories has not gone unanswered. Harvard physicist Luboš Motl called the Virginia and Oregon firings "acts of blatant ideological cleansing."[83]

In 2017, climatologist Judith Curry, serving as the chair of the School of Earth and Atmospheric Sciences at Georgia Institute of Technology, walked away from her tenured professorship, citing climate "craziness" and an untenable situation of "a battle of scientific integrity versus career suicide."[84]

"I have retired from Georgia Tech, and I have no intention of seeking another academic or administrative position in a university or government agency. However, I most certainly am not retiring from professional life," Curry wrote in January 2017.[85] "I'm 'cashing out' with 186 published journal articles and two books," she explained. "The deeper reasons have to do with my growing disenchantment with universities, the academic field of climate science and scientists."

Curry continued:

> My fall from the ivory tower that started in 2005 is now complete. The deeper reasons [for my resignation] have to do with my growing disenchantment with universities, the academic field of climate science and scientists. A deciding factor was that I no longer know what to say to students and postdocs regarding how to navigate the CRAZINESS in the field of climate science. Research and other professional activities are professionally rewarded only if they are channeled in certain directions approved by a politicized academic establishment—funding, ease of getting your papers published, getting

hired in prestigious positions, appointments to prestigious committees and boards, professional recognition, etc.

How young scientists are to navigate all this is beyond me, and it often becomes a battle of scientific integrity versus career suicide (I have worked through these issues with a number of skeptical young scientists).... At this point, the private sector seems like a more "honest" place for a scientist working in a politicized field than universities or government labs—at least when you are your own boss.[86]

Morano also tells the unfortunate story of Lennart Bengtsson, a well-respected climatologist at Britain's University of Reading. In 2014, Bengtsson submitted a paper to the journal *Environmental Research Letters* that was rejected after one reviewer found it "harmful" to the global warming cause. The study in question found that CO_2 emissions would cause less warming than the climate models had predicted. Once again, not the kind of results that are in line with the demands of anti-science climate pornographers.

"They've threatened him. They've bullied him. They've pulled his papers. They're now going through everything they can to smear his reputation. And the 'they' I'm referring to is the global warming establishment," Morano said in a 2014 TV interview on Fox News.[87]

Bengtsson was forced to resign from the board of an organization called the Global Warming Policy Foundation after he was subjected to what Morano described as "McCarthy-style pressure" from his warmist colleagues. The foundation's skeptical outlook toward climate alarmism made Bengtsson a pariah in their eyes.

The Times (UK) reported that the pressure was so intense on Bengtsson "that he would be unable to continue working and feared for his health and safety unless he stepped down from the Global Warming Policy Foundation's academic advisory council. He said the pressure had mainly come from climate scientists in the US, including one employed by the US government who threatened to withdraw as co-author of a forthcoming paper because of his link with the foundation."[88]

A German physicist likened Bengtsson's joining an outfit that rejects alarmist views on climate to joining the Ku Klux Klan.[89]

At a 2014 congressional hearing, UN IPCC lead author Richard Tol condemned "the hounding of Lennart Bengtsson," who has "won many awards in a long and distinguished career in meteorology and climatology." Because Bengtsson was not promoting climate alarmism, he "was insulted by his peers" and "a Texas A&M professor even suggested he is senile."

Tol explained that "other eminent meteorologists have been treated like Bengtsson was—[Judith] Curry, [Richard] Lindzen, [Roger] Pielke Sr., [Roger] Pielke Jr. [have] been mistreated too, merely for sticking to the academic literature, as reflected by the IPCC, that there is no statistical evidence that the impact of natural disaster has increased because of climate change."

Tol testified he'd "had my share of abuse, too. Staff of the London School of Economics and the *Guardian* now routinely tell lies about me and my work." Summing up, he said, "Academics who research climate change out of curiosity but find less than alarming things are ignored, unless they rise to prominence in which case they are harassed and smeared."[90]

Lysenkoism Back on the March

The late atmospheric scientist and hurricane pioneer Bill Gray noted in 2014, "I am just appalled science has been hurt greatly by this because the government has come in and dictated science, much like Stalin and the Lysenkoism—we have had many examples in history of when the best people in the field were wrong."[91]

Retired Princeton physicist Will Happer, founder of the CO_2 Coalition, knows this history inside and out. "There are honest climate scientists today who are trying to straighten out the contradictions between climate models and observations, just as there were honest biologists in the Soviet Union who had the courage to speak out against Lysenko's cult," Happer told me in an interview.

Trofim Lysenko was a biologist who directed the Lenin All-Union Academy of Agricultural Sciences. With the support of Soviet strongman Joseph Stalin, he dictated scientific results in step with the government's political agenda.

"Lysenko's biology was adopted as official truth by Stalin's Communist Party by about 1930," Happer said. He noted that the "falsifications" and "bogus proofs" used to prop up Lysenko's schemes are not dissimilar from the methodology at work today among climate activists.

Even as a "recalcitrant Mother Nature," in Happer's words, has refused to cooperate with dire global warming predictions, Lysenko-like efforts are being made to muzzle scientists whose studies do not produce politically desired results. More than three thousand biologists were dismissed from their positions, imprisoned, and even executed during the Soviet Union's Lysenko campaign.[92] Today's government-funded scientists, who have a financial stake in stirring climate hysteria, are applying their own strong-arm tactics.

Morano has kept careful tabs on the rhetoric of government-funded climate activists who would like to jail their critics. James Hansen, one of many taxpayer-subsidized climate activists, made it clear in 2012 while he was leading NASA's Goddard Institute for Space Studies that he had no problem demonizing dissenting voices. Living on a taxpayer-financed salary, Hansen warned climate-alarmism skeptics and energy company CEOs that "our children and grandchildren will judge those who have misled the public, allowing fossil fuel emissions to continue almost unfettered, as guilty of crimes against humanity and nature."[93]

What was the crime?

"They should be blamed because they have supported misinformation to the public about climate change," Hansen said. The NASA bureaucrat doubled down on his charge a few months later, noting that he had used the phrase "crimes against humanity" deliberately—not just for "dramatic effect," but because his statement is accurate, "given the enormous scale of the consequences to humanity" if current climate-change trends continue unabated.[94]

Many climate activists find the idea of jailing skeptics appealing. In 2014, the *Gawker* website declared, "Arrest Climate-Change Deniers" and "Those denialists should face jail." Calling global-warming skeptics "criminally negligent," *Gawker* argued, "It's time to punish the climate-change liars."[95]

Likewise, Canadian environmentalist David Suzuki has called for government leaders skeptical of global warming to be "thrown in jail."[96] "I really believe that people like the former prime minister of Canada should be thrown in jail for willful blindness," Suzuki said in 2016.

In 2017, climate activist John Gilkison at *EV World* accused Marc Morano of "crimes against humanity" for "retarding any meaningful action to mitigate climate change." Prison was later determined to be an insufficient punishment, as Morano was "sentenced to death" in trials imagined by Gilkison.[97]

A public appeal on the influential news website *Talking Points Memo* asked, "At what point do we jail or execute global warming deniers?"[98] As Morano observed, "*Talking Points Memo* often sets the agenda for the political Left in the U.S."

"So, when the right-wing fucktards have caused it to be too late to fix the problem, and we start seeing the devastating consequences and we start seeing end of the World type events—how will we punish those responsible?" *Talking Points Memo* declared in its 2009 article. "It will be too late. So shouldn't we start punishing them now?"[99]

After Morano's *Climate Depot* drew unwelcome attention to the *Talking Points Memo* article, it was pulled and the website published a retraction and apology. "But the sentiment expressed was stark and unequivocal, and it has significant support among climate-fear promoters," Morano said.

Here's another example: Peter Sinclair wrote for the climate-fear-promoting website *Climate Denial Crock of the Week*, "As climate impacts continue to become clearer to the general populace, fossil fuel executives, and climate misinformers who have played a part in this catastrophe, may sometime soon prefer a safe jail cell to the torches and pitchforks that are coming their way."[100]

On June 5, 2009, former Clinton administration official Joe Romm of *Climate Progress* defended a post on his website warning that climate skeptics would be strangled in bed for rejecting the view that we face a man-made climate crisis. "An entire generation will soon be ready to strangle you and your kind while you sleep in your beds," he warned.

Romm, too, pulled his comments after *Climate Depot* drew attention to them. "The original was clearly not a threat but a prediction—albeit one that I certainly do not agree with. Since some people misread it, I am editing it," Romm wrote.[101]

In the early days of Trump's second term, media platforms accustomed to spreading climate porn went into meltdown mode. Outlets seized on the phony concept of a widespread "scientific consensus" to denounce Trump's efforts to dismantle climate regulations and programs.

"Trump's 30-Day Climate Assault" screamed a February 2025 headline in *Politico*. "Trump has trounced Biden-era clean energy programs, decimated the federal workforce and dammed the flow of climate and infrastructure dollars—sometimes flouting court orders to reverse course," the article lamented. "He has fired hundreds of staff at the nation's already-strained disaster response agency and threatened to dismantle it entirely."[102]

Politico is entitled to champion bloated climate bureaucracies, given its leanings. But what it's really complaining about is Trump's early successes in delivering on what he promised voters.

Hopefully, these recent policy shifts amount to more than just a bump in the road. But no victory is permanent in American politics, which is why it's worth revisiting the lawfare tactics that were used against scientists, researchers, business leaders, and elected officials who did not comply with the climate agenda.

CHAPTER 5

RICO Prosecutions as a Weapon Against Climate Realists and First Amendment Freedoms

As we have seen, climate activists and their allies in government have sunk to smear campaigns, lawfare threats, and censorship to deplatform and discredit scientists challenging their cooked-up claims of a "consensus." Up until recently, at least, they had the wind at their backs. The Biden administration's "whole-of-government" approach to climate didn't leave much room for honest scientists to disagree.

How much success Donald Trump will have in reinstituting research practices that emphasize rigorous scientific observations over speculative modeling is an open question. Hopefully, there is some kind of permanent shift back toward research techniques that do not have their results decided before any data is captured. But in the event the Trump administration amounts to little more than a speed bump along the way to the installation of an international climate oligarchy, skeptics of climate alarmism ought to familiarize themselves with what has come to pass.

Al Gore and the State AGs Take Aim Against Industry

In an ostentatious display of moral vanity, former Vice President Al Gore joined with a coalition of seventeen state attorneys general gathered in New York in March 2016 to roll out an aggressive strategy for taking down the fossil fuel industry.

At their press conference, coalition members discussed what were essentially potential shakedown campaigns directed against energy companies. Then–New York Attorney General Eric T. Schneiderman, the coalition leader, suggested oil and gas companies were circulating misinformation about the climate that could be ripe for legal action.

"Our offices are seriously examining the potential of working together on high-impact, state-level initiatives, such as investigations into whether fossil fuel companies have misled investors about how climate change impacts their investments and business decisions," Schneiderman said.[103]

The coalition closely hewed to the climate-activist playbook in marketing itself to the public.

"As we all know, global warming, if not reversed, will be catastrophic for our planet," Vermont Attorney General William Sorrell said in a press release. "We, the states, have a role to play in this endeavor and intend to do our part."[104]

That role was not limited to just assaulting energy companies. A week or so after the New York press conference, Virgin Islands Attorney General Claude E. Walker, a coalition member, issued a subpoena against the Competitive Enterprise Institute, a free-market advocacy group based in Washington, DC, asking for "communications, emails, statements, drafts, and other documents" pertaining to CEI's work on climate change and energy policy. Walker also sought private donor information from CEI.

CEI, long known for its staunch advocacy of sound science and its skepticism of catastrophic climate-change narratives, fought back tenaciously. Sam Kazman, who served as a general counsel to CEI at the time, aptly described the subpoena as an "affront" to the First Amendment rights of free speech and freedom of association. He told the *Washington Times*: "If Walker and his allies succeed, the real victims will be all Americans, whose access to affordable energy will be hit by one costly regulation after another, while scientific and policy debates are wiped out one subpoena at a time."[105]

Fortunately, this particular instance of lawfare was short-lived.

The Virgin Islands' attorney general backed down sheepishly the following May after CEI waged an aggressive public campaign highlighting Walker's hostility to free speech rights. Walker withdrew his subpoena against CEI, as well as a separate but related subpoena against Exxon Mobil. He was the only independent among the seventeen attorneys general in the coalition; the rest were Democrats.

The coalition marketed itself as the "AGs United for Clean Energy." But Hans von Spakovsky, a legal analyst with the Heritage Foundation, punched through the propaganda and labeled Schneiderman and crew "AGs United to Silence Dissent." The coalition, von Spakovsky argued, was out to gut the free speech rights of climate skeptics.

Von Spakovsky drew a comparison between the AGs and another narrow-minded movement from a previous era. "The point is that these prosecutors, who have no expertise in science, are trying to treat one set of scientific views as absolute, infallible and above critique," Spakovsky wrote. "This has happened before—such as in Spain in 1478, when the Spanish Inquisition began systematically silencing any citizen who held religious, scientific, or moral views that conflicted with the 'truth' as seen by inquisitors. The AGs United for Clean Power are treating global warming theory the same way—like a religion whose blasphemers must be investigated and prosecuted."[106]

Senator Sheldon Whitehouse as the Ringleader

There's some history to this lawfare. One of the key players in the modern-day inquisition was US Senator Sheldon Whitehouse, a Democrat representing Rhode Island. Before opposing Trump's cabinet nominees in January 2025, Whitehouse popularized the strategy of using the Racketeer Influenced and Corrupt Organizations Act (RICO) to silence scientists and researchers who questioned theories of man-made global warming.

Congress had passed RICO in 1978 for the purpose of prosecuting mob crimes. But Whitehouse led efforts to morph RICO into a weapon against organizations, corporations, and scientists who are not convinced human activity is responsible for catastrophic climate change. He explained his legal rationale as follows: "In 2006, Judge Gladys Kessler of the U.S. District Court for the District of Columbia decided that the tobacco companies' fraudulent campaign amounted to a racketeering enterprise.... The parallels between what the tobacco industry did and what the fossil fuel industry is doing now are striking."[107]

The RICO effort reached its high-water mark on September 1, 2015, when twenty academics from across the country who specialize in climate change sent a letter to the Obama administration, asking it to pursue a federal racketeering investigation against "the fossil fuel industry and their supporters." They addressed the letter to President Barack Obama, Attorney General Loretta Lynch, and John Holdren, director of the Office of Science and Technology Policy.[108]

The "RICO 20," as the academics came to be known, argued that "corporations and other organizations…knowingly deceived the American people about the risks of climate change, as a means to forestall America's response to climate change." Many details about this and other elements of the campaign would never have been brought to light without the heavy lifting of Chris Horner, a master of the Freedom of Information Act. Horner obtained emails in his FOIA lawsuit against Virginia's George Mason University, demonstrating coordination between the academics and Senator Whitehouse, as well as green-group activists (some of whom discouraged the overreach). Horner, who was also an attorney at the time with the Competitive Enterprise Institute, had during that same period revealed how the state attorneys general were essentially taking stage direction from outside environmental activists. This work pulled loose critical details that helped spur congressional investigations.

George Mason was home to six of the academics who urged the Obama administration to prosecute individuals and organizations that resisted their climate agenda. The name at the top of the list of twenty belongs to Jagadish Shukla, a professor at George Mason University who specializes in atmospheric, oceanic, and earth studies.

In an October 2015 letter addressed to Shukla, Congressman Lamar Smith, Republican of Texas—then the chairman of the House Committee on Science, Space, and Technology—raised questions about how taxpayer funds were being used to finance a partisan, political agenda. He also issued subpoenas to the New

York and Massachusetts attorneys general and figures from eight environmental groups: the Union of Concerned Scientists, the Climate Accountability Institute, the Rockefeller Family Fund, the Rockefeller Brothers Fund, the Pawa Law Group, Greenpeace, the Climate Reality Project, and 350.org.[109]

The attorneys and the green groups all resisted the subpoenas, but there was no walking back the overt collusion among them, their taxpayer-funded institutions, and outside pressure groups, all advancing policies that would ultimately result in higher costs for those same taxpayers.

The Origins of the RICO Strategy

The RICO 20 credited Senator Whitehouse with proposing the use of the racketeering law against climate skeptics. But in reality, the seeds of this RICO strategy had originated three years before their letter was submitted, during a gathering of twenty-three left-wing trial lawyers, environmental activists, and academics.

Their meeting, held in June 2012 in the San Diego seaside neighborhood of La Jolla, was billed as a "Workshop on Climate Accountability, Public Opinion, and Legal Strategies." Its purpose was to devise a "strategy to fight industry in the courts" over climate change. Their specific targets were described as a "network of public relations firms and nonprofit front groups that have been actively sowing disinformation about global warming for years."

The workshop's significance to the climate-change movement can be gauged from its big-money donors, acknowledged on page two of the event's summary document: "This workshop was made possible by the V. Kann Rasmussen Foundation, the Mertz Gilmore Foundation, the Grantham Foundation for the

Protection of the Environment, and the Martin Johnson House at the Scripps Institution of Oceanography."

The Martin Johnson House, where the activists gathered, is an oceanfront cottage used by the Scripps Institution of Oceanography, a department of the University of California, San Diego. The assets of the three named foundations amount to more than half a billion dollars—$608.5 million—according to tax documents for 2013: $89.3 million for the Rasmussen Foundation; $125.1 million for the Gilmore Foundation; and $394.1 million for the Grantham Foundation. (This, of course, is just a small slice of what climate alarmists have at their disposal. They continuously pound away at "big oil," while a compliant media deflects attention away from their own vast resources and network.)

It was at the La Jolla gathering that the activists came up with the idea of using RICO against the fossil fuel industry. Richard Ayres, a Washington lawyer who is a cofounder and trustee of the Natural Resources Defense Council, first mentioned the RICO tactic as a possible weapon against fossil fuels, according to a thirty-six-page summary document of the meeting. Besides Ayres of NRDC, other workshop attendees included Peter Frumhoff, director of science and policy for the Union of Concerned Scientists, and Matthew Pawa, an environmental activist and trial lawyer who founded the Global Warming Legal Action Project.

In the workshop summary, "Establishing Accountability for Climate Change Damages," those attending acknowledged the precedent of the 1990s legal action against the tobacco industry, and they believed a similar legal strategy against fossil fuel companies "would present a number of different obstacles and opportunities." By opportunities, they meant litigation. The summary notes "widespread agreement among workshop participants" that some form of "cancer analog" for global warming, such as rising sea levels, had to be established.

Naomi Oreskes, a professor of the history of science at Harvard University, who played a key role in organizing the workshop, is quoted in the summary as saying: "When I talk to my students, I always say tobacco causes lung cancer, esophageal cancer, mouth cancer.... My question is: What is the 'cancer' of climate change that we need to focus on?"

The documents on tobacco litigation are collected in a searchable online repository called the Legacy Tobacco Documents Library. Workshop attendee Stanton Glantz, a professor of medicine and former director of the Center for Tobacco Control Research and Education at the University of California, San Francisco, runs the project.

In response to an email from the *Daily Signal* requesting comment, Glantz said he was "struck by the parallels" between the public relations tactics of the oil industry and the tobacco companies:

> The pattern of quietly financing public relations efforts and small "independent" groups of scientists in order to confuse the public about the overwhelming scientific evidence linking human activities—including energy consumption using Exxon Mobil—while privately using high-quality, accurate science that recognizes global warming to make internal business decisions is precisely the behavior pattern that got the tobacco companies into so much trouble for defrauding the public. The oil industry also uses a lot of the same individuals and organizations

as the tobacco industry. Such manipulation of science to defraud the public was a central element of the RICO case [against the tobacco industry].

That part about the "manipulation of science" deserves a hard look, because the RICO 20 have been caught engaging in some of the same practices they attempt to pin on others. (That's called "projection.") Moreover, contrary to what climate activists tell the public, the analogy between tobacco use and climate change does not hold. Theories linking human activity with rapidly accelerating dangerous levels of global warming are running up against fresh scientific observations.

Scientists Beyond Reach of Government Make a Stand

As mentioned earlier, hundreds of climate scientists from across the globe have contributed to reports of the Nongovernmental International Panel on Climate Change (NIPCC). Set up as an alternative to the IPCC, NIPCC calls itself an "international panel of nongovernment scientists and scholars, who have come together to present a comprehensive, authoritative, and realistic assessment of the science and economics of global warming." In contrast to the IPCC, NIPCC finds no consensus, no basis for predictions of future climate conditions, and no case for forcing a transition away from fossil fuels. The organization's reports demonstrate that an increasing number of scientists say natural variability, not human activity, is the primary driver of warming and cooling trends. In 2008, NIPCC joined with the Heartland Institute, a free-market think tank based in Illinois, to produce a report entitled *Nature, Not Human Activity, Rules the Climate*.

Bonner Cohen, a senior fellow at the National Center for Public Policy Research, told the *Daily Signal* that he sees vast differences between what occurred with the tobacco industry years ago and the scientific realities of climate change.

"The 1963 surgeon general's report linking cigarette smoking to a higher risk of lung cancer was a scientific finding, plain and simple, one which has withstood the test of time," Cohen said. However...

> Unlike "climate change," originally labeled "global warming," the surgeon general's report was never a part of a larger political agenda. From the moment man-made global warming was elevated to a problem requiring 'urgent' action at a well-orchestrated Senate hearing in 1988, the political class in the US and elsewhere has used the issue to increase its power and wealth.

Yet despite numerous international conferences, congressional hearings, untold billions of taxpayer dollars spent on climate "research," the blatant manipulation of data, and a vast PR campaign, alarmists have never succeeded in establishing a cause-and-effect relationship between man-made greenhouse gases and a warming of the planet.

Cohen continued:

> Such a relationship was established—and never seriously disputed—regarding the link between cigarette smoking and lung cancer. Alarmists have tacitly acknowledged this by claiming that the "science is settled on climate change." It isn't, and they know it, but they want to snuff out

all debate on the subject so we can get on to
the important business of eliminating fossil fuels
and replacing them with renewable energy. The
ultimate goal is to have a self-appointed man-
darin class of transnational bureaucrats dictate
how energy is to be rationed globally. This is a
far cry from warning people about the dangers
of smoking.

Four years after the 2012 meeting in La Jolla, Peter Frumhoff
delivered a presentation in New York to seven of the state attorneys general on the "imperative of taking action now on climate
change." The presentation was delivered just prior to their March
2016 press conference with Al Gore. That same morning, Pawa's
law office also briefed the attorneys general on climate-change
litigation.

This brings the history surrounding the RICO strategy somewhat full circle. But the money and organizational network
standing behind the La Jolla attendees, and their efforts to quell
dissent, remain active.

Exposing Big Green Inc.

Fortunately, Tom Pyle, president of the Institute for Energy
Research, is not letting them get away with it. IER operates
an online platform known as Big Green Inc., which tracks the
billions of dollars flowing out of left-leaning foundations into
the hands of various green pressure groups.[110] The funds support
aggressive climate litigation and the promotion of burdensome
anti-energy regulations. The La Jolla meeting figures into a larger

"Big Green" operation that helps explain how climate policies became so entrenched over the past few decades.

There is another added wrinkle to the RICO 20 affair.

Two groups devoted to openness and transparency in government sought to unravel the origins of the RICO strategy. The Energy and Environmental Legal Institute (E&E), based in Washington, DC, is devoted to "strategic litigation," "policy research," and "public education." The Free Market Environmental Law Clinic, based in Virginia, describes its mission as "to provide a counterweight to the litigious environmental movement that fosters an economically destructive regulatory scheme in the United States."

In July 2016, the two outfits took on Rhode Island Attorney General Peter Kilmartin with a FOIA suit, seeking information pertinent to the RICO strategy directed against opponents of President Obama's climate agenda. Apparently, the smallest state in the union had assumed an outsized role in efforts to corral climate realists. The two groups also filed a FOIA suit against Schneiderman's office.

They sought copies of correspondence from Gregory Schultz, a special assistant in the Rhode Island attorney general's office. Schultz was a person of interest in the suit, since he served as Kilmartin's representative in the preparations leading up to the press conference with Gore.

The central document at issue was the "Climate Change Conference Common Interest Agreement." Email records show Attorney General Kilmartin's representative signed it, in combination with the representatives of sixteen other state attorneys general. One of the emails Kilmartin's office begrudgingly released reveals that Schultz agreed to sign off on a draft version of the "common interest agreement" in April 2016.[111]

In the agreement, the state attorneys general said "they share common legal interests" in pursuing investigations in the name of climate change. They also agreed not to disclose certain information, prompting critics to label the document a "secrecy pact."[112] Kilmartin did not attend the meeting with Gore the previous month, but he did release a letter of support. Aside from its overt anti-free-speech impulses, what was most disturbing about the agreement was the effort made to neuter laws enabling the public to obtain government records.

Chris Horner, who was also an E&E legal fellow, saw the resistance to open records requests in Rhode Island fitting into a larger scheme. Kilmartin and other state attorneys general, Horner explained, were attempting to exempt themselves from open records laws. "They were giving themselves a 'Get Out of FOIA Free' card for discussions of certain subjects." If their effort had been successful, Horner warned, it could have enabled ideologically driven attorneys to create a privilege for what should be public records.

A spokesman for Schneiderman described the agreement as "routine" and dismissed critics as self-interested allies of the fossil fuel industry.[113] Still, the exposure from the FOIA litigation derailed the AG coalition's efforts to cloak their climate machinations from public scrutiny—at least temporarily. The self-appointed climate prosecutors who posed for pictures with Gore subtly but definitively stepped away from a campaign that had lost the moral high ground.

The RICO 20 affair helped answer some lingering questions. Why were academic and government figures so eager to silence scientific voices? Why did they work overtime to suppress mounds of evidence pointing to natural rather than human influences behind climate change?

83

Marc Morano, editor of the *Climate Depot* website, offers a cogent answer: "follow the money." Lurking behind the moral posturing over the supposed evils of America's carbon footprint is a financial racket.

Getting Rich Off Taxpayers in the Name of Climate

Let's begin with the RICO 20 ringleader, Jagadish Shukla, a George Mason University professor who heads up the university's Center for Ocean-Land-Atmospheric Studies. Ian Tuttle of *National Review* has accused Shukla of "getting rich" off climate-change research funding and "pocketing $5.6 million from taxpayers."[114]

If anything, that's an understatement.

That $5.6 million was funneled through the now-defunct Institute for Global Environment and Society (IGES), a non-profit outfit based in Rockville, Maryland, that listed Shukla as its founder and president. Apparently, the RICO 20 leader was "double-dipping" at taxpayer expense while leading the charge against climate skeptics who threatened his revenue streams.[115]

Since 2001, Shukla's IGES was the recipient of more than $63 million from US taxpayers, according to the *Washington Free Beacon*. The organization received 98 percent of its funding from taxpayers, with grants from the National Science Foundation, the National Oceanic and Atmospheric Administration, and the National Aeronautics and Space Administration. IGES has paid Shukla and his wife $5.6 million since 2001, according to his tax filings. His wife was listed as the business manager of the "nonprofit," and their daughter was assistant business manager and assistant to the president. That $5.6 million came in addition to Shukla's $314,000 annual salary from George Mason University.[116]

By double-dipping between his university salary and his nonprofit, critics say Shukla appears to have violated George Mason University's conflict-of-interest stipulations and rules that federal grant recipients who work for universities are expected to observe.

One of those critics is Steve McIntyre, a statistician noted for challenging the data and methodology used in UN climate reports, who also edits the *Climate Audit* blog. McIntyre provided a detailed analysis of Shukla's compensation and how it failed to square with university and government policies. As McIntyre points out, George Mason University, and the various federal agencies that funded Shukla, all supposedly have policies to prevent the kind of "double-dipping" that served to enable Shukla's RICO campaign.[117]

Just to be clear about what went down here: Taxpayer-funded college professors and researchers, who invoke climate change as a reason to impose costly regulations on those same taxpayers, also advocated against free speech rights and open scientific inquiry.

This was too much for former Congressman Lamar Smith, Republican of Texas, who served as chairman of the House Committee on Science, Space, and Technology. Smith sent letters to the inspector general of the National Science Foundation and to Shukla in the fall of 2015, listing his concerns.

"The committee's investigation has revealed serious concerns related to Dr. Shukla's management of taxpayer money," Smith wrote in his letter to the IG.[118] Smith made it clear that he thought an IG investigation was in order, since Shukla received tens of millions of dollars in taxpayer-funded grants to study climate change, in addition to his publicly funded salary. Smith cut right to the heart of what the climate movement is really about—money and political power.

"IGES appears to be almost fully funded by taxpayer money while simultaneously participating in partisan political activity by requesting a RICO investigation of companies and organizations that disagree with the Obama administration on climate change," Smith wrote.[119]

IGES played a prominent role in circulating the RICO letter to Obama administration officials. But as Smith noted in his letter, the IGES website was scrubbed of its participation in the RICO 20 campaign. On the plus side, the money trail remains open to scrutiny for posterity.

Five of Shukla's George Mason University colleagues also signed the RICO 20 letter, as did academics from the University of Washington, Rutgers University, the University of Maryland, Florida State University, the University of Texas at Austin, and Columbia University. All are publicly funded universities.

Thankfully, the times may be a-changin'. IGES supposedly closed in 2013. With Trump back in office, the assault against honest science has been put on hold. But the strategies and techniques used to silence dissent can be easily reactivated.

CHAPTER 6

Canadians Mull Carbon Tax Lessons as Trump Halts US Funding of Climate Activism

C limate pornography had dominated the conversation in the United States thanks to taxpayer-funded grants to universities...until Donald Trump entered the Oval Office in early 2025. Until then, taxpayers had been on the hook to fund research projects crafted for the purpose of raising energy costs by imposing climate regulations on those same taxpayers.

Not many in academia have been willing to speak out against this unsavory dynamic. But some did, and now perhaps just enough have.

Follow the money from grants for climate research beginning in the early 1990s, and the trail will lead you back to federal agencies that expect preordained results. From his office at Princeton University, Will Happer, the CO_2 Coalition founder, described the unfortunate dynamic that has been at work. Scientists in academia, Happer explained in his interview with

Freedom Research, have been put into a position where they must produce "politically correct research results" that are satisfactory to their government sponsors.[120]

"You have to maintain your family, so that means you need money," Happer said. "And the only way to get money is to agree to this alarmist meme that has dominated climate scientists now for several decades."[121] The large pool of government funding available for research that supports the idea that there is a climate emergency has had a corrupting influence, the Princeton physicist observes. Scientists who dissent are much less likely to be funded.

The Trump administration's early efforts to root out these twisted incentives sparked hysterical press coverage from the likes of CNN, the *Guardian*, the Associated Press, and *The New York Times*. It was a good indication the president was aiming his arrow in the right direction. The skewed coverage also offered up further proof that establishment media outlets are not inclined to report the news from the taxpayers' point of view.

In its April 2025 press release, the Department of Commerce detailed how the administration arrived at its decision to cut $4 million from Princeton University's climate research programs. The release made it clear that the federal government under Trump would no longer be in the business of funding climate alarmism. As the release explained, the cuts were made as a part of a larger effort to "right size" the government and save taxpayers millions of dollars.[122]

For the next several years at least, this means NOAA, which sits inside the Commerce Department, will no longer serve as a pipeline for climate fearmongering. The university's climate-modeling program came under particular criticism, much to the consternation of the press. Here is the key passage from the release:

> This cooperative agreement promotes exaggerated and implausible climate threats, contributing to a phenomenon known as "climate anxiety," which has increased significantly among America's youth. Its focus on alarming climate scenarios fosters fear rather than rational, balanced discussion. Additionally, the use of federal funds to support these narratives, including educational initiatives aimed at K-12 students, is misaligned with the administration's priorities. NOAA will no longer fund these initiatives.[123]

The *Guardian*'s report claims these statements were made without citing any evidence to show that climate modeling is flawed and unworthy of federal funding.[124] In fact, there is plenty of evidence to back up the department's concerns with the modeling process.

Kevin Dayaratna, the statistics expert at the Heritage Foundation, has warned that family incomes could take a severe hit and household electricity prices could jump dramatically if policymakers make faulty assumptions based on the "social cost of carbon (SCC)." After analyzing the Biden administration's updated modeling, Dayaratna determined that it could be used to sock it to American energy consumers.

Dayaratna is particularly critical of the Data-driven Spatial Climate Impact Model (DSCIM) the Biden team used to quantify the SCC. Because DSCIM is open to manipulation, Dayaratna warns, the modeling results could be used to justify heavy regulations on a wide range of everyday products such as cars, household lamps, and pool pump motors, to name just a few.[125] The Biden-era malfeasance is but the latest in a long line of statistical abuses where climate activism is concerned.

But reality is beginning to catch up with the wild prognostications. Happer pointed out the critical difference between actual scientific observations and models that proceed from false assumptions. The observational programs that include satellite measurements of Earth's radiation, cloudiness, and temperatures are of very high quality, in Happer's view. But the same is not true of climate models that received taxpayer funding—at least until recently.

"I don't think most computer models mean anything," Happer said. "It's a complete waste of money, but that's what's driving the public perception. So, the public is unable to look at model results, which are not alarming at all. But instead, what they see is graphic displays from computer computations which are not tied into observations. So, I think the money that's been spent on computers, and lots of it has been spent there, has been mostly wasted."

Defunding university programs designed to make the case for more government regulation of the private sector is an important piece of a larger strategy. The Trump administration has also begun to cut funding for the US Global Change Research Program (USGCRP), which produces the National Climate Assessment. It was President George H. W. Bush who signed the Global Change Research Act of 1990 into law, which calls for the administration to release the assessment every four years.

Although there was never any clear direction from lawmakers to suggest that the assessment be used to prop up alarmist theories, it has clearly moved in that direction. The next assessment is due by 2027, but at Trump's direction NASA has terminated its contract with ICF International, the consulting firm that convenes the USGCRP and coordinates with federal agencies to produce the report.[126]

A source familiar with the White House decision told the *Daily Wire* the ICF had become heavily biased.

"ICF has produced assessments riddled with worst-case scenarios, obfuscating the assumptions underlying dire predictions about what the planet will be like in 100 years," the administration source said. "The quality of the information is low, and the Administration is committed to basing decisions on realistic assumptions that comport with legal standards."[127]

A climate scientist who previously worked with the assessment, and who spoke on the condition of anonymity, said the ICF had been exerting "undue influence over the global change narrative and priorities presented by the federal government."

NASA's cancelation of the contract can be seen as another step in the direction of dismantling the "climate-industrial complex," along with overturning the endangerment finding and withdrawing from the Paris Agreement. The assault on the unelected administrative state in America has begun in earnest. Still, the power and influence the climate lobby has built up means there is a lot more waste to expose, unravel, and delete. And the situation is even a bit more dire in neighboring Canada, the United Kingdom, and the European Union.

Carbon Tax Lessons from Canada

Climate insanity reached its apex in Canada under former Prime Minister Justin Trudeau, who pulverized his constituents with carbon taxes that exceeded their monthly heating bills.

A member of the Liberal Party of Canada, Trudeau served as prime minister from 2015 until 2025. Mark Carney, the former head of the Bank of Canada and the Bank of England, who succeeded Trudeau as party leader and prime minister, was elected to a full term after prevailing in the April 2025 parliamentary election. But Trudeau's climate agenda still has Canadians reeling. Coming into office, Carney supposedly scrapped the carbon tax, but a carbon price on business remains in effect. Carney is also moving ahead with the Carbon Border Adjustment Mechanism, which is a carbon tax on imports. While the Trudeau-era climate plans might be hibernating, they are hardly dead and buried.

A carbon tax is best thought of as an artificial and arbitrary cost government officials impose upon any outfit involved with buying and selling energy sources that emit carbon dioxide and other greenhouse gases. The stated motivation is to force a corrective move in the energy market, where the supposed negative effects of carbon emissions on climate are not taken into account. By forcing energy consumers away from coal, oil, and natural gas, which supply about 80 percent of the energy used in the United States, the Canadian Left insists the problem of global warming can be abated.

A carbon tax is properly viewed as a tax on almost every human activity imaginable. Anyone who starts their car, gets gas, then drives to the supermarket to get cereal pays carbon taxes every step of the way. The policy goal is very much in line with the thinking of central planners, neo-Marxists, and anti-American globalists bent on puncturing holes in the capitalist system.

The usual drill is for climate activists in government to home in on an energy source early in the supply chain. That means oil refiners and coal plants get hit with the tax and then pass the cost along to the consumer. Since energy is the foundational component of modern life, carbon taxes inevitably raise the costs of any goods manufactured and consumed. The list of Canadians victimized by climate policies is voluminous.

Trudeau first implemented his carbon tax plan in 2019 with the initial carbon price set at $20 per metric ton of carbon dioxide. That was just the start. Trudeau's plans called for increasing the carbon price to $170 per metric ton by 2030. That translates into a 750 percent increase. The economic pain is coming fast and hard. In April 2024, the carbon price increased to $80 per metric ton of carbon dioxide.

An analysis of the Canadian carbon tax from the Institute for Energy Research showed it costing most residences more than $50 extra per month. IER seized upon several examples of Canadian citizens in various occupations and living conditions to demonstrate how damaging Trudeau's plan has been.[128] The owner of a relatively small mobile home equipped with a new furnace saw a December 2024 heating bill for gas of $20 with a carbon tax of $32. *Ouch!*

Up in Northern Ontario—where it gets frigid, to say the least, with temperatures that can drop to minus 20 degrees overnight—a young mother saw her household's December 2024 gas bill feature a $134 carbon tax charge. Revelers at local drinking holes don't get a break either. A pub in Peterborough, Ontario, had a natural gas bill with a carbon tax charge of $1,044.

Occasionally, a local official will push back on behalf of their constituents. In Saskatchewan, Premier Scott Moe declined to collect Ottawa's carbon tax on home heating, which costs anywhere from $50 to $80 per month for homeowners. IER also cites the example of a "working dad of twins" living in Edmonton Centre whose natural gas bill was saddled with a carbon tax of $136.[129] The father also had to pay an additional carbon tax on gasoline for his truck. As IER reports, "The carbon tax adds 17 cents per liter, and he uses 200 liters per week, totaling $34 a week extra, or $1,768 per year, to pay the tax."[130]

There is a rebate program known as the Climate Action Incentive Payment, set up as a tax-free direct payment to alleviate the carbon tax cost. It is aimed at mostly rural communities, with the rebate amount based on household size and income.[131] But the calculations from Canada's Parliamentary Budget Officer (PBO) do not seem very promising. The PBO estimates the carbon tax will cost the average Canadian household between $377 and $911 in fiscal year 2024–25, even when the rebate is taken into account.[132]

Looking ahead to 2030, the average net cost of the carbon tax for Canadian households will rise to $1,490 in Manitoba, $1,723 in Saskatchewan, $1,820 in Ontario, and $2,773 in Alberta. About 60 percent of the households in Alberta, Ontario, Saskatchewan, Newfoundland and Labrador, Nova Scotia, Prince Edward Island, and Manitoba will pay more in carbon taxes than what they received in rebates, according to a PBO report.[133]

Therefore, Canadians can expect to see their household incomes dwindle as heating costs go up along with the electricity needed to keep the lights on at night.

A growing movement organized through the Canadian Taxpayers Federation (CTF), a nonprofit advocacy group founded in 1990, is lighting a fire. With offices in Ottawa and six provinces, the CTF is bringing together citizen activists devoted to dismantling the carbon tax. The federation is committed to fighting government waste, profligate spending, and high taxation.

Kris Sims is the Alberta director for the CTF and knows full well how truckers who deliver goods and services across Canada are getting bulldozed. She estimates that truckers are paying

$200 extra in carbon taxes on diesel fuel to fill up their pickup trucks. That's on top of the sales taxes and other taxes.

Living just a few miles north of Montana, Sims finds that Trudeau's carbon tax costs the average Alberta household about $400 extra each winter. Despite all the taxes, Sims can't help but notice that Canada never reaches any of its publicly stated carbon-reduction goals.

"We're responsible for about 1.3 percent of global emissions," she told me in an interview. "If Canada ceased to exist from the face of the Earth, it would not make a dent in global emissions. This is all virtue-signaling."

Sims put her finger on the political motivations behind the carbon tax.

"If you can control people's energy use, and put them in a position of energy poverty, then you've got them by the neck, and that's the real purpose here. They don't give a darn about global emissions." An exercise in elitism is at work, Sims explained, since wealthy members of the political class and their benefactors can absorb extra costs at the gas pump while average working people cannot.

The other casualty, as Sims sees it, is genuine environmentalism and conservation, which have been usurped by climate extremism.

"As someone who grew up on Vancouver Island—that is so beautiful with rainforests, bears, and killer whales, you name it—the kicker is that with all this carbon reduction, climate-change hysteria has totally taken away from other elements of an environmental movement," Sims said. "We never hear about campaign efforts that say, 'go clean up your river,' or 'clean up a toxic waste dump.' I never see kids picking up litter. You never hear about it. But we do constantly hear about how we have to meet these carbon targets."

Now that political figures have been nailed with their own data showing that emissions keep going up, despite the imposition of carbon taxes and other climate measures, there is some tacit admission about what the goals really are.

"Now we see this fascinating shift where they say we are giving out rebates so poor people get more back than they pay in, and it's only the rich people who have to pay this," Sims observed. "So, they've turned it into a wealth-transfer narrative."

But it doesn't take much to put the lie to what the Canadian Left is telling its beleaguered taxpayers. Sims and crew have become quite adept at taking the government's figures and turning them back on whatever the carbon-tax narrative of the day is.

The PBO report release in October 2024 ought to be the death knell for carbon taxes in the post-Trudeau era. "The average household in each of the backstop provinces will see a net cost, paying more in the federal fuel charge and GST, as well as receiving lower incomes (due to the fuel charge), compared to the Canada Carbon Rebate they receive," according to the PBO.[134]

The Canadian Taxpayers Federation made the most of the dour news.

"Once again the PBO confirms the carbon tax costs average families hundreds of dollars more than they get back in rebates," Franco Terrazzano, CTF federal director, said in a press release. "This PBO report proves that politicians' favourite talking point is incorrect and it proves the carbon tax is making life harder for Canadians."[135]

The federation estimates the carbon tax will cost the average Canadian household up to $400 more in 2024 than the rebates. Apparently, it is not just high society that has to pony up for the carbon taxes. It's also important to keep in mind that the Canadian government charges its goods and services tax (GST) on top of the carbon tax. The PBO report shows that this multilayered system of taxation cost taxpayers about $400 million in 2024.[136]

Aside from the fact that the rebate is a mythical beast, there's another problem. It's expensive!

After reviewing government records, the federation determined that the cost of administering the carbon tax and the alleged rebate has risen to about $283 million since it was first imposed back in 2019. The bloated carbon-tax administration is not exactly on a downward trajectory. By 2030, those costs are expected to approach $800 million. Government records at the time also showed there were about 461 carbon-tax bureaucrats assigned with the job of administering the tax and the rebate.[137]

Terrazzano has the right perspective.

"It's magic math to believe the feds can raise taxes, skim hundreds-of-millions off the top to hire hundreds of new bureaucrats and then somehow make everyone better off with rebates," he said in a release.[138]

Remember how carbon taxes are essentially a tax on every human activity imaginable? Canadian truckers understand this better than anyone else. As Sims points out, everything people see in front of their eyes, like smartphones, clothing, and the shoes on their feet, is delivered in some way by trucks. There's a ripple effect. The additional costs of the carbon tax cannot be absorbed by industry, which means they are passed on to consumers.

The Canadian Trucking Alliance (CTA) estimates the carbon tax will cost the trucking industry about $2 billion in 2024. And the pain only becomes more acute over time. The CTA also estimates the carbon tax will cost truckers $4 billion annually come

2030, and by that time the carbon tax will have cost Canadian truckers a whopping $26 billion since it was put into place.[139]

There are also carbon-tax costs that come into the equation before any food is loaded onto trucks. Farmers know all about that, since the natural gas and propane they use to heat barns and dry out grain gets hit with a carbon tax. The PBO sees the carbon tax costing Canada's farmers $1 billion by 2030.[140]

There's no escape. Driving, eating, farming, and shopping all trigger carbon taxation.

The underlying agenda behind these climate policies is evident to anyone paying attention to the actions of government officials. Deidra Garyk, an energy policy consultant in Calgary, has twenty years of experience in the oil and gas industry. Garyk recalls seeing President Biden's motorcade moving through Ottawa back in 2023.

"I didn't see any EVs," she said. "Instead, it was a parade of SUVs using conventional oil and gas to get high-ranking government officials to where they are going. Clearly, politicians know their climate policies don't work in the real world. The whole agenda is really anti-capitalist and anti–free market. Whenever you see government officials flying off to one of their UN meetings, it's always in private jets. They obviously don't believe their own rhetoric."

Garyk understands the environmental, social, and governance (ESG) agenda that has taken hold in Canada and the United States, having worked in it for the last four years. ESG is essentially a classification system the Left uses to push a progressive agenda within private companies. Green activists have been primarily responsible for pushing ESG to the detriment of retirement savings and investments.

"Once again we see anti-capitalist and anti-development undertones folded inside the climate agenda," she said. "ESG has been very damaging to pensions across the country because of these bad green investments. ESG was sold to the public as this virtuous endeavor, but it's really about imposing a top-down approach that doesn't leave any room for the free market."

Canada's Warning for America

Canada should serve as a warning to America, Garyk said, since Canada has gone much farther down the road with ESG. But Garyk has identified an even bigger problem that should put US policymakers on high alert. There's more than just sound energy policy at stake. Climate activism also touches on questions of national security and national sovereignty, given its international reach. Whether it's ESG, carbon taxes, electric vehicle mandates, or some other climate scheme, there is clear evidence of foreign meddling that has given rise to harmful anti-capitalist policies.

"It's common knowledge that in the past few federal elections, Communist China has attempted to exert influence in Canada," she said. "There are some ongoing investigations that are finally getting some attention."

She cites the work of Sam Cooper, an investigative reporter who runs a Substack called *The Bureau*, and Andy Lee, an Alberta resident and former federal candidate who has tracked foreign interference on her radio program. A post from Cooper describes how a conservative candidate in Canada became the focus of Chinese electoral interference.[141] The candidate had to refrain from making public campaign appearances for a time in response to Chinese threats.

Lee has been doing her part on X, where she highlights the work of a Canadian special task force that has linked Chinese Communist Party officials with misinformation efforts aimed at Canadian voters.[142] Climate activists who work to shut down domestic energy production in the United States and Canada are doing the bidding of the regime in Beijing. Garyk suspects other countries could have their fingers in the pie too. She points to Russia and possibly Qatar and North Korea.

The goal is to make Western countries more reliant upon critical minerals that form the key components of renewable-energy platforms. It's not surprising, therefore, to find examples of climate activists either knowingly or unknowingly taking stage directions from China. And since Canada's Conservative Party candidates are more inclined to adopt a tougher stance against the Beijing regime, they tend to lose out when Chinese operatives burrow in.

The Canadian Security Intelligence Service has provided government officials with information detailing the extent of Chinese meddling. It's evident China interfered in the Canadian federal elections held in 2019 and 2021, when Trudeau's Liberal Party prevailed.[143] The Chinese efforts didn't necessarily alter the final outcome of either vote, but they did heavily support candidates with viewpoints that advanced the interests of the Beijing government.

Erin O'Toole, the leader of the Canadian Conservative Party in 2021, told members of the press that Chinese interference probably cost his party about nine seats.[144] No one willing to poke the Chinese Communist Party is immune. A lawmaker with Canada's left-leaning New Democrats discovered that once she'd taken a critical view of Beijing's Hong Kong policy, she was out of luck with swank invitations that were once forthcoming from the "politically influential ethnic Chinese Community."[145] Census figures from 2021 show there are about 1.7 million ethnic Chinese in Canada, which is almost 5 percent of the population.

Garyk, the Calgary-based energy consultant, continues to view Canada as an early warning sign for what might go down in America. The more Canada envelops itself in climate policies that curtail the use of reliable energy, she said, the more Canada plays into China's hands. Likewise with the United States.

Just a few weeks prior to his election in April 2025, Canadian Prime Minister Mark Carney made it clear he viewed China as a top threat in terms of electoral interference. He also expressed concern about China's presence in the Arctic and suggested countermeasures may be in order, though he did not specify what they would look like. But the only way for Carney to put his country on a stronger footing to confront China is by abandoning climate schemes that preclude Canada from making the most of its rich oil and gas deposits.

There is no area of national security that is not touched by climate activism in some way. There is a deliberate, orchestrated effort to restrict America's ability to project military and economic power, in a manner that benefits China and other top adversaries. That doesn't mean all climate activists are knowingly complicit in this effort. But they are complicit.

Thus, overreliance on climate models versus scientific observations can result in severe geopolitical setbacks. The steps Trump has taken to disrupt the corruptive influence of government funds in climate projects is encouraging. But there are other problems. Debbie Lesko, a former Republican member of Congress representing Arizona, has called attention to the problem of "rogue lawsuits as a national security risk."[146] She makes a compelling argument in favor of cutting off federal funds for states that pursue climate lawsuits against US energy companies.

Climate Lawsuits as "Political Theater"

Lesko credits Trump for instructing his Justice Department to take stock of state and local laws, policies, and legal actions that disrupt domestic energy development. While serving on the Energy, Climate, and Grid Security Subcommittee in Congress, she saw firsthand how abusive legal practices, done under the guise of "ESG" or "environmental justice," put American families, and the country as a whole, in a compromised position.

Now is a good time ask: Who benefits from the lawsuits, and who might be steering and directing them from locations overseas? Lesko recommends Trump cut infrastructure and energy funding to states that continuously sue US energy companies.

"These lawsuits are political theater," Lesko argues. "They're not about justice but about forcing a radical left-wing environmental agenda on the rest of the country through the courts, bypassing the checks and balances that make our constitutional system work."[147]

There's political theater for sure. But to the extent these suits are successful, they are also creating gaping holes in US national security.

CHAPTER 7

How Climate Change Policies Undermine US National Security and Boost Foreign Adversaries

I n the eyes of former NASA engineers, scientists, and astronauts spanning several generations, unvalidated climate models are a threat to US national security. Over the past few years, they have expressed concern that the US Defense Department has been establishing the wrong priorities, while China races ahead with a massive military buildup—the climate notwithstanding.

The Right Climate Stuff organization was established in large part to nudge policymakers back in the direction of the scientific honesty that had marked the Apollo era. Unfortunately, Trump's first term turned out to be little more than a slight delay on the way toward a "greening of the US military," a policy set in motion under Obama and reestablished under Biden.

The late Hal Doiron helped develop the Apollo Lunar Module's landing dynamics software during NASA's moon missions. While speaking on behalf of the Right Climate Stuff during a 2017 conference in Houston, Texas, Doiron went into some detail about the policy implications of climate alarmism and the "propaganda" lurking behind unsubstantiated climate models.[148]

The sixteen-year NASA veteran defined unvalidated climate models as those that do not agree with physical data. Public policy and military planning, he insisted, should be based only on models validated by physical data.[149] For example, he criticized the US Navy for "preparing for something that is unreasonable and would cost too much money," in the form of "extreme sea-level rise," which has not been borne out by rigorous scientific study.

The scientific method requires that any hypothesis be confirmed by physical data, Doiron explained. Unfortunately, climate activists who hold sway over policymakers are putting things into computer models that are not backed up by physical observations.[150]

"At NASA, we have a policy," Doiron told the audience. "You can't make a design decision on a spacecraft or rocket that is not validated. You don't make critical decisions based on 'garbage in, garbage out.' Yet our government has been doing that with respect to climate alarm, because too many academics in universities are writing papers, drawing conclusions from models that don't agree with physical data."[151]

The Right Climate Stuff has produced its own "rigorous, earth surface temperature model using conservation-of-energy principles" that operates similarly to the way the surface and internal temperature of a spacecraft is analyzed, according to information found on the group's website.

Doiron called for US policymakers to establish official data on two key metrics: "the true sensitivity of surface temperature to greenhouse gases" and a "reasonable projection of greenhouse emissions and [the] concentrations rise in our atmosphere." He also developed "a new metric" called "transient climate sensitivity," which measures how much warming can be seen with a doubling of carbon dioxide in the atmosphere in the "way that it's actually happening," based on a "very small amount of carbon dioxide." The advantage from a policy perspective is that Doiron's "new metric" is something that can be measured and verified against physical data.

The bottom line, Doiron informed audience members, is that when unvalidated models are juxtaposed against validated models based on physical evidence, the validated models predict much less global warming.

The conclusions of the Right Climate Stuff, based on empirical data, are neatly summarized on its website as follows:

> The warming of the atmosphere caused by increased amounts of CO_2 are small and insignificant, only about one degree centigrade for this century. Our further studies showed that the claims of climate change causing more frequent and more severe hurricanes, tornadoes, droughts, floods, sea level rise, forest fires, etc. are false. The actual measured data shows no increase in any of these serious conditions. Our conclusion is simple: Mother Nature is controlling the climate; CO_2 emissions are not. And more CO_2 is definitely beneficial to Mother Nature's work. There is valid proof of significant greening of the earth since the beginning of fossil fuel use.[152]

In Trump administration 2.0, there's an opportunity to make a clean break from the faulty premise that anthropogenic CO_2 emissions are tied in with catastrophic levels of global warming. The opportunity costs of time and resources spent on scientifically unsound projections about sea levels and global temperature plays into the hands of hostile foreign actors.

Some energy policy analysts have suggested that it might be time to junk climate models altogether. Steve Goreham, author of *Green Breakdown: The Coming Renewable Energy Failure*, makes a strong case. He notes there are more than forty climate models worldwide, with thirteen of the most prominent models located in the United States. The National Aeronautics and Space Administration in New York City; the National Oceanic and Atmospheric Administration in Princeton, New Jersey; and the Department of Energy in Boulder, Colorado; are charged with operating the US models. With budget cuts in motion under Trump, Goreham is calling on NASA "to stick to space exploration" and for NOAA "to stick to weather forecasting."[153]

There's a special urgency in having these agencies and others return to their core mission. Proposals aimed at restricting US carbon dioxide emissions that take inspiration from climate models have national security implications that are every bit as severe as the economic implications.

From Kyoto to Paris

International treaties such as the UN Paris Climate Agreement would greatly diminish US military readiness if they were strictly enforced. With a compliant US administration in place under President Biden, the Paris Agreement provided Communist China the ability to double down on its use of fossil fuels.

President Xi Jinping had initially pledged to reduce carbon emissions by 2030 at the latest. But in true communist form, Xi only feigned his willingness to comply with the Paris Agreement. It's now evident that since its inception, the Paris Agreement was all about constraining and restricting America's military and economic might. Xi stopped pretending back in July 2023, when he made it clear China would continue to cut its own path without yielding to outside parties. Xi's comments coincided with a visit from former Secretary of State John Kerry, who was serving as Biden's climate envoy at the time. Secretary of State Antony Blinken was also in town.[154] Interestingly, Xi became more emboldened in his anti-American policies the more he heard from Team Biden.

The Paris Climate Agreement emerged from a 2015 UN climate meeting in Paris, France. Under the agreement, participating countries pledged to reduce their carbon dioxide emissions through "intended nationally determined contributions," or INDCs, for the ostensible purpose of reducing "global warming."

But under close examination, the climate rationale does not wash. The late Fred Singer, an atmospheric and space physicist, unpackaged the economic motivations behind the Paris Agreement in an updated version of his book exploring the science and politics of climate change.

"The accord is mainly about money transfers and virtue signaling, designed to provide a legacy for Obama," Singer wrote. "Although it talks bravely about keeping global warming below 2 degrees Celsius, it never explains how to define and measure this (alleged) 'critical threshold.' It is simply a scheme for redistributing money from Western nations to developing countries, funding the IPCC and other UN bureaucracies, and *possibly* reducing emissions of GHGs [greenhouse gases]. The current plan is to revisit and attempt to tighten national commitments every five years."[155]

The Paris Agreement is about further burdening the American taxpayer with wealth transfers to third world nations. More insidiously, it is also about diminishing America's geopolitical position to the benefit of China.

Given the latitude the UN treaty gave participating countries to set their own goals, the Obama administration committed America to reducing its greenhouse gas emissions by 26 percent to 28 percent in the first ten years after the pact went into effect in 2016. Even if the United States were to somehow rid itself of all fossil fuels, the impact on the climate would be negligible, according to research done by Kevin Dayaratna, the chief statistician of the Heritage Foundation.[156] Obama's plan would only make a difference of two-tenths of one degree Celsius by 2100, Dayaratna explained in his correspondence with the EPA. This is all pain and no gain, but for what end and to what purpose?

Viewed through the lens of an "America Last" policy agenda, the climate initiatives begun under Obama and continued under Biden suddenly make sense. The United States has more combined coal, oil, and natural gas resources than any other nation in the world. America's dominance in the energy sector enables it to project military power in a manner that other countries cannot. China, on the other hand, has an effective monopoly over the processing of rare earth minerals that are needed to produce wind and solar power equipment.

By design, the Paris Treaty would compel America to abandon fossil fuel resources it has in abundance, in favor of rare earth minerals where China is dominant. America Last policies—rooted in a desire to shift the United States and other global economies away from American-dominant energy sources toward China-dominant energy sources—would pose significant threats to America's security and international influence, for obvious reasons.

As has already been discussed, the modest levels of global warming that have transpired in recent decades are not likely to result in any catastrophic upheavals. In fact, the recent warming trend will probably lead to environmental benefits. That's a major thesis of the CO_2 Coalition members, who see a "greening of the planet" at work that can be advantageous to the most vulnerable populations. That's not a finding the climate activists want out in circulation. As Gregory Wrightstone, the coalition's executive director, has often observed, "There's a lot of people who make a lot of money on the backs of the false notion of a pending climate crisis."[157]

A peer-reviewed study published in the scientific journal *Global Ecology and Conservation* concludes that Earth's "greening," resulting from increased CO_2 emissions, is an "indisputable fact." The heightened CO_2 levels have served as fertilizer of sorts for agriculture and plant life, which in turn benefits animal life.[158] Leaving aside for a moment how little or how much human CO_2 might contribute to global warming, the study blows a hole in the idea that humanity is a blight on the planet.

The Paris Climate Agreement, which is a treaty that should have been subject to US Senate approval right from the beginning, offers an ideal window into how climate policies threaten US national security, sovereignty, and economic prowess. A careful reading of the agreement's provisions shows that it provides ample latitude for belligerent foreign actors like China to deploy reliable energy sources while restricting US emissions. While the agreement does not include penalties for noncompliance, it provides leeway for globalists sitting in US positions of power to follow the UN's lead. But this can only happen if the president can find a way to circumvent Congress.

Barack Obama did. A little history is in order.

It was President George H. W. Bush who brought the United States into the UN Framework Convention on Climate Change (FCCC) during the 1992 Earth Summit held in Rio de Janeiro. The framework rests on the assumption that human CO_2 emissions are responsible for dangerous levels of global warming. Beginning in 1995, the countries that ratified the FCCC began convening as a Conference of the Parties, or COP, with the most recent meeting, COP30 being held in Belem, Brazil, November 2025 Rucker, the CFACT president, was in attendance as was California Governor Gavin Newsom who took the opportunity to take shots at President Trump. "Newsom seems to be the new rock star now for the UN climate meetings," Rucker told me. "He's displaced former Vice President Al Gore and Greta Thunberg." (For those who haven't been following, Thunberg is the twentysomething Swedish activist who has become a media darling over her high-profile climate protests.) Trump decided against sending a formal US delegation to COP30, leaving it to Rucker and crew to carry the mantle for climate realism. It would seem the COP meetings have passed their high-water mark in terms of influence and media attention.

The Paris Agreement emerged in December 2021 from COP21, making it arguably the most consequential of all the UN climate conferences. The agreement is a successor to the Kyoto Protocol, an international "cap and trade" treaty that was adopted in Kyoto, Japan, in December 1997. But that previous July, the US Senate, in a 95–0 vote, had passed a resolution against adopting the protocol or any other similar agreement. President Bill Clinton supported the protocol and signed off on it in November 1998. But knowing the climate treaty would not be ratified, Clinton never submitted it to the Senate. In 2001, President George W. Bush, to his ever-lasting credit, withdrew the United States from the Kyoto Protocol altogether.[159]

The globalists learned their lesson. After losing out with the Kyoto climate accord, Paris Agreement proponents were determined to circumvent the US Senate.

Barack Obama was only too willing to oblige.

Like its predecessors, the Paris Agreement operates under the auspices of the UN Framework Convention on Climate Change. The agreement's stated goal "is to strengthen the global response to the threat of climate change by keeping a global temperature rise this century well below 2 degrees Celsius above pre-industrial levels and to pursue efforts to limit the temperature increase even further to 1.5 degrees Celsius."[160] In eager compliance, the Obama administration pledged to "achieve an economy-wide target of reducing its greenhouse gas emissions by 26–28 per cent below its 2005 level in 2025 and to make best efforts to reduce its emissions by 28%."[161] But Team Obama was careful never to use the word "treaty" or "protocol" in its description of the Paris Agreement, in order to make an end run around the Constitution's senatorial ratification process for treaty-making.

At the time Obama adopted the Paris Agreement, Marlo Lewis, an energy policy analyst with the Competitive Enterprise Institute, made a compelling case that it was, in fact, a treaty requiring ratification under Article 2, Section 2 of the US Constitution.

Obama claimed the Paris Agreement was not a treaty, in part because its emissions-reduction commitments were non-binding. But, as Lewis observed in a report for CEI, this doesn't square with what went down at the UN, going back to the Rio

Summit. Emissions-reduction commitments made under the Senate-ratified UN framework agreement are also nonbinding. Yet participants widely recognized the framework as an international treaty.

"Far from being toothless, the Paris Agreement is the framework for a multi-decade global campaign of political pressure directed chiefly against Republican leaders, Red State voters, and the fossil fuel industry," Lewis wrote.

Calling the beast by its name—a treaty—the CEI scholar went on to identify three major goals of the Paris Treaty that should alarm proponents of American independence and sovereignty. Paris was designed, Lewis argued, to (1) discourage future presidents and Congresses from overturning the EPA's Obama-era "Clean Power Plan" and any future climate regulations, (2) apply pressure on US policymakers to continuously uptick commitments to CO_2 reductions, and (3) shift US energy and climate policy authority out of Congress and into the hands of unaccountable international bureaucrats.[162]

The Paris Treaty also had a mechanism in place to transfer $100 million from richer nations to "development," on an annual basis from 2020 to 2025. This was necessary, UN officials said, to help developing countries allay the costs associated with the international community's planned transition to energy sources that generate fewer emissions.[163]

In the first Trump administration, State Department officials persuaded the president to follow UN provisions while withdrawing from the treaty. The UN stipulated that a country could give notice of withdrawal three years after the agreement had taken hold. The United States had entered the agreement on November 4, 2016; Trump, therefore, gave notice on November 4, 2019. But by following UN guidelines, the withdrawal process took another year, making the real withdrawal date November 4, 2020, the day after the 2020 presidential election. America's separation from the Paris Treaty proved to be all too temporary, with Biden reinserting the United States into the agreement shortly after taking office in January 2021.

Fortunately, the Paris Treaty now can be spoken of in the past tense, since in his second term Trump moved quickly and decisively to withdraw from the Paris Agreement once again. But he did so in a more permanent manner without sticking so rigidly to UN bureaucratic protocols.

On his first day back in office in January 2025, Trump signed an executive order putting the UN on notice that the United States would be leaving the climate agreement, which he correctly views as an unfair, expensive burden on the American people. It will only take about a year for the withdrawal to become official. That's a much better deal than what happened previously. Trump's January 2025 executive order said the decision to withdraw would be "effective immediately."[164] The EO also had the added benefit of revoking any financial commitments under the UNFCCC.

But for climate activists, pending climate catastrophes do not lend themselves to democratic debate and deliberation. American constitutional government must be suspended, businesses shuttered, industries stalled, conventional vehicles immobilized, and those devilish CO_2 emissions curtailed, no matter what the cost. Whether it's "cap and trade" plans designed to reduce emissions or carbon tax schemes aimed at discouraging fossil fuel consumption, the climate emergency calls for instantaneous measures.

No doubt there are climate activists genuinely devoted to the idea that humanity is a cancer on the planet. But Freedom of Information Act litigation filed against the Obama State

Department in 2018 showed that at least some of them are also taking stage direction from foreign actors who are not exactly conservationists.

China's Role in Climate Activism

Which brings us back to the national security threat posed by such climate activism.

In a revealing chain of communications obtained through FOIA, climate activists with close ties to China were operating in an advisory capacity to Obama administration officials eager to bypass the US Senate. The FOIA results are instructive because the groups in question denied operating as foreign agents during congressional investigations.

The Institute for Energy Research burrowed into the actions of these environmental advocacy groups as part of its FOIA litigation. Email correspondence uncovered by IER shows the World Resources Institute and the Natural Resources Defense Council—environmental organizations closely tied to the Chinese government—were advising Obama State Department officials on climate-change policy. The Paris Agreement figured prominently in the correspondence between these Obama administration officials and the groups. Energy policy analysts and attorneys who have reviewed the FOIA records found a concerted effort to avoid describing the Paris Agreement as a treaty so the Obama administration could take unilateral action without obtaining Senate approval.

Tom Pyle, president of IER, summarizes their findings. "No less than a communist government effectively made use of pliable climate activists with close ties to the Obama administration to circumvent the US Senate's 'advise and consent' responsibilities and authority," he said. "As one of the most ecological destructive regimes on the planet, China does not exactly place a premium on the climate goals of Paris. But it does see geopolitical value in hampering US economic and military might via UN climate agreements."

The Natural Resources Defense Council, a well-endowed, New York–based environmental group, is one of several outfits that stands out in a series of email exchanges. Jake Schmidt, the NRDC's director of international programs, exchanged several messages with Obama State Department officials, including one Todd Stern, a special envoy for climate change at the time of correspondence in 2014 and 2015. Several messages are heavily redacted in the FOIA records, making it difficult to flush out key details.

But Chris Horner—an attorney for Government Accountability and Oversight, a nonprofit public interest law firm that filed the FOIA suit on behalf of IER—finds there is enough information to show that the NRDC had a hand in formulating the Obama administration's approach to the Paris Agreement.

"Paris is a treaty according to all historical and commonsense considerations," Horner says. "Pretending otherwise satisfies a publicly stated priority of the French hosts of the Paris talks, of the Obama White House and the Obama State Department, and of the NRDC, which emails suggest was the State Department's adviser on this issue."[165]

Of particular interest to Horner is the Circular 175 memo[166] that the Obama State Department used to enter into the Paris Agreement. This type of document outlines the legal process that department officials use prior to an administration's decision to join an international agreement or treaty. The memo is typically used as an action item by bureaus within the State Department to request authority from department leaders to "negotiate, conclude, amend, extend or terminate an international agreement."

As Horner observes, "Whatever the memo said about the Paris Agreement, it reflected NRDC's role and input and served as the justification for the Obama claim that an obvious treaty—adopted by all of our supposed models under their procedures for treaties, as opposed to agreements—was actually *not* a treaty, for US purposes."

Because the NRDC is lawyered up, it is adept at sidestepping FOIA requests, which would help to explain why so many of the documents IER requested in this case were so heavily redacted. But there's another outfit that was not quite as careful in how it handled its foreign relationships and its interactions with the Obama State Department, which were overt to say the least.

Enter the World Resources Institute, a Washington, DC–based nonprofit devoted to curtailing greenhouse gas emissions and promoting sustainable development.

The FOIA lawsuit IER filed in August 2018 sought records pertaining to Jennifer Morgan, once a global director for WRI's climate program. A press release from IER describes her as a "green group lobbyist" with close ties to China's National Center for Climate Change Strategy and International Cooperation.[167]

"Public records indicate the Obama State Department leapt to assist WRI's effort to aid the Chinese government even after being told precisely what the group had been asked to do and for whom," the release said. "The requested records would shed further light on what that help constituted, and what role Ms. Morgan and WRI played on behalf of China's government relevant to U.S. policy."[168]

The FOIA records point to a coordinated approach to climate-change policy in which Morgan, by her own acknowledgment, operated at the behest and encouragement of Chinese officials. An email dated April 15, 2015, from Morgan to Todd Stern, the State Department's special envoy for climate change, and Clare Sierawski, chief of staff in the office of special envoy for climate change, demonstrates how China turned climate activists into willing accomplices.

In her message, Morgan describes how she was "approached" by a Chinese government entity to "pursue a dialogue" that would bring American and Chinese officials together.

"We think the interest stems from Chinese recognition that this Administration is coming to an end soonish and their desire to open up channels in DC that are additional to the ones that are working well now," she wrote. "As you will see, they are also interested in long-term ideas that one could imagine being discussed with the next Administration (depending of course who it might be)."[169]

Morgan even names some of the Chinese officials who could be in on the conversations.

Morgan also tells State Department officials that her Chinese contacts were looking for an opening to "share ideas around the Paris Agreement" and to recruit think tanks in the United States for the purpose of examining what "different approaches or packages could look like for Paris."

The interlocking relationships are difficult to overstate. After leaving the State Department, Stern went on to serve as a distinguished fellow with the WRI.

It's evident China has an interest in seeing US fossil-fuel energy production curtailed through international agreements and is seeking American partners willing to do their bidding. WRI and NRDC were among several partners working to coerce the

United States into joining a climate treaty China never had any intention of observing.

Uneven Enforcement of the FARA Law

The Foreign Agents Registration Act dating back to 1938 had become an anachronism until the Department of Justice began to invoke the law against the Trump campaign and administration officials. Whatever the merits of FARA, it was only par for the course when two Republican congressmen—Rob Bishop, former chairman of the House Committee on Natural Resources, and Bruce Westerman, then-chairman of the Subcommittee on Oversight and Investigations—began sending letters to green advocacy groups inquiring about their compliance with FARA.

The letters were sent to the NRDC, WRI, the Center for Biological Diversity, and Earthjustice. Thus far, only Earthjustice has agreed to register under FARA, which it did back in September 2019. The letters raised similar questions and used similar language.

The NRDC's involvement in China spans two decades and represents a significant investment of time and resources. Their leaders regularly meet with senior Chinese and Communist Party officials, and their ability to work in China is dependent on the goodwill of the Chinese government. In their first letter to the NRDC president,[170] dated June 5, 2018, the congressmen detailed legal actions and advocacy campaigns the group had undertaken that may not have been in compliance with FARA. The letter noted that Chinese officials "work to control environmental information and news stories in an effort to counter the country's status as the world's largest polluter." The "severe pollution" tied to China's state-owned companies motivated government and Communist Party officials to "cultivate an image" that contradicted the reality of China's environmental record. The congressmen expressed concern about the NRDC's role in aiding China's PR efforts regarding pollution control and its international standing on environmental issues, in ways that might be detrimental to the United States.

More importantly, the NRDC's relationship with China has many of the criteria identified by US intelligence agencies and law enforcement as putting an entity at risk of being influenced or coerced by foreign interests. The letter pointed out that "the NRDC appears to practice self-censorship" and "generally refrains from criticizing Chinese officials." Regarding the Paris Agreement, the group "sought to shape public opinion" by working to "discredit those skeptical of China's commitment to pollution reduction targets." Similarly, the NRDC had never criticized or even mentioned China's "illegal and environmentally destructive island reclamation campaign.... Of note, the NRDC collaborates with Chinese government entities" working to "assert authority over the South China Sea in contravention of international law."

The House Republicans also highlighted NRDC litigation aimed at constraining US Navy exercises. The group filed several suits under the National Environmental Policy Act claiming US Navy sonar and anti-submarine drills are harmful to marine life. One case, which the navy ultimately won, went all the to the US Supreme Court.[171]

"We are unaware of the NRDC having made similar efforts to curtail naval exercises by Chinese People's Liberation Army Navy," Bishop and Westerman noted pointedly.

They concluded their letter by asking for the NRDC to provide documentation showing that it is registered under FARA or to explain why it is not. The NRDC settled on a strategy of explaining away its relationship with China, which worked under Obama and Biden.

But the past investigations by Bishop, Westerman, and others have opened the door for Trump's DOJ to begin its own probe into nonprofit advocacy groups that do the bidding of belligerent foreign adversaries. That's right in the wheelhouse of Attorney General Pam Bondi and anyone charged with enforcement of FARA. But it's just one small part of the profound policy shifts that the Trump team needs to set in motion.

Energy and National Security

The Heartland Institute released an eye-popping policy brief just prior to the COVID-19 pandemic. By becoming an energy powerhouse, the institute explains, the United States was able to build a powerful military. But the two cannot be separated.

"Proposals to restrict U.S. carbon dioxide emissions and impose expensive, jobs-killing energy sources on the economy present a clear and present danger to military strength," the brief says. "This is especially true because the Paris Climate Agreement and other international climate agreements target Western-style democracies and impose no similar carbon dioxide restrictions on many potentially hostile nations."[172]

The imposition of carbon dioxide restrictions on the US economy would undermine American military preparedness, Heartland argues. By doubling down on domestic energy production and freeing itself from international climate agreements that give a free pass to China, the United States will be better positioned to handle a range of national security challenges.

Ken Stiles, a former CIA analyst now in academia, is constantly looking at unconventional, devious methods China and Russia could use to exploit American infrastructure. As compelling as the economic and environmental arguments may be against offshore wind, there's a national-security component that should garner more attention. He explained why in an interview.

"The US Navy has good reason to be concerned with offshore wind because there could be interference with navy sonars," Stiles said. "Imagine a scenario where China and Russia could park their submarines in the seabed right outside the Chesapeake Bay because our sonars cannot operate as they should."[173]

Let's not forget that offshore wind turbines are becoming more reliant all the time on components and technology from China. So, there's more than just conjecture at work here. Apparently, a US Navy report going back to the Obama administration details how harmful offshore wind is to military exercises and national security. Among the groups trying to bring the report to light is the Virginia Energy Consumers Trust, a relatively new outfit committed to reliable, affordable, and secure energy for all Virginia consumers.

"Having a black-and-white report from the navy out there about the national security problems with offshore wind could help to reshape the whole debate," said Stiles, who is also a member of the new Virginia group.

As it is, information already publicly available highlights the navy's objections to offshore wind near the Norfolk Navy Base in Virginia. But that might be just a small part of a larger problem. I asked Stiles what exactly put him on to the potential connection between wind power and nefarious foreign operations. He reminded me about the Chinese balloon the Biden administration had let float across the country before it was shot down.

"The surveillance balloon is soaking up information as it's passing over cell towers, and it could be downloading information to those cell towers," Stiles observed. "It's a cheap, economical way of doing this kind of surveillance, and some of the cell phone towers are Chinese made. They don't need some kind of expensive spy satellite; instead, they can just use what's already there."

Further intrigued, I again asked my CIA friend what exactly led him to consider this new methodology of Chinese espionage, done on the cheap.

His answer: "That's how I would do it."

Okay, then.

There are points of vulnerability attached to wind farms that deserve urgent attention. The US Navy especially has been expressing these concerns. Fortunately, there finally seems to have been an awakening at the federal level. In August 2025, Trump's Commerce Department announced it was beginning a national security probe into the imports of wind turbines and their various components. Not a lot of details have been released. But we know the administration activated the probe under Section 232 of the Trade Expansion Act, which is designed to weigh the national-security implications of imports. That's an encouraging sign but not enough by itself to reverse what has already been implemented.

Even during the Biden years, the Defense Department released maps highlighting its concerns about offshore wind. The department identified four large sections of water off the coasts of Maryland, Delaware, Virginia, and North Carolina as "highly problematic" for locating wind farms.[174] The military was particularly concerned about the impact the wind farms would have on its Dare County bomb-testing range in North Carolina,

Naval Weapons Station Yorktown in Virginia, the Oceana Naval Air Station in Virginia Beach, and the Norfolk Naval Shipyard, also in Virginia.[175]

The US Navy and the Air Force both objected to planned wind projects off the North Carolina coast. The Bureau of Ocean Energy Management (BOEM) eventually removed the lease for the projects, once it became clear they would interfere with military exercises.[176] But the national security fallout from off-shore wind remains a problem in Virginia and in other parts of the country.

It was some time back in 2017 that the US Navy went into great detail about the problems offshore wind poses to military readiness. Apparently, BOEM has its own version of this report. The next step for opponents of these projects is to FOIA both the navy and BOEM for these documents, but that will almost certainly be a lengthy process. The reports potentially include enough bombshells to completely uproot offshore wind for reasons of national security.

But until they are released, there still is ample fodder to keep up the pressure against green schemes that make no sense economically or environmentally, while also creating avenues foreign powers can exploit. Much of that intrigue is taking place at the state level.

In Virginia, former Democrat Governor Ralph Northam initially attempted to bypass his General Assembly to impose carbon taxes by having his state join the Regional Greenhouse Gas Initiative, a multistate climate pact widely known as RGGI. Opponents correctly argued that only the legislature has the constitutional power to impose taxes. But after Northam's Democrat Party took over the General Assembly those arguments became moot, and Northam had Virginia join RGGI with approval from the state Senate and House of Delegates in 2020. There's been quite a back and forth here as Republican Governor Glenn Youngkin withdrew Virginia from RGGI in 2023 after describing the program as a "regressive tax on families and businesses."[177] A circuit court judge ruled in November 2024 that Youngkin's actions were unlawful. But the state has remained outside RGGI pending Youngkin's appeal of that ruling. This could all change now that Democrat Abigail Spanberger has become Virginia's new governor.

But the most critical state here may turn out to be Pennsylvania, home to the Marcellus Shale, a geological formation of sedimentary rock filled with oil and gas deposits that can be accessed through an innovative drilling technique known as hydraulic fracturing, or fracking. The Marcellus Shale cuts across a large portion of western Pennsylvania along with parts of New York, Ohio, and West Virginia.

In similar fashion to Northam in Virginia, Governor Tom Wolf, a Democrat, attempted to bypass the Pennsylvania General Assembly and join RGGI with executive actions beginning in 2019. But Wolf ran into a buzzsaw of legal action. In 2022, the Commonwealth Court ruled that Wolf's executive actions on RGGI resulted in an unconstitutional tax and illegally bypassed the legislature's constitutional role to levy taxes.[178] Wolf's successor, Governor Josh Shapiro, a particularly slick Democrat who postures as a moderate, expressed skepticism toward RGGI on the campaign trail. But he had no problem appealing the Commonwealth Court's ruling to the Pennsylvania Supreme Court. Although Pennsylvania is technically part of RGGI, it is not participating in any auctions pending the outcome of the litigation. In the meantime, Shapiro has been pursuing his own statewide climate initiatives. The governor's Climate Emissions

Reduction Act (PACER) and his Pennsylvania Reliable Energy Sustainability Standard (PRESS)—would result in an additional $157 billion in new electricity costs for Pennsylvanians over the next ten years, according to the Commonwealth Foundation, a free-market think tank based in Harrisburg, Pennsylvania.[179] Here again, we see another example where the people's elected representatives are cut out from exercising their constitutional role. Ultimately, that is what the climate movement is all about.

"Pennsylvania. occupies a unique, critical position," Erik Telford, the foundation's head of communications told me in an interview. "Pennsylvania has been described as the Saudi Arabia of North America. Energy independence leads into a stronger national security position. With the Marcellus Shale we have an abundance of clean and affordable energy supplies. But we have been hamstrung by progressive, liberal leadership. Whether through his pursuit of RGGI in court, or his PACER & PRESS legislative proposals, Shapiro is intent on forcing Pennsylvania into a cap-and-trade program. That will be very expensive for state residents. Shapiro is more of a show horse and less of work horse. He likes to take credit but hasn't shown any real leadership." [180]

Pennsylvania Pulls Out of Multistate Cap-and-Trade Plan

The lawmakers, industry representatives, and union leaders who all brought suit against Wolf's unconstitutional maneuverings achieved a significant victory in November 2025. That was when a state budget deal brought an official end to Pennsylvania's participation in RGGI. [181]

Daryl Metcalfe, the former chairman of a Pennsylvania House Environmental and Energy Committee, gave credit where it was deserved.

"I was thrilled to hear that RGGI has finally been defeated in Pennsylvania. During our battle over the years against this flawed policy that was going to harm our citizens, the CO_2 Coalition was a great ally in the fight," Metcalfe said in a statement. "I thank them for their continued work to protect our citizens and our economy from flawed policies that seek to reduce our ability to utilize our God-given resources to produce energy."

The victory here for constitutionalists and free-market forces is hugely significant. Pennsylvania was the only major energy exporting state that had been part of RGGI. Now that it is officially out, RGGI could be in the early stages of collapse. Shapiro's continued push for an internal, state-level cap-and-trade arrangement suggests he is working to placate progressive environmental supporters in anticipation of running for president. He's adept and skilled at having it both ways. But there's another problem here that could come back to bite proponents of multistate climate initiatives.

The environmental groups that back RGGI and other "cap-and-trade" type plans have palpable connections to Communist China. There's clearly strategy at work to hinder and constrain America's economic and military might while also eroding constitutional checks and balances. This brings us to the special case of California. In September 2025, that state's lawmakers passed a multipronged package of climate bills that will extend its own cap-and-trade program to 2045. That's terrible and painful for state residents. Unfortunately, we all have a stake in what happens with California.

CHAPTER 8

California vs. America on Climate Policy

Some of the most severe and pressing challenges to America's national and economic security come from not from without but from within.

We have already explored some of the more obvious examples, in the form of the Green New Deal and its supporters operating at all levels of government. Add to that the well-funded pressure groups, their benefactors, the media, and the academy, and you have a dire picture. But we're not done.

There is also the special case of California, which continuously attempts to set national policy. Nowhere is climate pornography more overtly on display than it is on the Left Coast, with Sacramento figures its leading purveyors.

, Under a provision of the Clean Air Act (CAA), the EPA is authorized to establish emissions standards for new motor vehicles. The agency can also grant California a special waiver to impose the more onerous regulations.

As a parting gift to Governor Gavin Newsom, the Biden administration in its final weeks granted California's request to receive a CAA waiver that would allow the state to enforce stricter tailpipe emissions requirements for its Advanced Clean Cars II program than what's in place at the federal level.[182] Several states have decided to fall in line with California's standards, which is permitted under the law. This would have the practical effect of prohibiting the sale of new gas-powered cars nationwide by 2035, enabling California to set national policy in a manner that reduces consumer choice while making all vehicles, old and new, more expensive.

California's Climate Power Grab

California's power grab is based on the Corporate Average Fuel Efficiency (CAFE) standards established and enforced through the Department of Transportation. The EPA enters into the regulatory process by calculating the average fuel economy levels and setting greenhouse gas emissions standards that operate in tandem with the CAFE standards.

The CAFE standards were initially enacted in response to the 1973 oil embargo, in an effort to curtail US dependence on Middle Eastern oil. But with the United States now the top oil and gas producer in the world, the original rationale for CAFE is anachronistic at best. That's why the EPA regulations were folded into the Biden administration's "whole-of-government approach" to climate change, with tailpipe CO_2 emissions targeted for reduction.

As it stood, California already had the largest congressional delegation in the country. But during the Biden administration it also had friends in high places.

Vice President Kamala Harris was a former US senator and attorney general for California, and she was firmly rooted in Newsom's climate agenda. The whole of point of the California waiver and the distortion of CAFE standards was to perpetuate self-dealing between the Biden-Harris EPA and Newsom's California. The California waiver is part of a concerted effort to gain political power and money, shrouded and wrapped in the language of climate activism.

But recently, California finally experienced some significant pushback in the form of a House resolution aimed at overturning the California waiver.

Under the Congressional Review Act (CRA), which became law in 1996, regulatory agencies are required to submit every new federal rule they make to both houses of Congress and the Government Accountability Office before they can go into effect. Congress then approves or disapproves the proposed rules. The CRA represents one of the more serious attempts to rein in the administrative state. But it's only under Trump that the CRA has begun to find serious expression.

EPA Administrator Lee Zeldin submitted Biden's last-minute waiver action to Congress for consideration under the CRA. The House responded on May 1, 2025, by passing a resolution providing for congressional disapproval of the California waiver. The vote was 246–164, with 35 Democrats joining with 211 Republicans in support of the resolution. In doing so, they quite correctly told the unelected bureaucrats in the GAO and the Senate parliamentarian's office, who tried to stifle the effort, to get lost.

Media reports pounced on elected officials in both chambers who favored the resolution, while falsely describing the GAO and the parliamentarian's office as nonpartisan. Arguments in opposition to using the CRA resolutions revealed a last-ditch effort to preserve California's ability to impose a nationwide electric vehicle mandate. Not only that, but Democrats made it clear they wanted to set a new precedent that would entirely neuter the CRA and once again outsource legislative functions to their allies in the left-wing bureaucracy.

Newsom's Pursuit of EV Mandates

Government officials at war with gasoline-powered vehicles, and who support an EV mandate, claim it would lead to environmental and economic benefits for all Americans. That's what Newsom and other blue-state governors have stated publicly. Newsom's effort to impose an EV mandate began with gusto in September 2020 when he signed an executive order requiring all new cars and passenger trucks sold in California to be zero-emissions vehicles. Here's what he said at the time:

> This is the most impactful step our state can take to fight climate change. For too many decades, we have allowed cars to pollute the air that our children and families breathe. Californians shouldn't have to worry if our cars are giving our kids asthma. Our cars shouldn't make wildfires worse—and create more days filled with smoky air. Cars shouldn't melt glaciers or raise sea levels threatening our cherished beaches and coastlines.[183]

Other blue-state governors following Newsom's lead used similar language. Here's what Governor Phil Murphy of New Jersey had to say in November 2023 while adopting the California standards:

> By filing the landmark Advanced Clean Cars II rule, New Jersey builds upon its standing as a national leader in climate action and its participation in the global Accelerating to Zero commitment. The steps we take today to lower emissions will improve air quality and mitigate climate impacts for generations to come, all while increasing access to cleaner car choices. Indeed, together with my Administration's continuing investments in voluntary electric vehicle incentives, charging infrastructure, and the green economy, these new standards will preserve consumer choice and promote affordability for hardworking New Jerseyans across the state.[184]

In pushing the EV mandate, Newsom and company ignore a host of negative impacts. IER plugged this lacuna with an analysis released in December 2024 that went into great detail about the higher costs, logistical challenges, and, yes, environmental fallout that occurs "When the Government Chooses Your Car." Since consumer preferences and economic factors continuously direct vehicle purchases, policymakers should know that any wide-ranging regulations will impose substantial costs across the economy.

The major takeaways from the IER report make this clear. For starters, the cost difference between the average internal combustion engine (ICE) vehicle and the average EV is stark. In fact, most Americans would be unable to afford the price of a new EV. IER found a 42 percent gap between the price of an average ICE and an average EV. Moreover, the replacement cost for EV tires is anywhere from $300 to $500 more than it is for ICE vehicles.[185]

The taxpayer-subsidized boost EVs are receiving from the political class doesn't begin to address the many problems with the technology. The Infrastructure and Jobs Act of 2022 allocated $7.5 billion for EV charging infrastructure. But as of the middle of 2024, only seven EV charging stations had become operational. There's also the problem of maintenance costs. EVs require longer repair periods than ICEs, and those repairs cost about 30 percent more than what they are for ICEs.[186]

That's not all. Perpetual charging and recharging quickly erode the EV's battery. The IER report finds that EVs can take a beating in winter conditions, losing anywhere from 10 percent to 36 percent of their range. The limited battery life is another important factor that makes the resale of EVs almost a nonstarter. When the replacement cost of the battery exceeds the car's value, there's not much point in buying a used EV.

The lack of flexibility, dexterity, and range of EVs is a large part of what discourages consumers who continue to purchase gas-powered vehicles in greater numbers. Despite all the preferential government policies, EVs remain just a tiny part of the vehicle market. Government stats show that in 2023, about 1.15 million battery electric vehicles were sold, which comes out to about 7.4 percent of all the vehicles sold that year.

The long-term reliability of the US electrical grid is another hurdle standing in the way of widespread EV deployment. In contrast to liquid fuel supply chains, which draw from multiple refineries, pipelines, and tanker trucks, the electrical grid is one interconnected system. That system is already greatly strained, as recent blackouts in California demonstrate. An accelerated growth of EVs will further exacerbate the problems of an already-stressed system.

IER points to other "growing demands for electricity," including from artificial intelligence, which show just how untenable EVs will become over the long term. Regulations targeting coal, oil, gas, and nuclear power make the challenges of supporting EV infrastructure all the more difficult. Let's not forget EV proponents are also fighting hard to eliminate these energy sources. EVs are likely to be one of the first casualties when the electrical grid goes belly up.

The climate and environmental rationale for EVs also runs into trouble. While it's certainly true that EVs produce zero tailpipe emissions, their overall carbon footprint—which includes battery production and electricity generation—is higher than that of conventional vehicles, according to life cycle assessments cited in the IER report. This is a reliable measurement, since the life cycle assessment is what car companies and industry consultants use to determine the carbon footprints of the materials used from the point of production until the vehicle's end of life.

A big part of the problem here comes from the emissions involved in the production of EVs—a process that includes mining, metal refining, chemical precursors, and battery modules. As it happens, these EV production emissions are significantly higher than what is released when a conventional car is assembled. IER found that an EV had a roughly 70 percent higher carbon footprint than a conventional car.[187]

EVs also have a penchant for catching on fire, and those fires are intense and difficult to put out. In 2023, the New York Fire Department reported more than 108 lithium-ion battery fires in New York City that injured dozens and caused thirteen fatalities. EVs, both bikes and cars, also tend to explode in a manner that makes escape impossible.[188] There is no slow burn, just an instantaneous explosion.

There are prominent examples of unsettling EV explosions from across the globe. South Korea appears to be out in front of this problem after what that country experienced in the summer of 2024. A parked Mercedes-Benz EV sedan "spontaneously caught on fire in an apartment complex in Anyang, Gyeonggi province on August 1, 2024," according to one report.[189] This prompted residents to ban EVs from their underground parking lot.

Another incident took place in Incheon, west of Seoul, where a parked EV caught fire in the first basement level of an apartment complex. The fire utterly destroyed forty nearby vehicles and damaged one hundred more.[190]

All this is more proof that the climate and environmental arguments made in favor of EVs have been knowingly fraudulent right from the beginning.

Reliance on EVs also poses its own set of national-security risks. When the Biden administration pushed the Orwellian-labeled "Inflation Reduction Act" and "Infrastructure Investment and Jobs Act"—including heavy taxpayer subsidies for EVs and EV battery manufacturing folded into the legislation—it ignored who dominates the industry.

So long as EVs continue to use electricity generated through wind and solar, China will be overseeing the supply chains. The hard reality is that China controls 80 percent of the critical minerals that are used to manufacture electric vehicle batteries. China also operates eight of the fourteen largest cobalt mines in the Democratic Republic of the Congo, which makes use of child labor to extract the minerals used to power electric vehicles. Even if the United States were to abruptly shift course and begin domestic mining and processing of the minerals needed for EVs, that would make for a time-consuming process that plays into Beijing's hands.[191]

As an alternative to EVs, some free-market policy analysts propose taking a hard look at hybrids, which still use fuels in addition to their batteries. IER makes a compelling case for this approach:

> Hybrids are a mature technology that is already widely accepted in the marketplace. There is no concern regarding vehicle range and refueling. There are no shortages of raw materials. There is no need to destroy the environment in developing regions through massive mining expansion. There is no need for child labor. There is no need to rely on China. There is no need to build renewable power plants or charging stations.[192]

Once again, the oft-stated climate rationale for EVs is a canard and cover for the real motivations. We also see further indications that the proponents of EVs know full well their plans will not work as advertised. By pushing for nationwide policies that will make America more dependent on Chinese supply chains, California politicians are knowingly doing the bidding of Beijing and lining their pockets in the process.

Newsom sometimes even says the quiet part out loud. He went so far as to proclaim August 8, 2024, "California Panda Day," to advertise continued Sino-California cooperation.[193] During one of his many visits to China, he signed a declaration and five memoranda of understanding regarding climate change.

"Building on our strong foundation of partnership and deep cultural and economic ties, I traveled to China last year to advance priority issues including climate action and economic development," Newsom later said in a statement. "We hope that the newly arrived panda 'envoys of friendship' will lead to further exchanges and cooperation between California and China."[194]

Not too subtle.

Money is changing hands while Newsom sells out California, and the United States as a whole. There are statistics that speak to Newsom's incessant dealmaking with the Communist regime in Beijing. China produces 80 percent of the world's solar panels and batteries, more than 50 percent of its EVs, and 60 percent of its windmills.[195] The climate agreements with China Newsom publicly celebrates are all about money and power, not the climate.

Unfortunately, they are also about espionage.

In May 2025, Reuters released a bombshell report about "rogue communications devices" found within Chinese-made solar power inverters. "The rogue components provide additional, undocumented communication channels that could allow firewalls to be circumvented remotely, with potentially catastrophic consequences," unnamed sources told Reuters.[196] The devices could potentially give China the ability to shut down the inverters remotely, alter settings, destabilize US power grids, and trigger widespread blackouts throughout the United States. If solar power can be used as an instrument of Chinese espionage, why not EVs?

The Brits are way ahead in sounding the alarm here. Beginning in the spring of 2025, British defense firms began issuing warnings about the potential dangers of connecting phones with Chinese-made EVs. Cybersecurity analysts quoted in the British press described the multiple avenues EVs have for passing along data to hostile regimes, including microphones, cameras, and Wi-Fi connections.[197]

The widespread use of solar inverters and EVs could greatly hinder America's ability to counter hostile actions from China. They also make the Biden administration's push to incorporate more Chinese-made green-energy products into US energy infrastructure look all the more foolish in retrospect.

This is why when Newsom and Chinese leader Xi Jinping exchanged pleasantries during the governor's October 2023 trip to China, it should have been carefully weighed from a national security perspective. In a press release highlighting his "achievements" during the visit, Newsom went into some detail about his climate agreements with Chinese provinces. He also touted a "first-of-its-kind declaration" that would see China and California partner "on subnational climate action like aggressively cutting greenhouse gas emissions, transitioning away from fossil fuels, and developing clean energy."[198]

Newsom's China trip included a visit to the Guangdong province where the city of Shenzhen gained international recognition for its first-of-its-kind, all-electric bus fleet. The city has sixteen thousand electric buses and forty thousand charging stations. A Chinese electric vehicle company known as BYD has a battery-electric bus manufacturing facility in Los Angeles County.[199] The Chinese strategy is as shrewd as it is dangerous, since California has been angling to set national climate policy in the United States for some time.

Coming Ever So Close to a Nationwide Ban on Gas-Powered Cars

This brings us back to the California EV waiver. The rule would have prohibited the sale of new gas-powered vehicles in that state by 2035, as part of a government-led effort to force the public into purchasing EVs. Since other states could adopt California's stricter emissions standards, and eleven had already done so, the waiver could have resulted in a nationwide ban on gas-powered vehicles. Gavin Newsom came precariously close to telling all Americans what cars they could or could not buy.

The Advanced Clean Cars II rule was only one of three California EV mandates the Biden administration withheld from congressional review. The Advanced Clean Trucks rule, calling for increased electrification of all medium- and heavy-duty vehicles, dated back to 2023, while the waiver for Omnibus NO_x rules for medium- and heavy-duty vehicles, which were designed to phase out diesel engine trucks, was paired with the waiver for the clean cars rule in December 2024.

EPA Administrator Lee Zeldin submitted all three waivers for congressional review in February 2025.

As a counterbalance to the California mischief, IER organized the Save Our Cars Coalition back in 2023, which now includes more than forty national and state-based organizations committed to safeguarding American consumers' freedom to choose the car or truck that suits their needs. The waiver enabling California to set stricter emissions standards for cars is of special interest to coalition members.

"What we had here was an abuse of the Clean Air Act," the IER's Tom Pyle told me in an interview. "The waiver process was not created to allow California to ban gas-powered vehicles across the country. That was never the intention. The waiver process was implemented so California could address its own special challenges with smog that affect parts of that state."

He nicely encapsulated what is at stake.

"In a nation as expansive as the United States, cars are not merely vehicles, they are integral to the American way of life. They play a pivotal role in our daily lives, especially in suburban and rural settings. This modern-day Prohibition would outlaw a product and a value—in this case, gasoline-powered cars and trucks that have created personal mobility on an unprecedented scale—that it cannot persuade people to forego themselves."

Senate Republicans Can Take a Bow

Fortunately, Senate Republicans found their spine and made use of the CRA to revoke the California waivers on a mostly party line vote in March 2025. But the history of that vote is worth revisiting. While the bureaucratic and partisan maneuverings seemingly involved dry, esoteric subject matter, the battle over the waiver was ultimately about restoring constitutional, limited government.

Pyle, the IER president, described the CRA as a "great piece of legislation," crafted for the purpose of "reining in a runaway bureaucracy in conflict with constitutional checks and balances." But true to form, anti-constitutionalist climate activists made every effort to gum up the works.

In response to a request from three Senate Democrats, the Government Accountability Office (GAO) issued a memo in March 2025 claiming the waiver did not meet the definition of what qualifies as a rule under the Administrative Procedures Act. Instead, the GAO argued, the waiver is "an adjudicatory order" that cannot be subjected to the CRA. Senate Parliamentarian Elizabeth MacDonough backed up the GAO's opinion.

Advocates for constitutional government told the unelected lefties to go pound sand.

"Neither the GAO nor the Senate parliamentarian is the final authority on what is considered a rule under the Congressional Review Act since the law is plain and simple," Pyle said. "If an agency sends a rule to Congress for review, elected members have the right to review it."

Daren Bakst, director of the Competitive Enterprise Institute's Center for Energy and Environment, observed that since Congress never authorized the EPA to ban gas-powered cars, the agency could not in turn give California any authority the EPA itself did not possess. In an analysis for CEI, Bakst detailed the "improper GAO meddling" and offered a robust defense for using the CRA to take down the California waiver. The GAO memo, Bakst explained, mistakenly omitted the fact that other states had already adopted California's standards.

"The EPA waiver, while granted to California, was known to be the green light for all the other states that had adopted the California standard," Bakst wrote. "Tell the people in those states that the waiver is just for California."

The desperate effort to block application of the CRA was never about logic, reason, sound science, or any genuine concerns about climate change. That much was made apparent by the lead signatory of the "request" to the GAO, Senator Sheldon Whitehouse of Rhode Island.

If climate activists in the Senate and GAO had succeeded in preventing elected officials from using the CRA to dismantle the California waivers, we would be staring at what might be called the "Whitehouse Rule." This would have neutered any effective use of the CRA, whenever climate activists wanted to preserve their anti-constitutional regulations.

For the moment, the CRA lives on.

But back in Rhode Island, Whitehouse's constituents are enduring climate schemes that benefit only a select few.

For example, the Revolution Wind project, located about twelve miles southwest of Martha's Vineyard, is expected to consist of about fifty wind turbines. The project would be over ten times the size of Rhode Island's current thirty-megawatt Block Island wind farm. President Trump did step in to potentially terminate the Revolution Wind in August 2025. In its letter halting construction, the BOEM agency cited national security as one of its top concerns.[200]

But the rebellion there against the climate activists continues—a modern echo of Rhode Island's proud history. Rhode Island was the first colony to foreswear allegiance to Great Britain on May 4, 1776, two months before the Declaration of Independence. Rhode Island was also the only state not to send delegates to the Constitutional Convention in Philadelphia in 1787, out of fear of a stronger federal government that had the power to tax. And for the same reason, Rhode Island was the last state to ratify the US Constitution, on May 29, 1790.

Given Rhode Island's prominent role in the history of American independence, now is a good time for a different kind of revolution. For nothing threatens that independence and American sovereignty more than the UN's globalist climate agenda—with wind power as the tip of their spear.

CHAPTER 9

Challenging "Unfounded Assumptions" While Reasserting American Independence

D espite the repeated denials from government officials and outfits like Greenpeace, the evidence linking whale fatalities to offshore wind has only strengthened over time. That's one reason CFACT activists in Virginia are holding out hope that the New Jersey petition on behalf of the right whale could put a stop to Dominion Energy's project off Virginia Beach.

While the litigation cites multiple federal laws, CFACT's suit is narrowly focused on the Endangered Species Act. Dominion has been named as a defendant along with several federal agencies. As of April 2025, Dominion Energy appears to be on track to complete construction on 90 monopiles out of the almost 180 that will be needed. However, no wind turbines have yet been erected, and the cabling is not yet finished.

After organizing a number of anti-wind, save-the-whale campaigns in Virginia and New Jersey, CFACT's president Craig

Rucker sees an opportunity to permanently gain the moral high ground against climate activists. He recalls how one hundred activists turned out in Cape May, New Jersey, in October 2024 to take part in the "Cairn Lighting Against Wind Turbines," complete with a giant whale tail that was lit up on the beach.[201] The demonstration was timed with similar events in Norway and Scotland.

From his perch off Virginia Beach, Rucker contemplates his next moves while the Trump administration reevaluates his case. The blurred distinction between the "takings" permitted under the Marine Mammal Protection Act are foremost on his mind. A Level A "take" can apply to serious injuries or fatalities and also includes any disturbance that has the "potential to injure" a marine mammal. Level B allows for some behavioral harassment but no enduring biological consequences.[202]

Up until now, as Rucker explains, federal officials have only allowed for Level B.[203]

What does this mean in practice? There's a lot of noise with Level B that can interfere with the whale's sonar. This is where it all gets a bit confusing, because Level B harassment could cause whales to collide with ships or beach themselves. Whatever separation exists between Level B and Level A is more than a little blurred.

In its most recent study detailing the reasons why offshore wind energy vessel surveys are responsible for whale and dolphin casualties, Save LBI drove home the point that elevated noise levels from survey devices occur in the same frequency range as whale hearings and vocalizations. Here's how the report describes the precarious situation for marine life:

> The vessel surveys do create the "potential to injure" or the "likelihood of injury." For

example, such Level B disturbances can lead to:
(1) avoiding the noise or "standing off" from
it in an undesirable direction or location, and
in a migratory setting, obstructing or blocking
it, (2) If the mammal is between the shore and
the vessel source, being driven towards the shore
seeking relief, with loss of its navigation capability and potentially beaching itself, (3) surfacing
(demonstrated experimentally) to seek a lower
noise level and becoming more vulnerable to
vessel strike, (4) the separation of mothers and
calves due to the "masking" of their normal communications, which would be fatal for the calf,
(5) the cessation of feeding or mating, (6) the
loss of energy and (7) the loss of its navigational
capability and the ability to detect predators or
oncoming ships.[204]

The correlation between increased vessel surveys and the
unprecedented spike in whale deaths figures prominently in
the study. While there's always room to argue that correlation
is not necessarily causation, no other plausible causes have been
brought forward.

The spike in whale deaths off New Jersey began in December
2022 and continued through March 2023. The number of
vessel surveys increased from two in November 2022 to six in
December 2022, when the spike began. There is no escaping
the fact that the time and place of whale deaths correlate with
the presence of survey vessels. Save LBI also claims the National
Marine Fisheries Service (NMFS) greatly underestimated the

amount of harm to whales that could result from noise generated through vessel surveys.

"The Agency authorizations for those surveys relied on arbitrary, scientifically unsupported assumptions resulting in a significant underestimation of noise extent," the study says, while citing an example from the Atlantic Shores project where NMFS relied on smaller, less powerful units to obtain estimated noise levels.[205]

Notice again how we are getting into "unsupported assumptions," which are not unique to offshore wind initiatives. In fact, they are ubiquitous across the climate movement.

Nowhere is that unfortunate trend more damaging to average Americans than in the climate-modeling process. And nowhere has the penchant of climate activists for manipulating data to suit their agenda been better exposed and discredited than at the Heritage Foundation.

During a May 2025 symposium at the conservative think tank, Kevin Dayaratna, its chief statistician, along with other noted scientists and researchers, dissected the three key assumptions lurking behind models that give rise to burdensome regulations.[206] The models are designed to estimate the social cost of carbon, or SCC, which can be defined as the measurement the EPA uses to calculate the economic impact of CO_2 emissions. The presumption, of course, is that increased CO_2 will be harmful to the environment and future generations. Specifically, the SCC measures the economic damages per metric ton of CO_2 emissions.

Following in line with this thinking, the so-called discount rate operates as one of the key assumptions. Modelers discount future costs and benefits of climate policies back to their present-day value. The process can be seen as the reverse of compounding. The discount rate makes it possible to compare future benefits of cutting CO_2 to the future benefits of alternative investments. Think of the discount rate as counting backwards. Lower discount rates will result in a higher SCC. This is how the Obama and Biden administrations justified more aggressive climate polices. Yes, the discount rate can involve dense subject matter, but David Kreutzer, a new retired energy policy analyst, wrote a piece for the Institute for Energy Research that can help all of us here. Apparently, it was during his wedding anniversary that the poor chap had to suffer through the 2019 film *Little Women*, a period piece that follows the lives of the March sisters—Meg, Jo, Beth, and Amy—in Concord, Massachusetts, back in the nineteenth century. Without probing any further, this does sound like a particularly excruciating chick flick, and we can all thank Mr. Kreutzer for taking one for the team:

> Period dramas, like this one, always have enough people with enough inherited money that the plot is not bogged down by too many people having to go to work. Nevertheless, there were plenty of bits in the movie to reference how poor the people of the mid-19th century were compared to today. The huge difference in incomes between 1861 (roughly when Little Women took place) and now helps illustrate the absurdity of calling for more and more costly climate policies to account for intergenerational equity.[207]

Kreutzer goes on to provide us with data that shows that per capita GDP in the US for 1861 (around the period the film is set) was $2,943 while the same data shows the per capita GDP in the US for 2019 was $58,056—that's a twentyfold increase in income. Sooooo...anything Meg, Jo, Amy, and Beth could have done back in 1861 to cut a ton of CO_2 emissions can be viewed as a climate investment and whatever mitigation in climate damage that cut produced for today can be viewed as the payoff. But let's great real. As Kreutzer explains:

> The world of *Little Women* was a harsher, poorer, and technologically cruder world than the one we live in today. In similar fashion, the next 160 years will likely bring increases in wealth and technology that are beyond our imagination. Using an inefficiently low discount to game the SCC estimates can in no way be considered a tool for greater intergenerational equity.

The discount rate is not the only problem.

Another assumption behind SCC modeling is the time horizon for aggregate CO_2 damages, which are set out almost three hundred years into the future. However, all kinds of variables are difficult if not impossible to forecast over the span of several decades, much less over centuries. The final assumption here is equilibrium climate sensitivity (ECS), which attempts to quantify what Earth's temperature will be in response to a doubling of CO_2 emissions. The ECS is very much open to debate because empirical observations, including those pulled into satellite data, show the climate models have greatly overestimated the amount of Earth's warming.

During the Heritage symposium, Dayaratna described the concept of "settled science" as an oxymoron. He noted that "science is consistently evolving over time, which is why new studies come to light."[208] One of those new studies was a central topic of discussion at the Heritage symposium. Willie Soon, the astrophysicist who heads up the CERES science group, delved into the major findings of his paper on solar activity, mentioned in an earlier chapter. The study also took a hard look at the "Urban Heat Island Effect," which can have a distorting influence on global data. Together with other CERES team members, Soon made a compelling case that the recent warming trends are driven mostly by natural influences. The CERES study also presented some evidence that a combination of natural and human influences could be involved.

Either way, the updated research suggested the widely heralded idea that human activity has put us on a path to catastrophic climate change is pure bunk. In fact, Dayaratna told me that the mild warming we have experienced since the mid-twentieth century could have some benefits for animal and plant life.[209]

"After making very reasonable changes to the assumptions to the social cost of carbon, those costs could become negative, meaning there are net benefits to society from increased CO_2 and even some warming," he told me.[210]

In other words, when the social cost of carbon moves into the negative, this means whatever costs are incurred by CO_2 emissions are outweighed by the benefits. Under this scenario, it makes very little sense to tax or restrict CO_2 emissions. In fact, one could make the argument that CO_2 emissions should be subsidized.

"I don't take the position that CO_2 should be taxed or subsidized," Dayaratna said. "What we are demonstrating is that these models are very open to user manipulation. That's why they should not be used as a policymaking tool."[211]

Dayaratna rejected the demonization of CO_2 that is central to climate narrative.

CLIMATE PORN

"Carbon dioxide is a naturally occurring substance that is critical to life on earth," he said. "The endangerment finding that is at root of so many of our regulations is based on faulty assumptions and should be repealed. I'm of the view that there might be some human contribution to global warming, but we are seeing mostly natural influences at work. There's a real debate about how much human influence is involved. But climate models that are most accurate are the ones that put the human contribution at the lower end."[212]

If anything, Soon's coauthors, Ronan Connolly and Michael Connolly, both independent CERES scientists, are even more skeptical. In their study, they carefully go through the methods used to collect temperature data and discuss the limitations of those methods. For starters, the weather stations that collect data for UN studies and other government studies leave out large portions of the globe.[213] The other problem, as the report points out, is that not all of the weather stations operate continuously, which means they could be missing months or even years of data.

These weather stations were not designed to study long-term changes, but instead focused on current weather trends.[214] Why does this matter? Because localized changes produce what the team calls "non-climatic" biases into the temperature record of a particular station. Some examples include changes in instrumentation, changes in thermometer shelter, station relocations, and population increases. These factors can have a distorting influence on the data.

This brings us to the "urban heat island effect," which the UN's IPCC appears to be lowballing. There are several factors likely responsible for the effect, which recognizes elevated temperatures in and around urban areas. Man-made materials store more heat from the sun than natural soil surfaces. Sunlight that hits concrete, pavement, and rock is converted into heat. By contrast, in rural areas with more plant cover, the sunlight that reaches plants is converted by photosynthesis into biomass instead of heat. The concentration of human activity and machinery in developed areas also figures into higher heat.[215] This is not an exhaustive list of what goes into the heat effect, but it's enough to demonstrate that the effect should be taken into account when trying to attribute causes of apparent rises in global temperatures.

Urban areas occupy less than 4 percent of the planet's land area, but most of the weather stations throughout the Global Historical Climatological Network are in urban areas. With this in mind, the CERES team sought to separate out the heat island effect. This was done by using data from rural weather stations and then comparing the data to temperature trends from both rural and urban stations.[216] What did they find? Not surprisingly, the rural analysis showed warming levels that were significantly less than the combined estimate.

The scientists concluded there was an overall warming trend of 0.89 degree Celsius per century when the rural and urban stations were analyzed together, versus an overall warming trend of 0.55 degree Celsius per century when just the rural stations were analyzed. That's a 40 percent decline in the observed warming. Another significant takeaway is that the rural station data point to a cyclical pattern of warming and cooling periods covering several decades since the late 1800s, as opposed to nearly unbroken warming trends of estimates using both urban and rural data.[217]

The question becomes, if human activity can create localized warming through the urban heat island effect, then can human activity also be tied in with global climate change?

Soon took us back to the *IPCC's Sixth Assessment Report*, which the UN completed in 2023. Apparently, the UN seized on just one of many TSI (total solar irradiance) changes when it drew its conclusions. That's problematic, to put it mildly, since a substantial quantity of TSI datasets available in the scientific literature delivers a different view of the TSI changes since 1850.

Soon delineated some of the reasons for pulling in as many different samples as possible, and some of the challenges in collecting that information. There are two steps involved in the process. One is focused on TSI measurements from the satellite era beginning in the late 1970s, while the other goes back to the pre-satellite era and makes use of what are called "proxies."[218] These include sunspots that give insight into how active the sun was in a particular period. Everyone is using the same proxies, but the satellite data get tricky because, as Soon's study explains, the missions only last for a decade or so. This means that to create a comprehensive record, researchers need to combine records from several missions.

Soon and company identified twenty-seven different estimates of the changes in TSI since 1850. Here's what they found:

Several of these estimates suggest that global warming is "mostly natural," and several suggest that global warming is a mixture of natural and human-caused factors. We therefore conclude that the IPCC was overconfident and premature in its detection and attribution statements. The scientific debate remains ongoing. In our opinion, the scientific community is not yet in a position to establish whether the observed temperature changes since the 1800s are "mostly natural," "mostly human-caused," or "a mixture of both." The scientific debate about how much global warming is man-made and how much is natural has not been resolved. We hope that in its Seventh Assessment Report, the IPCC will not continue with its scientifically weak approach.[219]

That *Seventh Assessment* is set to roll out in 2029. That's plenty of time for the UN team to properly adjust and account for solar data that give a more complete picture of natural influences on climate, a topic we'll explore in the concluding chapter.

But for the moment, let's consider what makes sense as a matter of policy, and what the challenges are for humanity. As Dayaratna explained to me:

> The common perception in the mainstream media is that the sky is falling due to climate change. But the Earth's climate has been changing for 4.5 billion years. The real question today is to what degree the climate is changing. The Left likes to portray those with a different viewpoint as saying that there is no climate change. But that's not the issue. No one denies the climate is changing, but the evidence is very much against any kind of climate catastrophe. But let's suppose for a minute that there is some kind of climate catastrophe coming. Will the proposed policies have any effect? No, they won't. Even when we use the IPCC climate models at the Heritage Foundation, this shows that if the US were to completely abate all CO_2 emissions, there would

be less than 0.23 degrees Celsius temperature mitigation by the end of this century.[220]

So even by their own metrics, the policies advanced by self-described climate activists do not make any appreciable dent in climate. But they do create a long list of victims, for all the reasons Dayaratna lays out.

"Reliable energy underpins the utilization of what many of us take for granted," he said. "Like turning the lights on and getting into the car to get groceries. If you restrict affordable, reliable energy there are going to be reverberations throughout the whole economy. Life expectancy is higher in countries that consume more energy, and there are lower rates of child mortality and lower deaths due to dirty air. I find it baffling, for example, that in parts of Africa, there is some hesitation to enable people to gain access to affordable energy."[221]

Hesitation is one word for it. But lust is another—lust for political power and lust for government control. The goal of the policies and programs is to drive money and power to progressive climate activists. For them, the United Nations, its Agenda 21 schemes, and the concept of sustainability are the perfect vehicles. And for them, an independent, free United States, with a Constitution devoted to limited government and the protection of natural rights, remains the greatest obstacle to this agenda.

The History of Agenda 21 and the Attack on Private Property

Agenda 21 is a byproduct of the UN Conference on Environment and Development, held as part of the "Earth Summit" in Rio de Janeiro, Brazil, in June 1992. The agenda was designed to spur action across governments with the common goal of achieving "sustainable development," which the UN defines as growth and development that satisfies contemporary needs without undermining the ability of future generations to meet their needs. An authority on what makes this all tick is Dan Eichenbaum, chairman of the Cherokee County Board of Commissioners in North Carolina, which operates the *Freedom Forum* blog and radio program.

"Everything that is being done in the name of sustainable development is being done to destroy America," Eichenbaum told me in an interview. "The goal is to eliminate private property, which is the first plan in the *Communist Manifesto*, and eliminate the need to travel unless by bike or public transportation. The other goals are to eliminate unalienable, individual rights, depopulate the planet, eliminate the middle class, redistribute wealth, attack the family unit and religion, overregulate industries and dumb down the schools."[222]

Much of Agenda 21, Eichenbaum warns, is "built on fear," calibrated to spur government action. He encourages people to go back and revisit the first Earth Day held on April 22, 1970.[223] Back then, pseudoscientists, with the assistance of the major media platforms of the day, warned of global cooling and a looming ice age.

"When earth's climate did not cooperate, their new crisis was global warming," Eichenbaum observed. "Both potential catastrophes were blamed on greenhouse gas emissions, specifically carbon dioxide."[224]

Earth Day immediately became an annual international day of activism devoted to contemporary climate initiatives in line with the UN agenda. But whether it's global cooling or global warming, the policy prescriptions remain the same. Eichenbaum fears that even in the Age of Trump, too many Americans remain blithely unaware of how much progress climate activists have made toward unraveling America's constitutional system.

At the national level, he points to an executive order President Bill Clinton signed in 1993 implementing Agenda 21's sustainable development initiatives as an example of something Trump should repeal. Such a move could disrupt the flow of taxpayer-funded grants to organizations supporting Agenda 21. Repeal would have the added benefit of delegitimizing the Agenda 21 schemes Eichenbaum has identified at the state level in Oregon, Washington state, California, New Mexico, and elsewhere.[225]

Getting the United States out of the Paris Treaty (and it is quite appropriate to call it a treaty rather than an accord) was a good first step for Trump's second administration. But if more Americans properly understood how diametrically opposed the UN was to their country's founding principles, they would be clamoring for the president to go a few steps further and withdraw from the UN Framework Convention on Climate Change, dating back to the 1992 Earth Summit in Rio de Janeiro.

Trump has made some incremental moves in this direction. In violation of the 1992 climate treaty, the Trump administration declined to submit an annual inventory of US greenhouse gas emissions by April 15, 2025. Secretary of State Marco Rubio has also eliminated the Office of Global Change, charged with overseeing US participation in the UN's annual climate conferences. Over at the EPA, Lee Zeldin is putting an end to the agency's gas-reporting program, which feeds into the inventory sought by the UN.[226]

A "Great Awakening" that leads to a rediscovery of what animated the American founding period is in order. Getting completely out of the framework agreement would be a great way to celebrate the 250th anniversary of American independence.

So is organized resistance against the globalist agenda. Climate activism, and Agenda 21 in particular, embodies the UN's collectivist approach to human rights. While the US Constitution is carefully calibrated to preserve God-given natural rights, the UN's approach to climate is structured to withdraw or restrict individual rights.

A careful read of the UN Declaration of Human Rights shows it's designed to control the individual for the greater good of a global community. The declaration bluntly asserts: "Rights and freedoms may in no case be exercised contrary to the purposes and principles of the United Nations." By contrast, the Declaration of Independence and the US Constitution protect and secure the individual rights we are born with—our unalienable natural rights. The famous phrase "that all Men are created equal, that they are endowed by their Creator with certain unalienable rights" makes clear why the ideals of the American founding are incompatible with the UN globalist agenda.

The premise lurking behind the UN climate agenda—that Earth is headed for destruction because of human activity, and that humans are the enemy—is gradually coming unglued. The globalist plan to alter the way we eat, travel, communicate, and live has finally overreached to the point where people are awakening to its true aims. The motivations behind wind-power plans that draw from foreign sources, often hostile—that enrich a select few at the expense of the environment, and that empower government bureaucrats and activists at the expense of the people—have become transparently clear. The honorable tradition of conservationism, which predates the command-and-control approach that became ascendant in the 1970s, is beginning to reassert itself.

The Outspoken Astrophysicist Makes Enemies

But the climate activists and globalists aren't giving up without a fight—and they are targeting those who have been uncovering their machinations.

For example, Willie Soon, the outspoken astrophysicist, has made powerful enemies by exposing the flaws in UN climate models and calling further attention to the natural influences driving climate.

Since climate activists found it difficult to assail any of Soon's conclusions, they pivoted to attacking him for his funding sources. First, *The New York Times* rolled out a report in February 2015 suggesting there were conflicts of interest in Soon's research, because he had received more than $1.2 million from the fossil fuel industry during his time with the Harvard-Smithsonian Center for Astrophysics. The *Times* claimed Soon did not disclose this contribution.[227] Greenpeace went a step further with a "case study" that showed Soon "has received substantial funding from the fossil fuel industry for most of his scientific career."

But the smears collapsed under closer scrutiny. Soon received less than $60,000 per year from the Smithsonian. Does that sound like a lot? Moreover, it turned out that the funds Soon did receive were part of a ten-year, $1.2 million grant from the Smithsonian, which took a 40 percent cut, without disclosing to Soon the donors behind the grant.

The Smithsonian has a "Statement of Values and Code of Ethics" that says the institution provides oversight to prevent any undue influence by outside parties (such as donors or sponsors) on any scholarship or publication that stems from externally donated funds. This is why the Smithsonian deducts anywhere from 30 percent to 40 percent of any external grant to cover its overhead costs. From what's left, the grantee pays their own stipend to cover any research costs. Under the Smithsonian's arrangements, Soon and other grantees did not have the authority to sign a research contract to receive a grant or decide the terms of any contracts.[228]

The Soon case is typical of how climate alarmists will throw up a nothingburger to attack a scientist who had the audacity to puncture their balloon. Furthermore, as seen during the RICO investigations, climate alarmists caught double-dipping at taxpayer expense are hardly in a position to criticize anyone's funding. But since they have raised the question of who's funding whom, we will now take up that baton.

Welcome to Big Green Inc.

CHAPTER 10

Foreign Agents, "Useful Idiots," and the Emergence of Anti-Population Ideologues

Victims can be found in surprising places, and sometimes they don't know they are victims. Even when they do, they may not be clear about who or what is responsible for their plight.

The media narrative about climate change fixates on the myth of "big oil" and those nasty, rapacious capitalists. But it's the incestuous relationship between government figures and anti-energy climate activists that really lays waste to ordinary people of modest means.

This is where the insight of someone with thirty years of experience as an intelligence official is invaluable. While members of the House were conducting investigations into green advocacy groups closely tied in with foreign actors, Ken Stiles, the former CIA official we previously encountered, was connecting the dots.[229] As it turns out, those who get caught in the crossfire of anti-pipeline protests and anti-fracking activism are not just victims of well-heeled special interests.

They are also very likely victims of espionage.

In a series of interviews, Stiles explained why this was the case and what he means by "agents of influence." There are three different types, he told me.

The first type, a "controlled agent," knowingly works for a foreign entity; but rather than stealing secrets, this agent tries to influence his country's public policy. Harry Dexter White, an economist and top Treasury Department official in the 1940s, is an example. White, who knowingly passed secrets to the Soviet Union, tried to convince US policymakers to provide interest-free loans to the Soviets to help them rebuild after World War II.

The second type, a "trusted contact," knows he or she is helping a foreign source but isn't necessarily gaining from it personally. He shares the goals of the foreign entity and is willing to help achieve them.

The third type, a "manipulated source," has no idea he or she is working for a foreign country.[230] (I still like the phrase "useful idiots" for that type.)

So where do the anti-pipeline, anti-fracking activists come into this? Mostly number three; but follow the money trail far enough and there has to be a "trusted contact" somewhere.

Agents of Influence

While key congressional figures were probing the connection between Vladmir Putin's Russian government, a Bermuda-based shell company, and grants from the Sea Change Foundation, Stiles was eyeballing groups in Virginia. This matters because the Sea Change Foundation gave a total of $2 million from 2008 to

CLIMATE PORN

2012 to an outfit named Virginia Organizing to "educate the public about climate and clean energy." This according to the Capital Research Center, a Washington-based think tank that tracks causes on the left.[231]

Pull the thread even further and we find that two anti-pipeline groups are listed as partners of Virginia Organizing. Preserve Montgomery County, based in Blacksburg, Virginia, was formed to "unite citizens" in opposition to "the intrusion" of the Mountain Valley Pipeline, according to the organization's website and to "work in cooperation with other regional groups to fight the pipelines and their assault on the environment." Nellysford-based Friends of Nelson County operates with similar motives, targeting the Atlantic Coast Pipeline.[232]

Stiles told me he defines espionage as "an operation that is planned and executed as to conceal the identity of, or permit plausible denial by, the sponsor." The purpose of espionage, he continued, "is to create a political effect upon an adversary. Covert operations aim to secretly fulfill their mission objectives without any parties knowing who sponsored or carried out the operation."[233]

There is "no question," Stiles said, that Russia's efforts to undermine natural gas development in the United States is "a form of espionage" made possible with "agents of influence." Because of their affiliation with Virginia Organizing, Stiles said, Preserve Montgomery County and the Friends of Nelson County have both either knowingly or unknowingly operated as "agents of influence" on behalf of the Russians—and Putin in particular.

If the Atlantic Coast Pipeline had been constructed, it would have originated in West Virginia and run six hundred miles underground across Virginia into North Carolina. But the project, a joint venture of Dominion Energy and Duke Energy, was

161

canceled in 2020 after the companies cited legal uncertainties. Those who would have benefited from the gas supplies drawn from domestic sources can thus be viewed as victims of Russian espionage.

The news is more encouraging for the Mountain Valley Pipeline, which originates in the northwestern part of West Virginia and is poised to run 303 miles underground into southern Virginia. The project, a joint venture between Equitrans Midstream, NextEra Energy Resources, and Con Edison Transmission, cleared a major hurdle in 2024 when it received approval from FERC to activate service and begin flowing gas. The company also filed an application in early 2025 to complete the project with an extension into North Carolina.

Supporters and opponents continue to clash over the proposed extension into North Carolina, known as "Southgate." Mountain Valley has support from landowners, business groups, and community members who would like to see North Carolina included in natural gas deliveries. Some of the groups that have popped up in opposition to the extension are Appalachian Voices, an environmental nonprofit headquartered in Boone, North Carolina; the Sierra Club; and the Chesapeake Climate Action Network, an activist group with offices in Maryland and Virginia.[234]

Despite all the opposition, rich supplies of homegrown natural gas seem guaranteed to lower energy bills for some residents, compliments of the Mountain Valley Pipeline. Unfortunately, the more expansive plans of the Atlantic Coast Pipeline have been put on hold for now. Energy consumers who are losing on additional supplies of natural gas from the Marcellus and Utica Shale deposits that cut across Ohio, Pennsylvania, West Virginia, and New York may not view themselves as victims of Russian espionage. But Stiles encourages his fellow Americans to take a broader view of what's happening.

"People must understand that this is not just a local issue," Stein said. "Geopolitically, this was an example of Putin's Moscow attempting to thwart America's efforts to gain energy independence and dominance and to help our allies get from underneath Putin's energy boot."[235]

The Russian problem is not exactly in the past tense, and certainly not since the invasion of Ukraine. But there are encouraging signs the European Union is working to free itself from dependence on Russian energy. Trump's plans to accelerate liquefied natural gas (LNG) exports to the EU is promising but could also be short-lived, depending upon what happens in the next election cycle. The elaborate money-laundering operation Russia has established has come under increased scrutiny, but it still exists. The Bermuda-based shell company known as Klein Ltd. has repeatedly denied being part of any Russian operation. Still based in Bermuda, it has officially been renamed the Sea Change Foundation International.

As for the San Francisco–based Sea Change Foundation itself, it does not deny receiving funds from overseas, and tax records show it continues to pump substantial amounts of grant funds into the coffers of left-wing environmentalist groups. Something else worth keeping in mind is that the Energy Foundation— ostensibly based in San Francisco but now renamed as the Energy Foundation China—has been the largest recipient of grants from the Sea Change Foundation.

Of all the hostile foreign actors that make savvy use of the climate movement in America, Communist China looms largest. Where China is concerned, this isn't just question of the financial ties that might exist between left-leaning foundations and climate activist groups. There is also the special challenge of "lawfare."

America's enemies are well-positioned to exploit litigious green groups and climate activists for their own purposes. There are strong indications this is already being done. The lawsuits filed against various branches of the military in the name of environmental protection, for example, likely have what some call a "white whale" standing behind them.

Our strategic competitors in Moscow and Beijing will continue these schemes until long-overdue changes are made to environmental laws at the federal and state levels. Until such time, the examples set by farmers, landowners, business owners, ranchers, ratepayers, car owners, beachgoers, medical patients, and anyone who enjoys traveling, will have to suffice.

The Interlocking Relationships Between Government and Greenies

That's pretty much all of us. But we will start with the example of Martha Boneta Fain, a former Virginia farmer and property-rights activist now serving in an advisory capacity to the Trump administration. Because Boneta Fain went toe-to-toe with well-funded, well-connected environmentalists, Virginians involved in property disputes with special interests are on a more level playing field. But to accomplish that, Boneta Fain needed to marshal her own resources, build her own alliances, and lobby lawmakers. Her travails are a case study in how to take on Big Green Inc.

Step one is to expose and highlight the relationships among government officials who are either appointed or elected to serve the public interest, but who instead carry the water for agenda-laced private interests. Step two is to make smart use of alternative media platforms willing to tell a complete story about the dispute. Step three entails carefully targeted open-records requests. Step four, unfortunately, involves money. That's where the progressive climate-activist movement is at a perpetual advantage, for the reasons already discussed. But as Boneta Fain demonstrated, average citizens who are willing and able to fight need only raise enough money to get their message out. They can also take advantage of a growing number of pro bono legal services.

Boneta Fain covered these bases very nicely while she was the owner of the sixty-four-acre Liberty Farm in Fauquier County, Virginia. According to a lawsuit Boneta Fain filed in the Fauquier County Circuit Court in the fall of 2013, the trouble all began with a zoning claim. The Piedmont Environmental Council (PEC)—a 501(c)(3) tax-exempt group, along with the husband-wife real estate team of Phillip and Patricia Thomas, who are members of the PEC—lobbied a zoning administrator and members of the elected Fauquier County Board of Supervisors to issue zoning citations against Liberty Farm. Headquartered in Warrenton, Virginia, the PEC had received hundreds of thousands of dollars in grants from left-leaning foundations, including the highly influential Tides Foundation, based in San Francisco.

The controversy revolved around what are called conservation easements. These were set up to benefit financially distressed landowners, who received tax credits in exchange for agreeing to preclude future development on their property. Typically, property owners enter into a legally binding agreement with a nonprofit group, such as a land trust or government agency. The owner who sells the easement is the "grantor," and the nonprofit group that receives the easement is the "grantee." The grantor maintains ownership but agrees to terms on the use of the property to ensure it will be conserved.

It sounds like a very benign arrangement, and that's how it was, until Big Green turned it into a premise for their lawfare. Boneta Fain bought the farm from the Piedmont Environmental Council in July 2006 with the easement already attached. In the years that followed, the PEC accused Boneta Fain of violating the terms of the easement. Boneta Fain in turn accused the PEC of overstepping its authority under the easement, to the point where they were trespassing on her property. Whatever the merits of the arguments, some peculiarities began to emerge during the litigation.

Boneta Fain, who is also an attorney in her own right, produced documentation that showed the PEC had filed an alternative version of the easement with Fauquier County officials, without her consent, prior to transferring the title of the property over to her. This alternative version provided the nonprofit land trust with rights and privileges that were not in the version Boneta Fain agreed to when she purchased the farm.

There were also all kinds of interlocking relationships Boneta Fain exposed with Freedom of Information Act (FOIA) requests. She obtained, for example, electronic messages and other written communications that showed Peter Schwartz, a county supervisor, and the PEC holding several meetings specifically to discuss zoning violations directed against her. As it happens, Schwartz is a former board member of the PEC.[236]

According to the Boneta Fain suit, the PEC and the Thomases made repeated attempts to convince the zoning administrator and local government officials, such as Schwartz, to cite Liberty Farm with zoning violations. In August 2012, the Fauquier County Zoning Board of Appeals voted to uphold a series of

$15,000-per-day fines against Boneta Fain, based on the amendments that were made to the county's zoning ordinance. The zoning board administrator claimed Boneta Fain had sold fresh fruit, beverages, and homemade handicrafts out of her on-site farm store, in violation of the modified zoning rules. In response, Boneta Fain said she had a retail farm store business license that "grandfathered" her into any zoning changes that were made. Nevertheless, she shut down the store.[237]

It was this zoning dispute that spurred Boneta Fain to become involved in the legislative process, where she secured significant policy changes. Boneta Bill 1 opened new economic opportunities for farmers, enabling them to sell more products while curtailing the reach of zoning ordinances. Boneta Bill 2 enabled landowners who are parties to conservation easements to seek assistance from the Virginia Land Conservation Foundation, a state-funded conservation entity, to mediate disputes with land trusts.[238] The idea behind the second bill was to prevent land trusts from operating as a judge and prosecutor without any oversight or transparency. Former Governor Terry McAuliffe, a Democrat, signed both bills into law after they received bipartisan support in the General Assembly.

"I think I represent many Americans who have to deal with egregious lawfare," Boneta Fain told me in interview in February 2025, just as the Trump administration was gearing up its regulatory relief efforts. "I'm sorry to see anyone having to go through [it]. But the good news: I'm seeing the Trump administration cleaning house, and making sure that the heavy hand of government and the Department of Justice is never used again to go after your political enemies. We are the United States of America, and we are the last bastion of freedom in the world, and we can't allow political operatives to use our court system to go after those who dissent from their agenda. This can never happen again."

The final part of Boneta Fain's successful strategy involved the emergence of the *Daily Signal*, a news site initially launched as a project of the Heritage Foundation. The *Daily Signal* now operates independently, but its mission remains the same: "to deliver news and analysis that cuts through the noise," so readers can make informed decisions. Rob Bluey, the news organization's president and executive editor, has the stated goal of "reaching the movable middle." He believes many Americans have lost trust in legacy media outlets, and there's a demand for something different. That's certainly true in Fauquier County, Virginia, and other parts of the country, where readers took notice of the incestuous relationship between green pressure groups and public officials.

It's why the *Daily Signal* sprang into action upon learning of Boneta Fain's story. It published more than a dozen stories that documented and detailed the controversy. The outlet provided a unique perspective that other media outlets outright ignored. Those stories had an outsized impact locally in Fauquier County but also helped expose Boneta Fain's story to a national audience.

"We created the *Daily Signal* to report on stories like Martha's fight precisely because other media outlets either willfully ignored it or skewed their coverage to advance an agenda," Bluey said. "We take pride in our storytelling and covering news that goes unreported."

Boneta Fain eventually reached a settlement with the PEC and the realtors, which advanced the cause of property rights. But it involved considerable time and expense. As an added insult, Boneta Fain was also audited by the IRS for tax years 2010 and 2011.[239] Margaret "Peggy" Richardson, who sat on the PEC's board at the time, previously served as the IRS commissioner under President Bill Clinton. Richardson has denied any involvement with the audits, and there's no evidence that she was involved. But it's very evident that green groups have burrowed deeply into all levels of government, most especially under Democrat presidents.

Getting the instrumentation of government back into the hands of "We the People" is a tall order. But Martha Boneta Fain is enthused by Trump's early moves, particularly at those agencies that previously served as platforms for Biden's climate activism.

"I see us becoming energy independent again, and the United States becoming an energy powerhouse," she said. "Independence and freedom go together. I think the second Trump administration benefits from obvious examples of policies that did not work under Biden, with the cost of everyday goods going up. The cost of eggs, food, oil and gas, and the cost of transportation. Everything went through the roof. By unleashing American energy, Trump is making basic needs more affordable again. What we are seeing is the ultimate comeback."

Even so, Boneta Fain remains leery of climate activists, who are lying in wait for a new administration that will enable them to reconstitute their power within administrative agencies.

The Piedmont Environmental Council also serves as an example of climate activism usurping traditional environmentalism. That part about trespassing on private property is an extension of what Piedmont calls "smart growth" and "green energy policy decision making"—all done to supposedly mitigate climate change. In 2023, the PEC created a "preliminary climate action platform document" for the benefit of Albemarle County, built around "sustainable energy," "smart transportation," and "land conservation"—to cite just a few seemingly benign policies that create more avenues for government intervention. The

PEC remains adept at forging key alliances in government. But Boneta Fain's saga at least offers an important case study in how to come out on top legally and even financially against the climate activists.

Ranchers Take on Greenies and Win

A second example comes to us from Jim and Sue Chilton, Arizona ranchers who faced down the Center for Biological Diversity (CBD) and won.

For decades, the Chiltons had owned and operated a ranch that sits just north of the US-Mexico border. Their saga began in 2002, when the center published what the Chiltons, their attorneys, and fellow cowboys viewed as defamatory material. In a press release, the CBD alleged that Jim Chilton had mismanaged the cattle on his federal grazing allotment, to the point where they were causing significant environmental damage. The Chiltons' lawyers asked for the CBD to remove the offensive material, but the activist group ignored the request, prompting the Chiltons to sue.[240]

Fast-forward to 2005, when an Arizona jury awarded the Chiltons $600,000 in actual and punitive damages. In awarding $500,000 in punitive damages, the jury concluded the CBD's conduct went beyond mere negligence and met the legal standard of "willful, malicious or fraudulent" behavior.[241]

Along the way, Jim and Sue Chilton uncovered a plot on part of the government officials in the US Forest Service, who were also members of the CBD, to manipulate the surveys they were responsible for performing. The Chiltons were required to renew their grazing permit from the feds every ten years. Before it could be renewed, the Forest Service had the responsibility of evaluating how well the Chiltons had operated as stewards of the land. But the Forest Service members in league with the CBD did not play it straight. Their goal was to have the Chilton's public-land grazing permit rescinded.

The techniques the green activists inside and outside government used to achieve this goal were taken from the same playbook climate activists use while cooking the books with their climate models. But this time around, the greenies ran into a buzzsaw of the truth.

Chilton's lawyers provided jury members with wider-angle photos of the same scenery the CBD had photographed, and showed that contrary to the CBD's depictions, there were in fact healthy trees and lush, green pastures.[242] It didn't take much to persuade the jury that the CBD photos were deliberately misleading.

Given where the Chiltons are located, it would be logical to assume that their greatest challenges would involve illegal immigration and smuggling exercises. But even when these problems were at their peak under Biden, Jim Chilton was mostly concerned about the enemy within.

"The smooth tracks of illegal immigrant traffic obliterates our cow-tracks and widens the trails," Jim Chilton said in a book detailing his ordeal. "Illegal crossers give us trouble, but none of these people are as dangerous as the anti-ranchers who use our country's environmental rules to try to steal our way of life. They have a head start and have been successful too long. Every day is Earth Day to ranchers, but we worship the Lord, not the Earth. These radicals use 'Earth first' as a slogan to run cattle off the public land with claims that cattle ruin the land."[243]

Although Boneta Fain and the Chiltons came out on top legally, politically, and even financially, the interlocking relationships between green activists and government agents have made it almost impossible for Americans with fewer resources to do the same. It's prudent to revisit some very unfortunate recent history to determine how we got to where we are, and what the implications of lawfare are today.

Dig a Pond, Go to Prison

Sometimes the green goons in government operate in sly, subtle ways. But occasionally they overreach and drop the mask.

Joe Robertson, a US Navy veteran from Montana, was seventy-eight when he was convicted, sentenced to eighteen months in federal prison, and ordered to pay $130,000 in restitution through deductions from his Social Security checks.[244]

His crime?

Robertson, whose business supplied water trucks to Montana firefighters, dug a series of small ponds close to his home in 2013 and 2014. The site was a wooded area near a channel, a foot wide and a foot deep, with two to three garden-hoses' worth of flow, according to court documents.[245]

The US government prosecuted Robertson for digging too close to "navigable waters" without a permit, in violation of the Clean Water Act administered by the Environmental Protection Agency and the Army Corps of Engineers.[246]

The navy veteran insisted that he didn't violate the Clean Water Act, because digging the ponds did not discharge any soil into navigable waters—the trickle in the channel hardly constituted navigable waters. The other problem with the federal case was that the largest navigable body of water anywhere near the Robertson home is more than forty miles away.[247] That's not exactly close.

The Pacific Legal Foundation (PLF), a public interest law firm that defends constitutional liberties, filed a petition on behalf of Robertson, asking the Supreme Court to review his case, which turns on the definition of "navigable waters."

Tony Francois, then an attorney with the PLF, provided some important background about Robertson's case. He pointed out, for example, that Robertson lived in a wooded area that was highly prone to fire, and therefore he had good reason to be concerned about the safety of his property. Robertson built the ponds so he could be prepared in the event of a fire. Seems reasonable. But the EPA and the Army Corps of Engineers pressed ahead with their case.[248]

Robertson was sentenced in 2016 and served eighteen months behind bars before being released in late 2017. He was still on parole for the next twenty months when he died of natural causes on March 18, 2019, at the age eighty.[249]

How did we reach a point where a patriotic American who served his country found himself imprisoned by a runaway federal government?

Congress initially passed the Clean Water Act in 1948, but lawmakers greatly altered and expanded it into its current form with amendments in 1972. The law "establishes the basic structure for regulating discharges of pollutants into the waters of the United States and regulating quality standards for surface waters," according to the EPA's website.

Under the 1972 amendments, it is illegal to discharge any pollutant from a point source into navigable waters without a permit from the EPA. The Corps oversees the permitting process and shares enforcement authority with the EPA. But a critical turning point came in 2015 when the Obama administration implemented its Clean Water Rule, widely known as the Waters of the United States rule, or WOTUS rule, which expanded the regulatory reach of the EPA and the Corps over bodies of water across the country.

The first Trump administration took steps to withdraw the Obama administration's rule and replace it with a new one that limits the regulatory reach of federal agencies. The second Trump administration is taking another shot at reforming WOTUS. At the EPA, Administrator Zeldin is pursuing an agenda that "reduces red-tape, cuts overall permitting costs, and lowers the cost of doing business in communities across the country while protecting the nation's navigable waters from pollution."[250]

Team Trump is taking inspiration from the Supreme Court's decision in *Sackett v. Environmental Protection Agency*, which stated that the Clean Water Act's use of "waters" encompasses only those relatively permanent, standing, or continuously flowing bodies of water forming streams, oceans, rivers, and lakes. The *Sackett* decision also made it clear that wetlands are only covered when they have a continuous surface connection to bodies of water that are waters of the United States in their own right.

As laudable as these efforts are, they came too late for Robertson.

After being convicted, fined, and imprisoned under the Clean Water Act for digging ponds to protect his Montana home from forest fires, Robertson finally had his name cleared in July 2019. The US Court of Appeals for the Ninth Circuit vacated Robertson's conviction in a legal victory that came posthumously, since the navy veteran had died four months prior to the decision.[251]

Climate Activists Hijacking the US Forest Service

While it's easy to view Robertson as an extreme example, he is not an outlier. In fact, there are several cases of federal agents stepping on property owners when climate activists have friends in high places.

One of the most recent episodes involves Charles and Heather Maude, who own and operate a fourth-generation cattle ranch and hog farm in South Dakota's badlands. Their troubles began on March 29, 2024, when the US Forest Service informed them that a hunter had issues with a "No Trespassing" sign on a part of their fence separating their ranch from the Buffalo Gap National Grassland, which falls under the jurisdiction of the Forest Service.[252] Supposedly, the hunter claimed that the Maudes' fence blocked access to federal land. In response to a directive from the Forest Service, the Maudes took down the sign.

Next, they met with agents of the Forest Service, who told the couple a survey was needed to determine their exact property line. Typically, this process takes about a year, but just a few days later, a special agent from the Forest Service popped up on the Maude ranch and began the survey.[253]

That's when events began to take an ugly turn. The couple discovered they were facing an indictment on June 24, 2024. Their crime? A Forest Service agent determined the Maudes "did knowingly steal, purloin, and covert to their own use... approximately 25 acres of National Grasslands for cultivation and approximately 25 acres of National Grasslands for cattle grazing."[254]

But that claim doesn't square with reality.

As one energy and environmental policy expert explains, the determination of property lines in the rough terrain of western

South Dakota is an inexact science. Moreover, the fence in question is one the Maudes inherited, and it's difficult to determine when exactly it was built. But it would have been sometime between 1910 and 1950, and it was done with survey equipment that is now highly antiquated.

The National Grasslands program dates to 1960. Since then, generations of the Maude family have repeatedly renewed their grazing permits with no issues.

But Biden's Forest Service was heavily bent on prosecution, which made it a much different creature than its previous incarnations. The hunter who filed the complaint was never identified, the Forest Service refused to release any details of its survey, and the couple was placed under a gag order, which meant they could not speak to the media.[255]

The Trump administration rode to the rescue, dropping the charges against Charles and Heather Maude in April 2025. But the motivations of Biden's Forest Service should remain the subject of continued scrutiny. Senator Mike Rounds, Republican of South Dakota, suggested that the Small Tracts Act of 1938 could be used to settle the dispute. Under the law, the Forest Service can trade or sell tracts of fewer than forty acres. It would seem this is an ideal solution.[256]

Rounds sent official correspondence to then-Agriculture Secretary Tom Vilsack, but he received no response. Apparently, the Maudes also offered to purchase small tracts during the May 1 meeting, but they were turned down.

The Biden administration's "all of the above approach" to climate lent itself to overzealous prosecutions. This was clearly a motivating factor in the legal assault against the ranchers. There is also the Left's incessant drive for more centralized planning at the expense of constitutional government. But going back a little further into history, there's an anti-population, anti-human mindset at work that views people as a cancer on the planet. Once that's understood, the contemporary climate movement comes into sharper focus.

The Anti-Population Mindset and Where It Comes From

No one rips off the cover of the climate activists better than Jerome Corsi, the author of some twenty-five books on economics, history, and politics, including six *New York Times* bestsellers. Corsi traces the current climate movement back to theories first promulgated by Thomas Malthus (1766–1834), an English economist and demographer who suggested that that world's population growth would outpace its food supply. This theory received added amplification from Harrison Brown, a nuclear chemist and political activist who authored *The Challenge of Man's Future* in 1954, where he affirmed the Malthusian view of limited supplies.

Brown made a couple of bold proclamations in his book that Corsi has revisited in his own research. "Brown left no doubt he endorsed Darwin's evolutionary principles to suggest we could perfect nature and advance the process of natural selection by engaging in eugenics once our scientific understanding of genetics had advanced," Corsi observed.[257]

Brown was also concerned that inferior people with limited intellectual capacities were quickly outbreeding superior people. Among some of the solutions Brown had in mind were the restriction of sexual intercourse, abortion, sterilization, and fertility control. Brown concluded that some form of world government was needed before population stabilization could become reality, and that independent, sovereign states were incompatible with his goal.

Picking up the baton from Brown was one John Holdren, a well-credentialed academic with expertise in physics and environmental science, who served as the senior advisor to President Obama on science and technology issues. Holdren shared Brown's views on overpopulation and married them to climate-change concerns. Holdren later joined forces with Paul Ehrlich, author of the 1968 book *The Population Bomb*, which advanced the Malthusian view that there were too many people and that the growing human population was a blight on the planet and its natural resources.

In 1977, Holdren coauthored a revised textbook with Ehrlich and Ehrlich's wife, Anne, titled *Ecoscience: Population, Resources, Environment*. It made the case for what Corsi aptly describes as an "authoritarian world government to aggressively limit population growth." Holdren and Ehrlich envisioned a "Planetary Regime" that would have the ability to control the world's population.[258]

Ehrlich famously lost a bet with Julian Simon, an economist who rejected Malthusian thinking and views humanity as the "ultimate resource." The bet centered on what the price would be in 1990 of any five metals Ehrlich selected. The objective was to see if the 1990 value, adjusted for inflation, exceeded or fell below the 1980 value. Ehrlich operated under the assumption that the metals would become scarce and, therefore, their prices would rise. In fact, all the metals Ehrlich selected became cheaper, vindicating Simon's view and punching a hole in the concept of limited resources.[259]

What's the critical takeaway from the collaborative efforts between Holdren and Ehrlich? They were ambiguous as to whether human activity was responsible for unnatural levels of warming or cooling. In the end, it didn't matter, because either way their policy goals were built around massive government intervention.

That's what the voting public needs to understand. The maestros of climate activism, dating all the way back to the 1970s, know full well that their policies do not work as advertised. From the get-go, they were in reality designed as an attack on capitalism, national sovereignty, limited constitutional government, and large families.

CHAPTER 11

How the Push for Decarbonized Health Care Intersects with the Abortion Industry and Anti-Life Measures

Nothing enables human populations like affordable and reliable energy, and nothing has done more to raise living standards across the globe than fossil fuels. This helps to explain the animus environmental activists have toward pipeline projects, and particularly those that can reach rural communities.

As lower energy prices coincide with higher disposable incomes, families are put in a position to have more children. For the Malthusians, this scenario is intolerable. This brings us back to the Mountain Valley Pipeline (MVP) in Virginia, which is encountering stiff opposition now that the company behind the project would like to build a thirty-one-mile extension—called Southgate—that would reach into North Carolina.

Let's recall that the main pipeline went forward despite opposition from the same groups now lined up against the expansion. The FERC agency, which is responsible for approving interstate pipelines, has been receiving comments both for and against the expansion plans.

MVP runs 303 miles from West Virginia through six Virginia counties and ends in Pittsylvania County. If constructed, Southgate would extend the pipeline into Rockingham, North Carolina. A broad coalition of landowners, residents, elected representatives, and business groups supports the expansion. On the opposing side is a large constellation of Big Green activists, including the Virginia chapter of the Sierra Club, the NRDC, the Blue Ridge Environmental Defense League, the Center for Biological Diversity, and Appalachian Voices.

But one particularly important player here is the Southern Environmental Law Center (SELC), a left-leaning litigation group that has consistently opposed energy infrastructure projects across the southern United States. The center's attorneys describe the Southgate proposal as "another attempt to commit the South to methane gas, a dangerous fossil fuel that worsens air pollution and accelerates climate change."[260] Construction, they argue, would be to the detriment of the climate and southern communities.

Mountain Valley counters that Southgate will deliver vital supplies of natural gas into communities that have been underserved. There are also compelling economic arguments weighing in favor of the extension. Proponents point to the 3,528-acre "mega site," jointly owned by Pittsylvania County and City of Danville, which stands to benefit from Mountain Valley's plans. Not only is it the largest industrial site of its kind in Virginia, but it's one of the largest in the southeastern United States.[261]

Anne Moore-Sparks, president and CEO of the Danville Pittsylvania Chamber of Commerce, has said that reliable and affordable energy is needed for the site to be an attractive investment for business leaders and for long-term economic development. Delegate Eric Phillips, a Henry County Republican who represents parts of Pittsylvania County, sees benefits in the form of additional tax revenue and new construction jobs.[262]

That might be another reason why all the usual suspects are lined up against the pipeline's expansion.

More Urbanization and More Government Control

Dan Kish, the free-market energy policy analyst who dissected the Climategate scandal, suspects there is an even bigger scheme at work on the part of progressive green activists and other leftists.

"Much of the green energy agenda is also aimed at more urbanization, with an eye towards driving people away from the rural areas because of greater distances," he said. "Any election map shows urbanization attracts more support for central controls by governments, and demographers and political analysts know this. Making energy deliberately more scarce and expensive limits opportunities in rural areas, where more energy is consumed just for daily life. The independence of people in rural areas is bothersome to those who see it as flyover country, appropriate only for vacationing."

It would seem the game plan is to herd all those irritating, independent-thinking, freedom-infested Americans into urban centers, where left-leaning government figures can exert greater control. This unsavory motivation should give locals further impetus to see the project come to fruition.

But on the flip side, are there not laudable motives behind any potential environmental fallout? What would they be?

Those are always fair questions to raise, if they are sincere and rooted in sound science. In its various environmental impact statements submitted to FERC and in its comments to the press, Mountain Valley has committed itself to a methane-abatement project, carbon offsets, erosion and sediment control, wetland protection, and strict compliance with the ESA. That's fine and dandy. But MVP is not making the best case for itself, and it spends too much time accepting the premise of what the opposition has to say about its project.

This brings us back to the so-called social cost of carbon (SCC), which is ripe for manipulation for all the reasons previously discussed. Climate activists have a vested interest in artificially inflating the present value of future climate damages by using very low discount rates that do not square with reality. Remember that discounting is simply compounding in reverse. The discounted value of the future cost/benefit, or present value, is the amount that would need to be invested today to generate the future value.

Mountain Valley gets back on solid ground by calling attention to the safety record of pipelines and the minimal environmental impact of pipelines in comparison to other projects— including the wind and solar boondoggles that greenies embrace. On its "Safety and Environmental Commitments" website, Mountain Valley informs readers that "natural gas pipeline network has the best safety record of any energy delivery system according to the National Transportation Safety Board and the US Department of Transportation (US DOT)."[263] Moreover, pipelines are the safest way to transport natural gas over long distances. The alternative transportation methods such as ships, trains, and trucks all involve a bigger environmental footprint and are more prone to accidents and mishaps.

The SELC litigation group and its allies are essentially telling residents who stand to benefit from Mountain Valley's extension that they need to suck it up. They argue that by accepting costly new regulations today, the people of Virginia and North Carolina can deliver a more pristine climate to future generations. That's a debatable proposition, to say the least, and one that can be easily dismissed by plugging reasonable assumptions into the SCC.

Dig a little deeper into what makes SELC tick and the motivations become clear. There are eleven seats on the law center's board, and three of those belong to leftist billionaire Fred Stanback, who has been characterized as a "known proponent of anti-humanist environmentalism."[264] In addition to SELC, other groups that have received at least $1 million in donations from Stanback in recent years include the Sierra Club Foundation, any number of Planned Parenthood funds, the Rocky Mountain Institute, and the Southern Alliance for Clean Energy.

The law center's commitment to Malthusian-type initiatives has attracted other like-minded donors. From 2017–2019, SELC received $750,000 from the WestWind Foundation, an outfit that funds pro-abortion and anti-life environmentalist groups. Edward M. Miller, who sits on SELC's board, is an investment manager at WestWind.

That's hardly the only interlocking relationship worth mentioning here. Planned Parenthood also fits into this equation.

You might ask: What exactly does the country's largest abortion provider have to do with opposition to natural gas pipelines? The short answer is: everything. The long answer goes all the way back to 1921 when Margaret Sanger, a member of the Socialist Party and the American Eugenics Society, founded the American Birth Control League. In true Malthusian fashion, Sanger vigorously advanced initiatives aimed at curtailing and limiting the human population. Her group was renamed Planned Parenthood in 1942.[265]

The overriding goal back then, as it is now, was to cull human populations that in some quarters were viewed as inferior. In a nutshell, the eugenics mindset is based on the idea that selective breeding can root out negative traits, with an eye toward racial purity.

Connecting the Abortion Industry with the Climate Movement

Hayden Ludwig, the director of policy research at Restoration of America, a right-of-center advocacy organization, has taken a deep dive into the alliance between Sanger and eugenicists. In 1921, Sanger authored an article titled "The Eugenic Value of Birth Control Propaganda," where she argued that "the campaign for Birth Control is not merely of eugenic value, but is practically identical in ideal, with the final aims of Eugenics."[266]

Ludwig went into further detail about the connection between the abortion industry and the modern environmental movement in an interview:[267]

> The abortion and environmental movements seem unrelated at first blush. But history shows they're siblings born a century ago from the same twisted, anti-human ideology that still shows itself in their behaviors today—just expressed differently. It's called "population control": the desire to limit the number of children born, out of the belief that humans are a blight on the planet who consume too many resources and destroy their own natural habitat. It's also manifested as eugenics, a pseudo-scientific effort to "beautify" the human race by limiting who

reproduces, so only "superior" individuals are born, improving the gene pool (or so the theory goes). In both cases, there's an obvious hatred of mankind fueling this desire to play God. I believe it's rooted in a deeply twisted version of the Christian teaching on original sin—that we're fundamentally evil and can never be redeemed, so deserve death.

As Ludwig explains, there is also a common denominator between pro-abortion campaigns and climate activism.

Both the abortion and climate activist networks try to hide their ugly origins, but it's obvious they are siblings. It's why Greenpeace condemned the Supreme Court's decision to overturn *Roe v. Wade* even though it had no effect on the environment, and Planned Parenthood champions "climate justice" initiatives that have nothing to do with abortion.

He added:

While eugenics fell out of fashion after the Nazis, you still see population control everywhere in the rhetoric of "green" and "reproductive rights" organizations. The United Nations Population Fund, for instance, meddles in developing nations by encouraging poor Africans to abort their unborn children to combat "strengthening storms and rising sea levels," supposedly resulting from climate change. The UN Population

Fund is heavily funded by the Bill & Melinda
Gates Foundation, one of the top funders
of abortion advocacy and politicized climate
science in the world. The Gates Foundation
pours a fortune into the Population Council, a
group created in the 1950s by top eugenicists
to depopulate Africa, India, and much of Asia
through birth control and even forced sterilization measures. They were deeply concerned
about the impact of "overpopulation" on the
environment and food supplies, something we
now know is bogus. Birth control later morphed
into abortion. In the 1990s, the Population
Council provided seed funding for developing
mifepristone, the drug used in the abortion pill
and now mailed to women for DIY abortions in
their own homes, no doctor oversight needed."

After this exchange, I probed a little further with Ludwig to
see how these seemingly disparate elements of left-wing, progressive activism fit together, and why the same financial network
stands behind global warming campaigns and elevation of lifestyle choices over innocent human life. Once again, his insight
is priceless:

I don't think anyone really believes that global
warming is inextricably linked with contraception or "a woman's right to choose." Yet that's
what both Planned Parenthood and its allies in
the environmental camp argue. I see two reasons
why.

First, the American Left is run by the activist groups that dominate Washington, not voters or Democratic politicians; and the Left is totally captured by Marxist intersectional ideology, which teaches that every issue is connected to every other issue in this imaginary matrix of oppression. That's why leftists frame every issue as "climate justice," "reproductive justice," "housing justice," "food justice," and so on. It's all meant to advance their goal of fundamentally transforming every aspect of our nation. In the 1960s, when this capture began, radicals explained it like this: "The issue is never the issue, the issue is the revolution."

The second reason is more practical. In the 1920s and '30s, these groups were far more divided into smaller factions—Margaret Sanger's American Birth Control League, the American Eugenics Society, the Socialist parties—that didn't really work together. Sanger, who really represented each camp, helped fuse them into a single bloc. She likened the birth control and eugenics movements to a person's left and right hands, respectively. Birth control advocates were concerned with *how many* babies are born while eugenicists were concerned with *who birthed* them.

Next, Ludwig quotes Sanger, who famously wrote:

"Birth Control is not contraception indiscriminately and thoughtlessly practiced. It means the release and cultivation of the better racial elements in our society, and the gradual suppression, elimination, and eventual extirpation of defective stocks—those human weeds which threaten the blooming of the finest flowers of American civilization."

As Ludwig observes, the name of a particular campaign may change over time, depending upon what is politically fashionable at the moment. But the progressive Left's antipathy toward growing human populations has an immutable quality:

Put together, population control represented the socialist dream of liberation—women's liberation from dying in childbirth, the working class's liberation from having too many mouths to feed, and society's liberation from the mentally and physically "unfit" dragging it down. A century later, the Left may have abandoned her talking points, but they've very much maintained Sanger's principle about political cohesion—which is why disparate groups stick together even on issues they apparently have no interest in, such as climate change.[268]

There you have it. Any discussion of the "Big Green" network that does not include Planned Parenthood can't help but lowball the amount of money and resources made available to progressive environmental advocacy groups, and to the climate activism those groups enable.

A *Restoration News* analysis of financial records in 2023 showed the Planned Parenthood empire, including its international and national affiliates, generated $1.5 billion in revenue that year. Planned Parenthood receives funding from both private and governmental sources.[269] So taxpayers who oppose abortion best pay attention.

Trump's "One Big Beautiful Bill" (OBBB), which became law on July 4, 2025, prevents Planned Parenthood, and other abortion providers, from receiving Medicaid funds for the next decade. That's a critically important step. Although federal law already says it is illegal for taxpayers to fund abortions, any taxpayer funds that go to Planned Parenthood allow the organization to fund abortion with other resources.

Some states have taken steps to reduce taxpayer funding of Planned Parenthood, and the federal legislation Trump signed into law could prove to be a critical turning point. Unfortunately, it's also possible that the changes made in the OBBB could prove to be all too temporary. As it is, a federal district judge moved quickly to issue a temporary injunction against the Medicaid cuts impacting Planned Parenthood. But let's suppose the Trump administration ultimately prevails in court. Anti-population zealots will continue to fall back on the Planned Parenthood Action Fund, the group's official PAC, and the various international affiliates that are operative in almost 190 countries.[270]

For now, let's just focus on Virginia. Planned Parenthood Advocates of Virginia has actively supported candidates opposed to the Mountain Valley Pipeline. Although the group's website and campaign literature are primarily loaded with references to "reproductive rights," its vast financial resources are also put to use when anti-pipeline activists come calling. If MVP's expansion plans go down to defeat, Planned Parenthood can rightly claim partial credit.

At the same time, the abortion group's support for anti–fossil fuel policies and reduced carbon emissions raises some interesting questions from a health-care perspective. Planned Parenthood California Central Coast has embraced a strategic plan that draws a connection between "health equity" and "climate mitigation."[271] Apparently, climate change can have an impact on "reproductive health," since "climate related disasters" create additional difficulties for people attempting to access health care. Anyway, that's their argument. So, it's only fair to ask what kind of impact the climate-change policies Planned Parenthood advocates will have on health care.

Hospitals Get in on the Climate Act

Suddenly, hospitals are turning into "climate change fighting machines." They are also limiting water with "timers for operating room sinks," investing in "more Earth-friendly drugs," and reducing "anesthetic gas." Those are some of the major takeaways from a report *Politico* filed on the "greening of American health care" in and around San Diego in 2023.[272]

The health care industry is responsible for more than 8 percent of US emissions of greenhouse gases, including carbon dioxide, in comparison to 4.6 percent of total greenhouse gas emissions for health care on a global basis, according to the report.[273] This figure is viewed as an intolerable rate that will make it virtually impossible for the United States to reach emissions reductions goals set by international institutions.

So, what are the recommendations? If you're going under the knife and looking for anesthesia, you might be out of luck.

"The drive to reimagine anesthesia is part of a broader if belated effort to decarbonize U.S. health care, from the operating room to the cafeteria to the gardens and grounds," *Politico* reports. "It's a push spurred on by both medical professionals and Washington policymakers, who feel increased pressure to act amid the dangers of climate change and who acknowledge health care has been slow to engage on sustainability."[274]

One climate culprit here is an anesthetic gas known as desflurane, which green activists object to since they are convinced it lingers in the atmosphere for far too long.

"One hour of that volatile agent [desflurane] is equivalent to driving a car 250 miles, a gasoline car," Joanne Donnelly, director of the nurse anesthesia program at the University of Minnesota, is quoted as saying in the article. "Extrapolate that across an urban area, a region, a nation," and "it's an incredible impact," she added.[275]

Politico's report makes it clear that the hospitals themselves are in the crosshairs of climate activists since they are the biggest sources of emissions in the health-care sector. On Earth Day 2022, Biden's Health and Human Services agency unveiled a "climate pledge," for the purpose of getting the health profession to take climate action of some kind. About 116 health organizations representing 872 hospitals and other health-care institutions signed the pledge, which committed them to cut emissions by 50 percent in 2030 and to cut net emissions by 100 percent come 2050.[276]

Evidently, it's not just the unborn who are threatened by climate activism. Anyone with health-care needs will have to develop a higher threshold of pain, since that pesky anesthesia supposedly does damage to the atmosphere.

Marc Morano, who runs the *Climate Depot* website, raises a pertinent question in response to this new movement against anesthesia. He would like to know how much we are willing to suffer in exchange for accommodating the demands of climate activists.

We are not talking hypothetically here, as Morano cites a new study that recommends "lowering the flow of anesthetic gas" in patents to save the planet. The study estimates that one hour of surgical anesthesia is equivalent to driving about 470 miles.[277] Medical professionals moonlighting as climate activists insist that it's possible to lower the flow of anesthetic gas without sacrificing patient care. (But you, dear readers, can go first.)

After all, climate change is going to do us all in before anything else, including cancer. At least, that's what the climate cult would like us all to believe. Go back to 2020, when a study in the *American Cancer Society Journal* expressed alarm, not over cancer, but the "carbon footprint of cancer care." Here's an excerpt from the study:

> To date, no studies have estimated the carbon footprint of cancer care.… The energy expenditure associated with operating cancer treatment facilities and medical devices, as well as the manufacturing, packaging, and shipment of devices and pharmaceuticals, contributes significantly to greenhouse gas emissions in cancer care.… Some cancer treatment facilities have begun to consider their own carbon footprint and started a process to achieve carbon neutrality.

Morano stands ready with the appropriate questions for the American Cancer Society. "If you need cancer treatment, would you go to a cancer treatment center that was worried about its carbon footprint? Or one that was worried about delivering the best possible modern care possible?"

It's not the people occupying elite positions who ever need to ask those questions. They'll make sure they get the best care. It's the "vulnerable populations"—the ones we are told are most susceptible to the dangers of climate change—that need to ask hard questions about those difficult tradeoffs. The more effective a cancer treatment might be, the bigger a carbon footprint it is likely to have. That means cancer patients are expected to make a sacrifice.

Climate pornography can cost lives. When cancer treatment is suddenly taking a back seat to propaganda-driven "net zero" policies, it's time to take a hard look at what the medical establishment is up to—not just in professional settings but also in academia.

Climate Change Politics Prioritized Over Human Health

In 2023, a medical school committee with Harvard University voted to insert "climate change" into the school's curriculum. What does this entail? Students have been examining "the impact of climate change on health and health inequality," according to the *Harvard Crimson*.[278] Students are told that physicians and health institutions must advance certain climate solutions. Since graduates of Harvard Medical School move on to serve in high-level positions within the medical profession, the motivations behind the new curriculum are fairly obvious. Climate considerations must come first, before any medical care is prescribed. Students who don't toe the line probably should not expect to move on to any leadership positions.

Climate change has also found its way into the emergency room. Never mind what the ailment might be or how old a patient is; they can suddenly be diagnosed as suffering from climate change. This happened in 2021, when a patient came into the Kootenay Lake Hospital in Nelson, British Columbia.[279] At the time, that part of Canada was in the midst of an intense heat wave that had begun impacting older residents, like the patient in question. She suffered from asthma and lived in a trailer with no air conditioning. The ER doctor grabbed hold of the patient's chart and wrote "climate change" as the cause of her ailments.[280]

So, should elderly patients be concerned about climate change? Or about the impact climate-change policies might have on whatever medical treatment they receive?

How far does this go? On his X account, Morano posted photos and videos of hospital staff taking part in a climate protest of some kind, featuring death certificates listing climate change as the cause of death.[281] The protest chant went something like this: "Cutting down on carbon will stop our bodies droppin' / Leaders should be yearnin' to stop the planet burnin'." A new episode of *The Twilight Zone* is in order.

The opportunity cost of climate activism in the medical profession, versus the time and effort that should be put into an accurate diagnosis, is difficult to quantify. But it's clear that anyone in need of health care is in some jeopardy of becoming a victim of climate activism. Unfortunately, this could be the case before even reaching the hospital.

That's because climate activists see a need to shrink the carbon footprints of ambulances. Time is certainly a factor for anyone in desperate need; but remember that the planet's health is the priority, and human beings are a blight on the planet. Since the medical establishment seems inclined to accept the premise of catastrophic climate change, it's not surprising to find there are several studies that measure the carbon footprints of emergency medical services.[282]

What kind of alternatives to quick, efficient ambulance transportation might climate activists come up with to save the planet? Sustainability in emergency services could be coming. Electric ambulances that have trouble charging and arriving promptly could be in the mix.

But there's no reason why we need to go down this road. Ehrlich's doomsday-scenario predictions linking environmental catastrophes with larger human populations have not materialized. Living standards have improved around the world, since human ingenuity has made it possible to reduce pollution while extracting natural resources in a responsible and efficient manner. The facts and evidence are not on the side of population-control advocates, who view birth-control measures including abortion as a vital necessity. But they still have ample money and organization.

In 1968, Ehrlich founded a group called Zero Population Growth (ZPG) that left no room for misinterpretation about its agenda. Possibly because the doomsday predictions did not materialize, the group rebranded itself as Population Connection in 2002. At one point, the nonprofit group, headquartered in Washington, DC, had adopted the motto "Stop at Two," aimed at persuading Americans not to have more than two children.[283] Population Connection pounds the drums for "climate action" and fixes the blame on Western countries, most especially the United States. As it says on its website:

> Climate change is closely linked to population growth. In high-income countries especially, each additional person causes significant emissions throughout their lifetime. High consuming

lifestyles in the most affluent countries result in much higher per capita emissions than in middle- and low-income countries, where most of the world's population lives and is projected to grow.[284]

Add water, mix, and stir. There's nothing unique about how Population Connection floats long-discredited screeds on climate hysteria. But what does stand out here in its discussion of the "injustice" of the "climate crisis" is how the anti-population activists give away their game:

> One of the many unjust realities of the climate crisis is that those who have contributed the least to historical emissions are now the most threatened by its impacts. In addition, the most vulnerable communities have an urgent need to increase their living standards, but the processes of industrialization that have historically facilitated increases in quality of life, overall health, and economic growth in affluent nations are making it harder to achieve a sustainable future.[285]

Despite how the preceding is couched, there's tacit acknowledgment here that climate policies will fall hardest on "the most vulnerable communities"—those most in need of new opportunities, affordable energy, and free-market policies. They are up against an anti-population climate-activist movement working to suffocate humanity at every turn. Population Connection has been a long-standing partner of Planned Parenthood and other pro-abortion outfits. Its affiliated organizations include the Population Connection Action Fund and the Population Connection Action Fund PAC.

One way to prevent "the most vulnerable" people from improving their station in life is to see to it that they are immobilized and unable to do the kind of traveling that's necessary to gain an education and conduct business. Unfortunately for them—and for all of us—the climate activists know just where to aim their arrow.

CHAPTER 12

Climate Credit Cards as a Tool to Constrain Human Movement

A round 2021, Mastercard got in on the climate act with a new CO_2-monitoring credit card that began to gain notoriety. The card came complete with a feature that enabled the tracking of "carbon footprints" with every purchase.

The credit card company partnered with the UN when it launched "Doconomy," for the purpose of allowing "all users to track, measure and understand their impact by presenting their carbon footprint on every purchase." The credit cards featured the slogan "DO. Everyday Climate Action." They also had a personal pledge on the back that read, "I am taking responsibility for every transaction I make to help protect the planet." Some critics have aptly described it as a "Chinese-style social credit card system," complete with a UN global action logo.[286]

The World Economic Forum cut to the chase in explaining how Doconomy could exert control over all of us big spenders: "While many of us are aware that we need to reduce our carbon footprint, advice on doing so can seem nebulous and keeping a tab is difficult. DO monitors and cuts off spending, when we hit our carbon max."

That's right—the climate activists are calling the shots once your spending hits a certain limit. What the limits are is not exactly clear.

But Mastercard and its UN partners very likely took guidance from an August 2021 study in the journal *Nature* that touted COVID-19 lockdowns as a model for the future. The basic idea is that COVID restrictions, smart meters, and tracking apps can all be used as a vehicle to develop what the authors call "personal carbon allowances," or PCAs. In their own words:

> We argue that recent advances in AI for sustainable development, together with the need for a low-carbon recovery from the COVID-19 crisis, open a new window of opportunity for PCAs. Furthermore, we present design principles based on the Sustainable Development Goals for the future adoption of PCAs. We conclude that PCAs could be trialed in selected climate-conscious technologically advanced countries, mindful of potential issues around integration into the current policy mix, privacy concerns and distributional impacts.[287]

What's coming next? Climate passports? Don't laugh! The concept is already out there. Activist groups that continue to see a looming climate crisis, which never comes to pass, view tourism as a big part of the problem. Apparently, the tourism industry is responsible for "one-tenth of the greenhouse gas emissions that contribute to the climate crisis."

A CNN report unpackages the general idea. "The idea of a carbon passport centers on each traveler being assigned a yearly carbon allowance that they cannot exceed," the report explains. "These allowances can then 'ration' travel."[288] CNN informs us that the concept is not exactly new, but because it has been viewed as extreme it has had difficulty getting off the ground. The UK Parliament proposed a similar concept back in 2008 in the form of "personal carbon trading."[289] At the time, the public didn't bite. But we are warned that unless "sustainable travel" becomes the norm, those vacation plans will continue to have a negative impact on the environment.

An organization identified as Intrepid Travel published a report in 2023 that said the tourism industry cannot hope to survive without carbon passports. The report sets a date of 2040 for when carbon passports are likely to become mainstream. Once again, Americans and other Westerners are the primary villains. The average annual carbon footprint for those living in the United States is 16 tons and about 11.7 tons for the UK, according to the carbon-footprint calculus environmental advocacy groups use. Even the lower UK rate, we are informed, is "more than five times the figure recommended by the Paris Agreement to keep global temperature rise below 1.5 Celsius (2.7 Fahrenheit) above pre-industrial levels."[290]

Cruises and air travel are also expected to come under the gun. The drive for reduced emissions could possibly result in higher ticket prices, along with limited services and a paucity of choices. The goal here is to dictate when, how, and where we all travel.

Give the UN crew credit for identifying the right strategy for controlling behavior and traducing societies that celebrate human freedom.

Here is how Doconomy markets itself to banks:

> Every individual financial transaction represents
> a choice that impacts both personal wellbeing
> and environmental sustainability. As consum-
> ers increasingly vote with their money, choos-
> ing products and services that align with their
> values, banks have a unique opportunity to
> facilitate positive change. But this opportunity
> comes with a challenge. While transaction data
> provides powerful insights into environmental
> impact, data alone cannot drive change. Data
> itself will never save the planet, only humans
> can do that, and data can serve as a tool to help
> guide their behaviors.[291]

But who is in charge of that guidance, and who is giving
stage directions to travelers and consumers?

Doconomy is a Swedish "fin-tech company" that has earned
praise from the UN for taking the initiative with credit cards
designed to limit the climate impact of their users. That's the
stated goal. The real goal is to alter behavior to the point where
it becomes easier to extend government control over everyday
activities. Doconomy, for instance, suggests that a family of four
switch to vegetarian meals and that this step alone could save
around twelve euros per day. Possibly, this could be enough to save
for their children's future expenses, including housing needs.[292]
That sounds enticing, but Doconomy leaves out the part about
how climate policies could greatly reduce future housing opportunities and raise living expenses along the way.

The UN's "certified green projects" serve as an example for some of the behavioral changes that climate activists within financial institutions are now working to effect. These projects include the use of "cleaner-burning cookstoves to wind-generated electricity to clean waste disposal—all projects that contribute to global emission reduction."[293]

UN Climate Change Executive Secretary Patricia Espinosa laments that the Paris Agreement is just not enough to achieve the international body's climate goals. Instead, private companies like Mastercard will need to step in and combat climate change "through responsible consumption and passionate collaboration."[294]

Scroll down a bit, and it doesn't take long for Doconomy to get into the benefits of ESG investing, a politically fashionable practice discussed earlier. Just to review, this stands for environmental, social, and governance investment, and if the movement hasn't quite died out yet, it may be in its death throes.

Yet the Swedish firm behind Doconomy makes this astonishing claim: "Many green funds are outperforming the S&P 500 Index as ESG investing becomes increasingly widespread. Whether customers are looking for investment returns or a green portfolio, banks must present these investment products at the optimal points in the customer journey."[295]

The part about green funds outperforming the S&P 500 cries out for verification, since major firms have been backing away from ESG for at least the past year or so. But maybe the real question is how ESG-friendly funds do in comparison to funds that are rooted in more traditional sources of energy? Another question—one some of our Canadian friends touched on previously—is: How many prospective retirees have lost out on solid investment returns because corporate officers prioritized political activism over their fiduciary responsibilities?

BlackRock Surrenders on ESG—Maybe

In August 2024, BlackRock, the world's largest investment firm, announced it was pivoting away from ESG. That's significant, since BlackRock oversees something to the tune of more than $10 trillion in assets. But prior to this about-face, Larry Fink, BlackRock's CEO, had been one of the most vocal climate activists, leading the charge for various "sustainability" measures, based on unfounded alarmist positions.[296]

The other major firms that have been complicit in ESG schemes, namely State Street and Vanguard, both appear to be hanging on to ESG but in a less pronounced fashion. Free-market-oriented outfits like the Heritage Foundation, the American Legislative Exchange Council (ALEC), and the National Center for Public Policy Research have been instrumental in exposing the deleterious effects of ESG investing.

Add to this list stiff resistance to ESG on the part of Republican governors and Republican-leaning state legislatures, and lefty shareholder activists may have finally met their match. Both Heritage and ALEC have advanced model legislation to uphold fiduciary duty requirements for asset managers, to ensure that they remain focused on generating returns for their states' funds, rather than playing footsie with ESG activists.[297]

The other important piece of this countermovement involves the National Center's Free Enterprise Project, "which engages corporate CEOs and board members, submits public comments, engages state and federal leaders, crafts legislation, files lawsuits and directs media campaigns to push corporations to respect their fiduciary obligations and to stay out of political and social engineering."[298] In other words, the project brings conservatives and libertarians into shareholder meetings so they can apply pressure from the other direction.

All positive moves for sure, but there is no recapturing the money drain the ESG movement has precipitated. This means recent and pending retirees can be added to the ever-expanding list of Americans who have been victimized by climate policies.

Media figures who spotlight senior citizens as potential victims whenever there is any serious discussion of entitlement reform suddenly head for the tall grass when ESG enters into the equation. Wouldn't it be interesting to see a study on what the opportunity cost has been for recent and pending retirees—all herded into ESG investments that laid an egg? After the results come in, a follow-up study could provide a list of all the media outlets that declined to publish the results.

Instead, media reports operate under the premise that the Trump administration's Medicaid and Medicare reforms will somehow diminish health care for the needy and elderly. Efforts to root out fraud, while requiring able-bodied, younger Medicaid recipients to work, are portrayed as heartless and rapacious. NPR lists "5 ways Trump's megabill will limit health care access." Immigrants and rural residents are particularly hard hit, according to the NPR piece.[299]

The *American Prospect*, a magazine that describes itself as a "independent voice for liberal thought," insists that the Trump-inspired One Big Beautiful Bill will lead to "mandatory sequestration," resulting in a "half trillion in Medicare cuts," with the implication that the elderly will find themselves destitute.[300] Nothing is said about the Trump administration's efforts to root out fraud and slow the rate of entitlement spending, which redounds to the benefit of prospective retirees. The fact that entitlement spending is responsible for a growing and unsustainable national debt is also omitted by "reports" solely devoted to vilifying Trump.

There are compelling reasons to be concerned about the financial well-being of seniors who are beyond the working age. But try going in search of reports that identify seniors as victims of ESG investing, and a paucity of results will show up. And they are victims: victims of climate policies that obsequious asset managers and corporate board members have chosen to accommodate.

Anytime a politician who is unwilling to talk honestly about entitlements launches a new "mediscare" campaign, that would be a good time to ask what kind of relationship that same politician has with ESG—and then let voting seniors know how their nest egg has been impacted.

Stone Washington, an astute energy and environmental policy analyst with the Competitive Enterprise Institute, fears that "ESG is still alive," even as many firms have publicly backed away. He sees left-wing shareholder activists moving underground while adopting "guerrilla tactics."[301]

"The aim in guerrilla warfare," Stone explains, "is to wear the more powerful enemy down by depleting their time, manpower, and resources with constant asymmetrical skirmishes. The aim with ESG is not so different. In guerrilla ESG, the major institutions provide the impression of a full retreat from controversial environmental and social causes in the face of noteworthy red state divestment and lawsuits targeting ESG funds."[302]

What we are witnessing are just head fakes that enable managers and proxy advisors to continue propping up ESG shareholder proposals. Adding further credence to Stone's well-reasoned concerns is the fact that the two proxy advisory firms (ISS and Glass Lewis) occupy 97 percent of the market, and both have a record of supporting ESG.[303]

Still, there are palpable indications ESG has passed its high-water mark and will find itself operating at the margins, so long as free-market shareholder activists remain engaged. There's also a golden opportunity to continue wrapping ESG around the necks of climate activists, who have done us a great favor by once again showing their hand.

Obviously, the purpose of ESG is not to maximize profits but to create new avenues for anti-capitalist policies. Corporate officers who are willing to find their spines should continuously drive home the point that climate activists are knowingly pushing policies that do not work as advertised. Scratch the average investor and they are not opposed to a healthy climate, any more than they are opposed to good weather and rainbows. But explain to them that climate proposals that pop up in boardrooms are a financial loser and that wind and solar schemes integral to proposals are often bad for the climate, and it's not difficult to take down the worst of what green activists have to offer.

Michael Faulkender, chief economist at the America First Policy Institute, makes a compelling case that ESG is simply an updated version of long-standing techniques climate activists and other progressives have adopted to implement policies they know would never pass muster through the legislative process. That's because climate activists are always searching for ways to bypass democratic bodies and enshrine far-reaching social changes without broad public input.

As Faulkender puts it, "Progressives have struggled mightily to implement their radical environmental and social agenda through the levers of government. Thus, they are partnering with far-Left investment managers to achieve through financial markets what they cannot achieve through the legislative process. Many progressive elites have captured the private retirement savings of the American people to force through an agenda that erodes our national, energy, and economic security. It is essential that policymakers at all levels of government identify and halt this dangerous transformation of our Nation."[304]

The Future of Shareholder Activism

Even with the ESG movement losing steam, climate activists and other progressive elements still maintain the advantage with shareholder activism. The countermovement on the right remains in its inchoate stages, while far-left shareholder proposals continue to come in a torrent. That's why it's important to go back and review what was in motion under Biden and what could still materialize under a President Gavin Newsom beginning in January 2029.

The House Judiciary Committee, under its Republican chairman, Jim Jordan of Ohio, presented evidence in the summer of 2024 that a "climate cartel," comprised of lefty environmental activists and several financial institutions, had joined forces to coerce American companies into accepting decarbonization plans that would put them on a path toward net zero.

Who are we talking about?

The committee identified Climate Action 100+, a group of investors from across the globe; the Net Zero Asset Managers initiative; the Glasgow Financial Alliance for Net Zero; blue state pensions, with the California Public Employees' Retirement System sitting at the top of that list; and nonprofit green groups like Ceres. Not surprisingly, the "climate cartel" also included the firms complicit in pushing ESG—BlackRock, State Street, and Vanguard, along with the leading proxy advisory services.[305]

The House Judiciary Committee determined that the "climate cartel" had "escalated its attacks on American companies" and was forcing those same companies "to slash output of products and services that are critical to Americans' daily lives." Chairman Jordan and crew also warned about a "Global World War" on behalf of net zero and against American companies.[306] That war has been put on hold with Trump in office, but the infrastructure for the climate cartel remains in place, and the cartel members still have friends in high places.

When those friends include people in the White House, deals are cut and favors are meted out. The climate-risk disclosure rules Biden's SEC first unfurled in March 2022 were crafted for the purpose of benefitting billionaire businessman Michael Bloomberg.

How do we know? Bloomberg—who ran for president in 2020 as a Democrat, and who serves as the UN secretary general's special envoy on climate ambition and solutions—was also chairman of the Task Force for Climate-Related Financial Disclosures, or TCFD, a panel that figures prominently in the SEC rules. A *Daily Signal* analysis of the proposed rules found 243 references in which the Securities and Exchange Commission pointed to the Bloomberg-run climate task force as the source of inspiration.[307] There was no denying any of the incestuous relationships.

Bloomberg is also the founder of Bloomberg LP—a financial, software, data, and media company headquartered in New York City—and of Bloomberg Philanthropies. The idea seemed to be for Bloomberg LP to create new revenue streams for itself, if subscriptions to a product called Bloomberg Terminal became the preferred source for SEC compliance.

During his time with the UN, Bloomberg has remained committed to achieving net-zero greenhouse gas emissions, in step with the goals of the Paris Agreement. The Financial Stability Board, an initiative of the G20 nations, established the climate task force during that UN conference and named Bloomberg as chairman. In June 2017, the task force issued its final recommendations, which served as the basis for UN "pilot projects" involving banks, investors, and insurers.

On November 18, 2021, Bloomberg LP announced it was working to become the "financial industry's first port of call for ESG." Bloomberg's company also introduced "climate transition scores," designed to provide oil and gas companies with "benchmarks" for measuring progress toward net-zero emissions, in comparison to those companies' own targets.[308]

The Biden SEC's proposal would have required companies to disclose three different types of emissions:

- Scope 1 emissions, which are direct greenhouse gas emissions owned or controlled by a particular company.
- Scope 2 emissions, which are indirect greenhouse gas emissions resulting from the generation of electricity, steam, heat, or cooling purchased or otherwise acquired by a company.
- Scope 3 emissions, which aren't directly produced by a particular company and don't result from the activities of any assets it owns or controls. Instead, they are the result of what occurs "upstream" and "downstream" of a company's activities.

The most controversial part of the SEC proposal involved the Scope 3 portion, where larger companies would be required to provide soup-to-nuts calculations of their carbon emissions, including those from thousands of their suppliers operating across hundreds of countries.

A *RealClear Investigations* report explained this very well with a scenario involving Cocoa Puffs cereal. Had the climate-disclosure rule gone into effect, General Mills might have had to calculate the emissions from "cocoa farms in Africa, corn fields in the U.S., or sugar plantations in Latin America. Then thousands of processors, transporters, packagers, distributors, office workers, and retailers join the supply chain before a kid in Minnesota, where General Mills is based, pours the cereal into a bowl."[309] Yes, that's every bit as nuts as it sounds.

Tammy Nemeth, an energy policy analyst based in the United Kingdom, told me in an interview that Bloomberg created the Task Force for Climate-Related Financial Disclosure to bring the United States into regulatory arrangements where companies are required to disclose the relationships between their business activities, their emissions, and what kind of climate risks they might encounter.[310]

Nemeth is host of *The Nemeth Report*, a podcast focusing on energy and geopolitical issues, and the author of a recent report on global financial disclosure standards affecting hydrocarbon companies in Canada. She has been carefully monitoring the status of ESG policies in the United Kingdom, Canada, and the European Union. She is concerned that US companies doing business in any of these countries may need to accommodate themselves in some way to foreign climate-disclosure rules.

Meanwhile Bloomberg, who continues to serve as a UN special envoy on climate, has not only recently taken over from

Mark Carney the leadership of the Glasgow Financial Alliance for Net Zero, he has also made it clear he intends to serve as a foil to the Trump administration. He has pledged to continue to pursue efforts to ensure that the United States lives up to Paris Agreement commitments, even without official American participation. The globalist is making use of his own philanthropic group and what he calls "other U.S. climate funders" to make certain this happens.[311]

The good news is that, at least for the time being, Bloomberg cannot draw on any special favors from the White House. In March 2025, Trump's SEC voted to end its defense of the climate-disclosure rules.

That decision came on the heels of intense opposition to the climate rules from congressional leaders, trade associations, state attorneys general, and business representatives.[312] This means that for now, the United States can cut its own path at the federal level. But it does not mean US companies are completely free of what Bloomberg and the international climate cartel are trying to put into place. Governor Newsom's California has its own climate disclosure rules, which speak to the importance of keeping him out of the White House.

And there are also the various international entities that Nemeth has been monitoring from across The Pond.

CHAPTER 13

How UK and EU Climate Clampdowns Serve as a Warning to America

Step inside any one of the Passyunk Avenue "dive bars" in London and you just might think of South Philly. What began as a modest food truck some time in 2015 now includes five locations throughout the United Kingdom's capital city. The owner and operator is an expat from Lawrenceville, New Jersey—a diehard Philadelphia sports fan, an expert restauranteur, and an old friend.

On a Friday afternoon in early June 2025, while it's still somewhat cold and rainy by American standards, we meet up at his Fitzrovia location. Since I arrive a bit early, I take in the scenery, including Philadelphia Phillies and Eagles memorabilia all over the walls, plenty of neon Budweiser signs, televisions blasting out American baseball, plenty of pickup from on tap, and a menu replete with Philly cheesesteaks and Italian-themed dishes.

One of the first items that catches my eye is Mike Schmidt's number 20 jersey hanging on the wall. That brings back memories of some of the greatest Phillies teams from the late 1970s and early 1980s. I remember Schmitty firing off those shots at Vet Stadium, a place that doesn't exist anymore.

J. P. Teti is a bit more attached to the 2008 World Series championship team. After he walks in, we pick up right where we left off during our time together in New Jersey, talking sports and politics.

Since Major League Baseball now plays games in London, fortunate fans can run into some of the current players at the various Passyunk locations when the Phillies are in town. J. P. is getting famous among local Brits who want to experience some of the American dive-bar scene. J. P. also has ambitions to continue expanding but acknowledges it's not always easy to do business in London, with the costs and regulations. They certainly hit a high-water mark during the COVID-19 shutdowns in 2020.

"It was brutal," he recalled. "I can understand during the first wave, when it wasn't entirely clear how lethal it was. But we were still shut down months later, even after it became clear that the mortality rate was low and it was not that lethal.[313]

"I began to develop home products and made use of online selling and shipping," he continues. "But I also had to make deals with landlords, furlough staff, and take out loans. I'm still paying down COVID debt."

J. P. is keenly aware of the "heavy climate regulations" in and around London. Just to cite one example, he mentions a "congestion rule" that is enforced in the name of climate, to prevent people driving into certain areas on certain days, based on their license plates. He's also fairly certain there are any number of "climate rules" that work to inflate the bills he receives.

J. P. describes the property tax in London as a "killer" for him and other small business owners. He also recognizes that the

COVID regulations that sullied his operation for months on end took inspiration from climate-change policies.

"Is it really true," he asks, "that there is a study that says it's indisputable that the science backs man-made global warming, and we have to change our lifestyle?"

I tell them it's "really true" that updated scientific research says this is most certainly not the case.

The conversation turns to Willie Soon, my astrophysicist friend, who has a new study pointing to natural influences as the primary driver of warming and cooling trends. J. P. isn't surprised to hear that there's fresh data linking solar cycles with global warming and cooling. But the science debunking alarmist claims, he informs me, has not made its way into the public mind in the United Kingdom, and certainly not into the European Union.

J. P. views both major parties as a failure. "The Tories are a dead party," he says. "But the Reform Party is gaining some ground. I expect the Labour Party to stay in power for some time. Both parties are all in with green activism. I don't see either offering regulatory relief, and certainly not with climate policies and all the rules that make it harder to do business. The Reform Party seems to have a heartbeat. We'll see."[314]

J. P. is also not a fan of Brexit.

"The British have turned themselves into second-class citizens on their continent with Brexit," he continues. "It used to be they could travel anywhere in the EU, and live anywhere in the EU, and do business anywhere in the EU. But now they need these stamps, and the process gets cumbersome. I already see some incremental steps being made away from Brexit."[315]

So that's one vote against independence, at least as it relates to the European Union. But what's most intriguing is how COVID policies compelled folks to open their eyes to abusive government policies, and how they relate to the climate agenda. What's most disappointing is that, aside from a few voices in the UK Reform Party, there are no climate realists gaining serious traction politically, as there are in the States.

J. P. is off to one of his other restaurants, and I linger for an hour or so with one those Philly cheesesteaks. On my way out, there are dollar bills lining the walls with inside jokes I think only people my age would get. One says: "Rocky Won the Cold War." Another is "Superbowl LIX" and "Let's Go Eagles." The downstairs of this particular Passyunk location is a tribute to Nick Foles, the winning quarterback for the Eagles in Superbowl LII.

As a passing thought, I'm wondering if my Philadelphia teams are somehow complicit in advancing these climate schemes that trip up J. P.-type entrepreneurs. I pull out my phone.... I'll just take a look at the Phillies first, and do a search on climate.... Let's see, let's see....

The first headline that pops up for me is TV news video, "Red Goes Green: Phillies Fight Climate Change Through Initiatives at the Ballpark."[316] Apparently, back in 2008, the Phillies became the first MLB team to join an EPA "Green Power Partnership" program, which involved purchasing "green power" to save on electricity. The Phils, we are told, "offset" 100 percent of their electricity usage. This was done by buying renewable energy credits that represented energy generated by wind and solar power.

The "Red Goes Green" sustainability program says my favorite team did what was politically fashionable at the time. But by becoming complicit in efforts to vilify more reliable forms of energy, the Phillies' management have not only made it more expensive and cumbersome for their fans to get to their stadium. They also have that silly policy of everyone using their credit or debit cards for purchases in the stadium, instead of just using cash. Seems like that's a leftover COVID-19 policy. The very laudable goal of a clean environment is folded into the baseball team's sustainability campaign. But here again, it would seem, we see another example where "fighting climate change" is really a stand-in for controlling human activity and behavior.

Still, at least back in the States, climate skepticism has a heartbeat. During the May 2025 summit at the Heritage Foundation, Sarah Elliott, Lady Elliott of Mickle Fell—the director of the UK-US Special Relationship Unit at the Prosperity Institute in London—discussed the divergent paths the two countries have taken on energy. The problem in Britain, she explained, is that both major parties are complicit in climate schemes that have raised energy costs.

"The political class has turned the UK into a test bed for radical climate policies," she told audience members. The fallout from new government edicts has had a significant impact on the everyday routine of average British citizens. Elliott pointed to examples where people had to sell their cars because they did not meet what she called "the ultralow emissions standards" now in place.

Elliott is also familiar with the predicaments of older citizens, confronted with higher electricity prices at the same time the new Labour government has decided to do away with what she called the "special winter subsidy fuel allowance."[317] How do Britain's seniors cope?

"Some of them just sit in the cold," Elliott said. "Or they go out, so they don't have to be at home. My mother-in-law recently checked her energy digital display, and it had gone up to two pounds. At five o'clock in the afternoon she turned out all the lights on the entire family. So now we are all monitoring our energy with these smart meters in our homes."

The key culprit here is the UK Climate Change Act of 2008, which Parliament passed in anticipation of the UN climate conference held in Copenhagen the following year. Initially, the act set an 80 percent reduction target in greenhouse gas emissions by 2050. But under the Conservative Party, this target was raised to eliminate 100 percent of net emissions by 2050. The change was made after just an eighty-eight-minute debate in the House of Commons. "No wonder why the conservatives lost," Elliott observed.

The false narrative of a dramatic and sustained drop in the cost of renewables was a major selling point of the Climate Act. But reality has caught up with the political rhetoric.

"The UK's decision to adopt net zero was based on false claims about the cost of offshore wind and wishful, even nonsensical thoughts about the economic consequences of net zero," Elliott said.

It was during a virtual UN climate summit in December 2020 that then–Prime Minister Boris Johnson spoke of turning the UK into the Saudi Arabia of wind power. By equating the "production of a commodity that yields more government revenue than any other" with one that requires "more inputs of labor, capital, and land to produce less energy," Johnson was engaging in a delusional exercise, Elliott said, and one that the UK cannot afford.

"This is a story of massive deception by environmentalists, leading to the biggest resource misallocation in British history, done in the name of saving the planet—which large emitters like China and India have no intention of emulating," Elliott added.

What does this mean for the United States?

In April 2021, the Biden administration followed the UK and set the goal of completely decarbonizing electricity generation by 2035 and achieving an economy-wide net-zero target by 2050.

"The UK offers a preview of what aggressive decarbonization would have looked like if President Biden had succeeded in doing by regulation what even a Democratic Congress refused to pass between 2021 and 2023," Elliott continued. "Thankfully, President Donald Trump is rolling back these regulations." The example set by the UK's "disastrous energy policies" should serve as a cautionary tale for America, she warned.

"Even before the recent surge in energy costs in 2020, Britons were paying about 75 percent more for electricity than Americans, and during the energy crisis in 2022, electricity rates for British businesses were more than double the average paid by US businesses," Elliott said.[318]

Apparently, only the wealthiest in Britain can absorb the financial fallout of net zero, while ordinary British citizens struggle to keep their homes and their cars. As an added insult, the net-zero policies exacting so much economic pain are doing nothing for the climate.

The Heritage Foundation has a climate calculator. It shows that even if all of Europe stopped using all fossil fuels immediately, this would only make a difference of one-tenth of one degree Celsius by 2100. For the United States, the calculator shows this figure is three-tenths of one degree Celsius.[319]

Some encouraging events have intervened to spare the American people and hopefully spur serious course corrections in the UK and the across the EU.

"The bursting of the wind power bubble came too late for the UK," Elliott said. "But it has come just in time to save America from making a similar error."[320] While growing political pressures could spur the UK to reverse course, Elliott acknowledged it will "take time and political will."

The Battle Against Big Wind Continues in the US

Meanwhile, back in the States, the battle against Big Wind continues to rage up and down the East Coast. There are currently five projects under construction, running up against lawsuits aimed at stopping them. There's Revolution Wind off the coast of Rhode Island and Connecticut, Sunrise Wind off New York's Montauk Point, Empire Wind off New York and New Jersey, and the Coastal Virginia Offshore Wind Project.

The biggest victory to date for citizen activists has come against Atlantic Shores Offshore Wind. That's the partnership between UK-Dutch oil company Shell and France's EDF Renewables in North America. Atlantic Shores petitioned the New Jersey Board of Public Utilities to terminate its Offshore Renewable Energy Certificates while citing economic and political headwinds. So at least there's an effective countermovement in the United States against climate schemes that do nothing for the climate, thanks to the moxie and legal savvy genuine conservationists have shown. It's fair to say that the Jersey project has been halted for the moment, while others face stiff resistance.

But as UK energy policy analyst Tammy Nemeth warns, Americans still have good reason to be concerned about the machinations of climate activists in Europe and Canada. They maintain global ambitions for climate-disclosure rules that impact private companies. Even as ESG takes a step back in America, the EU has found a way to keep it afloat with its own special requirements.

On May 24, 2024, the EU officially adopted what's known as the Corporate Sustainability Due Diligence Directive (CSDDD), a law that went into full effect on July 25, 2024. All twenty-seven EU countries are required to incorporate the CSDDD into their national laws by July 26, 2026, at which time they will be individually responsible for enforcing the rules.[321]

"Even if a company is not headquartered in the EU, they will still need to become involved with emissions accounting, and they will need to provide this data to the EU if they are doing business in the EU," Nemeth said. "This is a very intensive reporting requirement that can affect a company's entire supply chain. There's also the possibility of a company being audited, and if the EU agents find out you're not providing the right information and providing the right estimates, a company can be fined upwards to something like 10 percent of its global value. Each member state is required to have its own accounting people to verify emissions requirements have been met."[322]

This is where the direct assault on US sovereignty, free markets, and individual liberty comes back into play, with climate activism as the preferred vehicle for globalists. Nemeth explains how this dynamic works with the CSDDD.

"Suppose your company is from outside of the European Union, and you're in the US or Canada," she said. "Well, you're going to have these foreign bureaucrats from the EU coming in, and they want to see all your data, and how you are reporting this data. Then, they will want to know how you are getting this data. Then, they will say we need to calibrate and check and see that you're actually reporting this properly. This is really a form of extraterritoriality, where you have these foreign bureaucrats coming onto your soil to tell you whether you are accurate within the EU's preferred methodology."[323]

Globalists, by definition, are not content with just the EU. Canadian Prime Minister Mark Carney has his own innovative approach toward controlling emissions, and for that matter, all of humanity. That's why Nemeth describes him as "the most dangerous man in the world."[324]

Carney, along with Mike Bloomberg, has proposed a worldwide system of "high integrity" voluntary carbon offsets based on, among other things, investments in nature. The basic idea is to require companies or individuals to buy and trade credits, so as to offset the "hard to abate" part of their carbon emissions. The revenue generated here is meant as an incentive for communities, and landowners in particular, to protect and upgrade forest areas. Or something like that.

When he was running for office, Carney told voters he was going to set up new nature parks in Canada—not only to meet Canada's commitments under the Kunming-Montreal Biodiversity pledge, but also for this very purpose. Others have taken inspiration from Carney. In January 2025, former US Senator John Kerry, the special presidential envoy for climate under Biden, made a big announcement at the World Economic Forum in Davos, Switzerland: the Democratic Republic of Congo would be setting aside jungle forest areas—also for this very purpose.

This movement fits in perfectly with the EU's CSDDD schemes, and it's where Nemeth sees an angle for the UK to reinsert itself back into the EU. She expects Britain to roll out its own emissions disclosure standards sometime in 2026, along with a "carbon border adjustment" mechanism in 2027. And in May 2025, the UK agreed to relink its Emissions Trading System with the EU.[325]

What's the rationale?

"The UK wants to take advantage of the EU's desire to rearm," Nemeth explained. "When you're building up your own defense infrastructure, you want to do it within your own borders. So, while you may purchase defense items from another country, it will be fabricated to some extent within your own borders to keep the money within and to have jobs. The UK wants to participate in this rearming of the EU and have a piece of this pie."

But the ESG investments so integral to the carbon emissions regulatory regime typically have very tight rules and restrictions against investment in defense companies. So, this gets complicated.

"In the UK, there's been a debate about the government asking these large funds to waive those rules, because there's an existential threat of Russia," Nemeth said. "Therefore, with these funds, they need the money to be able to support these companies to build weapons. So, there's a need to relax these rules. That's an interesting twist."[326]

It's no wonder operatives from China are all in with ESG. Not that they will implement it themselves, but they can cajole foolish Westerners into accepting that agenda. Taking a deeper dive into what the globalists have in mind, Nemeth references the Financial Street Forum of 2024 that took place in Beijing, where the Bank of China assumed a prominent role.[327] Participants in the panel discussion included the former governor of the People's Bank of China, Zhou Xiaochuan; the former governor of the Bank of England and chairman of Brookfield Asset Management, Mark Carney, who was poised to become Canada's prime minister; and the former governor of the Swiss National Bank and vice chairman of BlackRock, Philipp Hildebrand. The discussion centered on "Diversifying Financial Support for Global Green Development."[328]

All three panelists were identified as "well-known leaders in carbon reduction, low-carbon development, and green development." Xiaochuan, who was up first, indicated that even if climate change is no longer a government priority, the carbon market and carbon pricing could be used through a range of entities to achieve certain results. Put another way, if the climate rationale no longer works to extend government control over the private sector, another rationale can be used to advance the global carbon-trading market.

Up next was Carney. His comments are worth reviewing in full, since he unpackaged the three elements global activists need to bring free-market economies to heel:

> Two things are true at the same time: there's been tremendous progress in building sustainable finance, but it's still not moving fast enough. That's the first point. The second, as Governor Zhou indicated, is this interplay between finance and policy—particularly a carbon price. Finance can't do the job on its own; it needs the policy framework. Where are we on climate finance as a whole? I'd say we have three gaps right now. We've made a lot of progress, but three gaps remain.
>
> The first is around data—starting with climate disclosure. It's a great pleasure to be here in Beijing, with China leading not just as co-headquarter of the ISSB [International Sustainability Standards Board], but also with its 2027 implementation here. Globally, more than 50 percent of GDP and

emissions will be covered by mandatory climate disclosure standards based on the ISSB. The gap is we need to get it to a higher level—including the United States and other jurisdictions in the emerging world. That's the first aspect of the data gap.

The second aspect is that everyone has a right to that data—freely available, open-source, around the world. By this time next year, the world will have an open-source data platform with over 10,000 companies—including financial institutions—making all their data available to every individual [UN Net Zero Data Public Utility]. Those are the two elements of the data gap. The second gap is around action. One thing I learned from Governor Zhou, Governor Hildebrand, and others during the financial crisis was: when you're in a crisis, a plan beats no plan. We're in a climate crisis—you need a transition plan at the national level, and you need it as a financial institution and a company. We're in a position now with transformation plans here in China being put in place. Including BlackRock, Brookfield, and others, 500 of the top 700 financial institutions in the world—over $100 trillion in assets—will have climate transition plans by the end of this year. These help them put money to work, but we need all institutions to move.

Third point—I'll just list the issues, not explain
the solutions, though we may come back to
them—of course, this is all about investment.
There's been a sharp increase in investment, but
we have clear gaps globally. First, the so-called
hard-to-abate or heavy-emitting sectors—like
steel, aluminum, and heavy-duty transport—
face an $800 billion-a-year investment gap. We
know what needs to be done, but more must be
done to accomplish it. Secondly, there's a gap for
the emerging and developing world—outside of
China—reaching about a trillion dollars a year.
There's a multifaceted set of solutions around
that, including reform at the international
multilateral development banks and others. As
Governor Zhou alluded to, a properly function-
ing carbon market is key.[329]

Particularly ominous from Nemeth's perspective is the emphasis Carney put on repackaging climate disclosures as data that
could be freely available and uploaded to the UN's net-zero data
public utility. For good reason, Nemeth views this strategy as
a worrying sign that global climate activists remain intent on
making countries inside and outside the EU bend to their will.

For his part, Hildebrand cited research indicating that about
$2.5 trillion will need to be invested per year to achieve the
desired climate goals by 2050 or 2060. "What will determine
the pace of decarbonization?" he asked. The cost of capital and
production, and the perpetual problem of making renewable
energy attractive for producers and investors. That hasn't happened, but Hildebrand continues to attach high hopes to electric

vehicles. He pointed to government policies in the form of taxes, subsidies, regulations, and market pricing.[330]

"The reality is we won't have one common policy standard across the world," Hildebrand said. "The U.S. is very unlikely to have a carbon tax, so you hope other regulatory measures come in."[331]

Keep in mind, the conference took place a few months before BlackRock's announcement that it would be pulling back on ESG investing in the United States. But it's evident that BlackRock is not letting go of ESG-type schemes globally, even as an independent, free America remains an outlier under Trump.

The part about "regulatory measures" coming into the United States should be of particular concern to younger Americans, who have been victimized by policies that have made it more difficult to enter the job market. Diana Furchtgott-Roth, the Heritage Foundation scholar who directs the think tank's Center for Energy, Climate, and Environment, and her coauthor Jared Meyer, a fellow with the Manhattan Institute for Public Policy, go into detail about the dilemma millennials face in their recent book titled" *Disinherited: How Washington Is Betraying America's Young.*

They make a compelling case that Washington politicians have "disinherited" younger people most in need of economic opportunity. This has been done through occupational licensing requirements designed to protect public safety but that insulate private businesses and owners at "the expense of everyday consumers, entrepreneurs, and young workers." At the same time, Furchtgott-Roth and Meyer write, these rules "make many promising career paths prohibitively expensive or time consuming to enter."[332]

That's just one piece of a larger picture: No discussion of the regulatory state is complete without delving into climate policies.

And no book about the victims of climate policies is complete without highlighting the climate-porn indoctrination that takes place in the classroom. Jerome Corsi, the political scientist and author we met previously, explains what is at stake as he offers his own definition of climate porn. "We are talking about something that's grotesque and in your face," he told me in an interview. "With sex we are talking about a certain immaturity that undercuts what the sexual act is really about. With climate, these exaggerated claims about the impact of carbon fuels are meant to stir up images of a dystopian future and all the nightmares that come with them."

CHAPTER 14

Climate Porn in the Classroom, on Screen, and in Your Face

P arents who would prefer not to have their sons and daughters subjected to political activism masquerading as science have a friend in the CO_2 Coalition and its online learning center. They also have a stake in the ever-growing school-choice movement.

One of the most beneficial unintended consequences of the COVID-19 school shutdowns has been the emergence of a vibrant parental-rights movement. While investigating COVID policies, parents who became skilled practitioners of open-records requests gained insight into the radical curriculum practices infecting their children's schools. Climate-change propaganda fits into this equation, along with a long list of other objectionable, taxpayer-funded ideological exercises.

The intersection of the transgender movement with material promoting the LGBT agenda in public schools is what spurred parental activism. But climate pornography has also been on vivid display in classrooms across the country. Millennials in danger of being "disinherited" by policies rooted in "junk science" have a huge stake in efforts to reintroduce the scientific method into educational settings, where it is most needed. The good news is that it does not take much to puncture the climate balloon when genuine scientists and honest researchers find expression.

Joining the Battle at the Grade School Level

That's why applause is in order for the CO_2 Coalition, which has been hitting climate pornography where it hurts the most—at lower grade levels. The coalition's online CO_2 Learning Center has several effective videos and "Fun Facts," and we'll just go through a few of the basics here.

Fun Fact #1 says, "There are a lot more polar bears alive today than when your grandparents were young!" Go ahead and "Click to Learn More," and students find that "In 1960, the estimated polar bear population was about 10,000. The latest estimate is about 32,000, the largest ever recorded."[333]

This brings back memories for me. Former Vice President Al Gore was out in front of climate propaganda campaigns that claimed man-made global warming was responsible for polar bear drownings. The basic idea was that melting ice from global warming left less of a platform for polar bears to thrive. Pushing back on this claim was my long-time friend and ally John Berlau, the director of finance policy at the Competitive Enterprise Institute (CEI). He was having none of it.

Gore famously received an Academy Award for his documentary *An Inconvenient Truth* in 2007, which argued that human emissions are responsible for dangerous levels of global warming. But as Berlau explained to me, Gore's flick doesn't live up to the Academy's basic "Rule 12" standards for truthfulness in the use of animation. This rule states that nontraditional documentary devices, such as animation or reenactments, may be used but only "as long as the emphasis is on fact and not on fiction."[334]

The scene at issue is the famed cartoon of a polar bear drowning. The sequence does not come close to approximating the reality of the study from which it is based. While Gore refers to "significant numbers" of polar bear drownings, the study only reported four bears' bodies floating in the sea. And the study attributed these deaths to an abrupt windstorm, not a lack of ice due to global warming. Yet nowhere in *An Inconvenient Truth*'s polar bear sequence is there a citation or even a mention of a storm.[335]

And why would there be, when you're trying to propagandize the public? For a detailed analysis of Gore's film, nothing compares with the takedown Marlo Lewis, an energy and environmental policy analyst with CEI, performed in "Al Gore's Science Fiction: A Skeptic's Guide to *An Inconvenient Truth*."

Lewis dishes, derails, and dismantles a long train of "one-sided statements," "misleading statements," "exaggerated statements," "speculative statements," and "wrong statements." Here's just one in the category of misleading statements—Gore's film "implies that, throughout the past 650,000 years, changes in CO_2 levels preceded and largely caused changes in global temperature, whereas the causality mostly runs the other way: CO_2 changes followed global temperature changes by hundreds to thousands of years."[336] And so on.

There's a timeless quality to what Lewis has produced, since climate realists skeptical of alarmist claims skeptics have clearly gained the upper hand in the past few years, with updated research that points to more natural rather than human influences on climate change. But at the time Lewis produced his rejoinder to Gore, he was running upstream against Hollywood, the news media, and the political establishment.

In some ways, he still is. But the terrain has shifted sufficiently to the point where detached, dispassionate scientific research (divorced from government funding) can transcend the climate establishment. One person who recognizes this tectonic shift is Calvin Beisner, the president, founder, and spokesman for the Cornwall Alliance—a network of Christian theologians, natural scientists, economists, and other scholars. Beisner told me the discredited alarmist predictions, along with the rising costs associated with climate activism, are now registering with the broader American public.

"Poverty is a far greater risk to human health and longevity than anything related to weather," he said in an interview. "We know this means human beings are not better off by fighting global warming. We are much better off by growing richer, which enables us to protect ourselves from all kinds of challenges, like extreme weather and changes in the climate. The fact that the human mortality rate due to extreme weather events has fallen by over 98 percent over the past one hundred years, during the same time we've had this warming trend, indicates that whatever kind of harm warming brings—and that's increasingly debatable—our increase in wealth has enabled us to protect ourselves to the point where we can greatly reduce that harm."[337]

Beisner also notes that more scientists are willing to speak out openly against what media organs long insisted was the consensus view on the science of global warming.

"The empirical research and the evidence are getting more and more difficult to ignore," Beisner continued. "The alarmist side has essentially depended on speaking on the output of models. Whether it's about global average temperature, or about the frequency and intensity of extreme weather events, they are dependent on speaking about the output of models—and they are being quiet about the fact that it's the output of models, and not real-world observations, that alarmists use to communicate with policymakers and the general public."

But because "real-world observations" are constantly falsifying alarmist claims, Beisner suspects we are sitting on the cusp of a profound shift within the scientific community. The fact that global temperatures have been rising at less than half—perhaps less than a third or even less than a fourth—of what average models have predicted, is an inescapable truth. The empirical data Beisner references also show there is no upward trend in the frequency and intensity of storms, be they hurricanes, floods, wildfires, tornadoes, or what have you.

"I think we are going to see more and more fruit coming from this rising number of scientists who are willing to speak up publicly without getting destroyed in their careers, which I know has happened in the past," Beisner observed.

That's good news for policymakers who are willing to carefully weigh the trade-offs that are naturally a part of any consequential decision. It's also good news for the public that has paid the piper for climate propaganda and for students who have to live with the consequences of policies that are now being shaped.

School Choice Opening the Door to Climate Realism

Getting back to the kiddies: I'm not so sure the climate pornographers have the field quite as wide open to them as they did just a few years ago. As we've learned, the COVID-19 shutdowns opened the eyes and ears of parents to what was being taught with their tax dollars. This circles back to the unintended and largely unexpected but benevolent consequence of using open-records requests to probe into education policy. The growing and accelerating school-choice movement just might be what the doctor ordered to get science back into the classroom. The "Fun Facts" delivered through the CO_2 Coalition are making heads explode in the education establishment—and that spells fun.

Here's another Fun Fact from the CO_2 Learning Center: "Carbon Dioxide is plant food. More is better!" Well, that's certainly "an inconvenient truth" for climate activists in government. When little tykes click on "Learn More," they will find that plants need three things to grow: water, sunlight, and carbon dioxide. Students also learn that "More CO_2 means plants grow faster and bigger and provide more food for us. Some people say that breathing on plants makes them grow better. Your breath has very high levels of CO_2 so more CO_2 could help them grow."[338]

Once again, it's more than evident that the attack on CO_2 is an attack on humanity itself.

That attack is often focused on students. Like many other parents, Rob Pluta, a former school board member in Lawrence, New Jersey, became politically active when he saw what kind of curriculum LGBTQ activists were pumping into public schools. As a business owner with a stake in his community, Pluta continues to push back against what he views as very harmful material circulating in the classrooms.

It was in late August 2025, when I visited Pluta's restaurant, just on the brink of another school year. This is when he tells me about a "gay pride parade" the Lawrence Intermediate Schools held the previous June. This would be for fourth-, fifth-, and sixth-grade students. The parade was the culmination of a month-long celebration of sorts promoting the LGBTQ agenda, which didn't have any relation to reading, writing, math, or anything that might be of value to middle-school students.

"Parents likely had no idea about any of this," Pluta informed me. "These pornographic exercises have been going on for years, and with money from taxpayers who don't support this radical agenda."

Under a 2019 New Jersey state law (N.J.S.A. 18A:35-4.35), LGBTQ+ inclusive material became mandated in schools without enabling parents to opt out. But the times, they are a-changin', thanks to the 2025 US Supreme Court ruling in *Mahmoud v. Taylor*, which said Montgomery County Public Schools in Maryland violated the First Amendment rights of parents by not allowing them to have their children opt out of instruction involving LGBTQ-themed storybooks. The high court ruling will most certainly foster long-overdue policy changes to secure parents' rights throughout the country. But it does mean parents will need to remain engaged.

"The material that I have seen in textbooks, online, and on videos that have been directed to children are highly pornographic, coercive, and damaging to children at a formative age," Pluta said. "We need to have a conversation about what's age-appropriate, and what really qualifies as education rather than just indoctrination."

Pluta is hardly operating at the margins on these questions. He's part of a growing majority. Protect Your Children NJ represents thousands of residents across the state, including parents, teachers, school board members, concerned taxpayers, mothers, fathers, church leaders, Christians, Orthodox Jews, Muslims, and Coptic Christians who are united in opposing LGBTQ curriculum in schools.

"There's no question the Supreme Court ruling is a godsend for all of us, but it also means parents are going to need to be more active than ever," Pluta said. "From being on the school board, I already know activists will try to find work-arounds so they can slide in their agenda. So, it's up to all of us to be sure the law is being enforced and our children are being protected."

Pluta is a devout, practicing Catholic and views the Supreme Court ruling in *Mahmoud* as a significant victory for religious freedom. But he's quick to point out that the presentation of pornographic material at the grade school and middle school levels should concern all parents, regardless of their religious convictions. "Children at the developmental stage," he said, "are not prepared for complex and highly emotional subject matter."

Thanks to the internet and smartphones, pornography is pervasive and easily accessible. From the Catholic perspective, pornography is a grave sin that "offends against chastity" and "does grave injury to the dignity of its participants." The other problem, according to the Catholic catechism, is the commodification of the human person, who becomes mere property and an object of abuse, profit, and violence.[339] The pornography industry, the church warns, perpetuates numerous horrible injustices, including human trafficking and sexual exploitation.

There ought to be some kind of consensus among school board members about what is age-appropriate for students, and what qualifies as education. While they're on that subject, they should also take a hard look at the pornographic influence climate propaganda has on students. The now widely discredited idea that there is a "consensus" on climate should be thrown out, along with results-oriented lesson plans that ignore the scientific method. Unfortunately, my home state and others have a long way to go on that front.

Before leaving the school board, Pluta became acquainted with a key component of the 2020 New Jersey Student Learning Standards (NJSLS), which made Jersey the first state in the nation to include climate change in all content areas of education. As the state education department website says:

> These standards are designed to prepare students to understand how and why climate change happens, the impact it has on our local and global communities and to act in informed and sustainable ways.[340]

Put another way: Students need to be sufficiently propagandized so they change their behavior in step with what climate activists seek. There's more:

> Districts are encouraged to utilize the NJSLS to develop interdisciplinary units focused on climate change that include authentic learning experiences, integrate a range of perspectives and are action oriented. While the 2016 NJSLS-English Language Arts (ELA) and Mathematics do not have specific climate change standards, districts may want to consider how they can design interdisciplinary climate change units that incorporate relevant ELA and mathematics standards. Likewise, it may be helpful to review the 2020 NJSLS documents to identify other relevant standards that might be incorporated as well as to understand the role of core ideas, performance expectations and practices in curriculum development and lesson planning.

When it comes to lesson planning, teachers can click on the appropriate "grade band" to see how they can reference climate change, which will be incorporated into: Visual and Performing Arts; Comprehensive Health and Physical Education; Science; Social Studies; World Languages; Computer Science & Design Thinking; and Career Readiness, Life Literacies and Key Skills.

Nothing is left out. That's why students in Jersey, and throughout the country, stand near the top of the list of victims of climate-change policies. They are essentially being told there is no room to debate or question the premise of anti-energy policies that will raise their costs of living and subtract from their opportunities.

But it doesn't have to stay that way.

Trump's "Tear Down This Wall" Moment

President Trump may have had his "Tear Down This Wall" moment, at least in terms of domestic policy, on July 29, 2025. That was the day his EPA issued rulemaking to withdraw the 2009 Endangerment Finding for greenhouse gases. At the same time, Trump's Department of Energy released a report giving a fresh rundown of the science behind climate change. Here we find for certain that there is no hard consensus and that natural influences on climate change must be taken into consideration.

As discussed at the outset, it is the Endangerment Finding that has served as the edifice for some of the most burdensome climate regulations currently in place. The legal and scientific rationales for the finding, which were always dubious, are finally coming under intense scrutiny. Trump's move could be the masterstroke that frees the economy, while also reinserting scientific rigor into the policymaking process.

Tom Pyle—the free-market activist who helped expose the money and influence behind "Big Green"—explains what's at stake. "For a decade and a half, the EPA has used the 'endangerment finding' as authority to reject permits, shut down projects, and deny Americans access to reliable, affordable energy and transportation choice," Pyle said in a press release. "It has reshaped investment and infrastructure to our country's detriment and has been used as a vehicle to push a political agenda."[341]

He added:

> The longstanding legal and scientific issues with the endangerment finding are finally going to be addressed under the leadership of President Donald Trump, EPA Administrator Lee Zeldin, and Secretary of Energy Chris Wright. Congress never granted EPA authority to regulate greenhouse gases under the Clean Air Act—legislation written specifically for harmful pollutants, not global emissions—and yet the endangerment finding has been used as a justification to repeatedly do exactly that.

If Zeldin is successful in his efforts to repeal the finding, the EPA estimates the American people will save about $54 billion annually, while the repeal will also unleash more than $1 trillion in long-term economic value and boost GDP by as much as $440 billion annually.[342] There's no limit to how the Endangerment Finding's CO_2 regulations restrict the use of cars, trucks, power plants, airplanes, along with oil and gas operations. The legal and economic case against the Endangerment Finding is well-established; but what about the environmental and scientific aspects?

Since 2005, US emissions have dropped more than 20 percent thanks to good, old-fashioned American ingenuity and the shift away from coal to natural gas.[343] Putting the emphasis on market-based solutions rather than federal mandates is clearly the way to go.

As to the science, the Energy Department's report—released in tandem with the EPA proposal to rescind the Endangerment Finding—presents a comprehensive rejoinder to what students have been told at all grade levels and in higher education. The report is the handiwork of five well-credentialed scientists who make several key points. Here are just a few taken from the executive summary:

- "The combination of overly sensitive models and implausible extreme scenarios for future emissions yields exaggerated projections of future warming."
- "Most extreme weather events in the U.S. do not show long-term trends. Claims of increased frequency or intensity of hurricanes, tornadoes, floods, and droughts are not supported by U.S. historical data."
- "Attribution of climate change or extreme weather events to human CO_2 emissions is challenged by natural climate variability, data limitations, and inherent model deficiencies. Moreover, solar activity's contribution to the late 20th century warming might be underestimated."
- "Both models and experience suggest that CO_2-induced warming might be less damaging economically than commonly believed, and excessively aggressive mitigation policies could prove more detrimental than beneficial. Social Cost of Carbon estimates, which attempt to quantify the economic damage of CO_2 emissions, are highly

sensitive to their underlying assumptions and so provide limited independent information."

Those are just snippets from a very comprehensive report that will have a long shelf life. But policymakers do not have unlimited time to make decisions with economic, environmental, and national security implications. The updated scientific research now in circulation makes a powerful case that climate-change policies are ultimately more harmful than climate change itself.

CHAPTER 15

Saving Environmentalism from Climate Activism, with National Security as the Ace in the Hole

F rom her rooftop in Harvey Cedars, Long Beach Island, Brook Folino tells a story about her encounters with marine life. She's had her home here for decades. Before the summer season began here in May 2025, she's was contemplating a move she did not want to make, but one that will be unavoidable if somehow the Atlantic Shores program is reactivated.

"The offshore wind will destroy the views, disrupt marine life, and erode our property values," she tells me. "This is a special place; we love it here. I can see the dolphins coming through, the birds, and the whales. There was a humpy that came through last year, and it was so close that if I was in the water, I could have reached out and touched it."[344]

That's what the locals call humpback whales—"humpies." For the surfers audacious enough go out into the ocean forty feet or so, or even farther, they have their own close encounters. But those of us who are a bit more timid and who just like to hug the shore are not left out. That spout coming out of water in that southern part of the island? That is no boat! It's another humpy chasing after some fish. That's fun, and that's the Jersey Shore.

But the dead carcasses that wash up have an unsettling story to tell about what makes the climate movement tick.

There comes a point on the pages of *Moby Dick*, Herman Melville describes all the different kinds of whales. Some might find that part tedious; I find it brilliant as he builds up to his point. Those who have read and reread *Moby Dick* might recall how Melville goes into some detail about how the dead whales on the beach do not capture the majesty and might of what the creature is in the ocean. The live version is a beast to behold, a behemoth that laid waste to those rickety boats the whalers used to try and harpoon them back in the day. When dump trucks show up in Atlantic City and Long Beach Island to cart off the dead whales—compliments of climate activists pushing their wind farm schemes—it's time for the genuine conservationists to go on offense.

As it turns out, they are.

Linda Bonvie joins in the conversation in Beach Haven. She's someone I met at a press conference on Long Beach Island in July 2024 when the "Save the Whales Movement" seemed to be back on its heels. As an investigative journalist probing into health and environmental issues, Bonvie has one of the sharpest, most cutting-edge Substacks pertinent to what's going down along coastal communities.

While we're enjoying the view from Folino's rooftop, Bonvie tells me how, during the Biden administration, neither Atlantic Shores Offshore Wind nor the federal Bureau of Ocean Energy Management (BOEM), which initially approved the project, had presented any study looking into the level and impact of the airborne noise that would be generated during the construction and operation of the two hundred enormous wind turbines.

"Remember, each of these is more than three times the height of the Statue of Liberty, and some of them are only about eight miles from the beach," Bonvie tells me. "The underground sonar and the large reverberations that come from the pile-driving for the steel monopile foundations in the seabed are where we get into problems with marine life."[345]

As to the human population, Folino informs me that once fully operational, the wind turbines could be so damaging to human senses that people simply could not remain on the beach. "My research showed that the rate the blades rotated was actually antithetical to the human body's rhythm, and it would be very uncomfortable to try and watch them turning, and would cause one to look away," Folino explains. "Their very existence, between the sound, the blinking lights, and the rotation, would keep people off the beaches entirely."[346]

Bonvie has consulted with Robert Rand, an acoustics expert based in Brunswick, Maine, to take a deeper dive into what Atlantic Shores had in mind, and what it would sound like for local residents. If the project were completed, it would come out to a total of 357 turbines.

"My estimate, based on working in acoustics for four decades, is that it will be a rumbling, thumping, low-frequency noise coming from the ocean, especially during the night," Rand explained in his conversation with Bonvie. "That's with new, fresh blades. When the blades are no longer smooth, that creates a lot more noise."[347]

Given how harmful offshore wind is to the environment, wildlife, and human health, the question becomes: Who exactly is benefiting?

"Just follow the money," Folino says. "The politicians, and anyone in industry supporting the project, have a financial stake—from Governor Murphy on down. Even when they are all forced to acknowledge the obvious environmental damage and degradation that will result, they fall back on 'climate' as their major rationale. Everything is subjugated beneath climate, and we are told it's such an emergency, we have to accept a certain level of damage now to head off a climate catastrophe in the future. That scenario is becoming less plausible all the time, and this is really just about narrow special interests, including foreign interests, lining their own pockets."

Fortunately, there are elected officials willing to go against the grain and fight against Big Wind. Congressman Jeff Van Drew, a Republican representing the shore areas in the Second District of New Jersey, took part in that same LBI press conference where I first met Bonvie. He made it clear he would help lead the charge against the Atlantic Shores project. Since then, Van Drew has compiled significant wins on behalf of his beach-dweller constituency. He had important input into Trump's executive order that began to turn the tide against offshore wind. The congressman has continued to press hard against what he calls "Green New Deal-style projects," such as wind turbines.[348] He's also been a persistent opponent of the net-zero policies former Governor Murphy pursued in New Jersey.

"Everyone wants a cleaner energy future, but it has to be done in a way that is realistic, sustainable, and affordable," Van Drew said in a press release. The congressman went on to say how families in his state are paying some of the highest energy bills nationwide and offered an alternative to Murphy's climate machinations.

"We need to act quickly but carefully to bring real relief with practical solutions," Van Drew said. He urged moving ahead with designs for a new nuclear power plant while reopening another one. "We also need to invest in new natural gas plants to maintain energy reliability and affordability as we transition," he added.

Van Drew and other like-minded elected officials have the facts on their side. They also have an opportunity during the Trump administration to cut the legs right out from under the climate movement. The whole point of an environmental impact statement is to compare a particular project against a base scenario where the project is not built. But under President Biden, the BOEM agency in its environmental impact statement admitted that its entire plan for offshore wind would have only "limited" impact on climate change.

Dismantling Wind Power Myths

In a June 2025 technical report, Save LBI made considerable hay out of this point with "science-based facts and common sense." They released the report as part of an effort to "clear up misunderstandings and explain how these projects impact the environment, local shore communities, and the cost of electricity."[349] The report sets about debunking a series of "myths" that windpower proponents have circulated, attached to "facts" countering those myths. Here are just the first two.

Myth 1: Offshore Wind Projects Reduce Global Warming

FACT: These full-scale industrial projects have virtually no effect on climate change. Proponents of offshore wind make vague, unsupported statements of "addressing," "tackling," or "dealing with" climate change but have yet to issue a report demonstrating how offshore wind projects mitigate climate change. In contrast, the federal Bureau of Ocean Energy Management (BOEM)—the agency responsible for regulating and managing offshore energy development—plainly states in its Environmental Impact Statement (EIS) for the 200-turbine Atlantic Shores South project that it will have a "negligible" impact on climate change. The agency uses similar language in the draft EIS for the Revolution Wind project off the coast of Rhode Island and, in the EIS for the Vineyard Wind project off the coast of Nantucket, wrote: "Overall, it is anticipated that there would be no collective impact on global warming as a result of offshore wind projects, including the Proposed Action alone."[350]

Myth 2: Offshore Wind Projects Reduce Regional Greenhouse Gas Emissions.

FACT: Claims of reductions in greenhouse gas emissions are oversimplified and misleading. In Final EIS documents for multiple OSW [offshore wind] projects along the East Coast, BOEM offers no evidence to support the claim that offshore wind farms reduce greenhouse gas (GHG) emissions on a regional scale. This assertion is clearly disputed in the 2017 report, "Evaluation and Comparison of US Wind and Skipjack Proposed Project Applications," submitted to the Maryland Public Service Commission. On page 92, Levitan & Associates wrote: "The market response that will displace 372 megawatts of planned onshore wind resources in western and central PJM—Pennsylvania, Jersey, Maryland Interconnection—*will cause carbon emissions to increase* [emphasis added] in western and central PJM due to increased coal generation." On page ES-25, the report calls US Wind's estimate of reduced power-plant air emissions "an oversimplistic assumption that ignores the fact that Maryland is integrated into the PJM [regional electric transmission] system." The same situation exists for Atlantic Shores, which is also part of the PJM grid. Contrary to statements made in BOEM's Final EIS for the Atlantic Shores South project, regional greenhouse gas emissions could actually increase.

If reducing GHG emissions is the goal, there are many less expensive and more effective ways to achieve reductions, including numerous measures that conserve energy while saving money. The "Global GHG abatement cost curve..." chart on page 4 of the full report, which shows the cost of removing one ton of GHG for 39 different abatement possibilities, confirms this. Building massive industrial wind farms in our oceans is far and away the most expensive of all.[351]

In July 2025, Save LBI sent correspondence to the most well-funded, self-described environmental advocacy groups, which cuts to the heart of where we are in the climate debate. In a letter addressed to the executives of the NRDC, the Sierra Club, and more than dozen others, Save LBI president Bob Stern asked them all to reconsider their support for offshore wind.

Stern directed their attention to the June 2025 report that showed how the risks of offshore wind outweigh its purposed benefits. Perhaps this will be a critical turning point. If the established environmental groups insist on moving forward with a project that's not good for the environment and does nothing for the climate, then the unavoidable questions that arise include: What are their goals? Who are they really working for? What are the implications for genuine environmentalists and conservationists?

Save LBI's petitions to federal agencies asking them to create a safe migration corridor along the East Coast to save the North Atlantic right whale from extinction could be a game changer. Environmental advocacy groups are faced with an either-or choice. Either they will join with local conservationists to save the whales, or they will prioritize offshore wind plans. It can't be both.

Whales as Pawns

Maybe in the end it's the whales that will save us, since their example can help put the lie to the climate movement and expose what really makes it tick.

When the US Navy was conducting advanced sonar exercises with an eye toward China and their enemy submarines, the green groups were all in with saving whales. Remember, the US Supreme Court dismissed a case from the NRDC against the navy on sonar use, citing a lack of evidence showing any harm to marine life. Still, it wasn't so long ago that the NRDC and other green activists seemed to care about the whales—or at least said they did. But suddenly, many of the same groups that sought to constrain military exercises because the sonars were supposedly harmful to the whales, now deny that offshore wind has any impact on marine life. That's quite the turnabout.

Consider what else Save LBI has to say in its highly detailed report:

> MYTH 9: There is "no evidence" that offshore wind-vessel surveys were the cause of recent increases in whale deaths.

> FACT: There is substantial, credible evidence that increased whale deaths are strongly correlated with the increased presence of wind-energy vessel surveys, which use high intensity noise devices to map the seabed.

> A statistician working with Save LBI has provided highly compelling statistical evidence that offshore wind activity was the primary cause of

the rapid increase in whale mortalities off the coast of New Jersey in early 2023. A statistically significant 12-fold increase in the mortality rate of humpback whales in the region coincided with a sharp increase in wind-survey-vessel traffic, which nearly tripled from an annual average of 58,895 vessel miles (2015–2022) to 171,440 vessel miles in 2023. During the same period, general shipping traffic rose an insignificant 9%, from 1,800,359 to 1,973,891 vessel miles per year—too small to account for the sharp increase in fatalities.

The same "no-coincidence" correlation is illustrated in the Save LBI report, "Impact of Vessel Survey Noise on Marine Mammals," which also documents numerous overseas incidents linking mammal stranding to the use of air guns in oil and gas surveys. Though the air guns used for these surveys propagate noise mostly downward and are louder at their source, the effect is similar to the "sparker" units used for wind-energy surveys, which also propagate noise energy horizontally where the animals are—meaning the correlation with mammal stranding and the harmful noise produced by both devices cannot be ignored....[352]

Craig Rucker, the CFACT president, describes his group as a "Greenpeace of the Right," since the climate activists present a clear and present danger to the environment and its living creatures.

"I find it interesting the way the large environmental activist groups are only concerned about whales when it comes to navy sonars, and other US military exercises that boost our national security," he observed in one of our many interviews. "But when it comes to offshore wind, they don't care about the whales at all. In fact, they are actively supporting these environmentally degrading wind turbines that studies show threaten whale populations, and that are responsible for an increasing number of whale deaths. I think it's obvious who the real conservationists are, and it's not the Big Green groups."

Whatever concerns the Big Green activists had about the whales was feigned and not real, since the overarching purpose of their litigation was to disrupt US military exercises. That creates an opportunity for Team Trump. If the environmental and economic arguments by themselves are not enough to scuttle the offshore wind project, then perhaps it's time to elevate national-security concerns.

Save LBI touches on this issue in another part of its report. Apparently, wind turbines can impair the ability of radar systems used in the defense of American air space.

In its 2020 "Radar Interference" study, BOEM reviewed seventeen Atlantic Region radar installations. But it overlooked the ARSR-4 air defense radar system in nearby Gibbsboro, New Jersey, which is part of the North American Aerospace Defense Command (NORAD) early-warning system. The agency did, however, analyze the impact of New York's Empire Wind project, located fifteen miles off the coast of Long Island, on the NORAD radar system in Riverhead, New York.

BOEM made two very disconcerting discoveries: Return signals from small and large aircraft would be obscured by numerous false targets created by turbine operation, and smaller aircraft flying just above the turbines, including drones, would not be detected. In December 2020, the Department of Defense advised BOEM that the Atlantic Shores project will undermine NORAD's missions by degrading air surveillance radar performance.

Is there more at work here than just poor judgment when it comes to the impact climate initiatives have on national security? Or is this by design?

Following the Money Back to Communist China

When you follow the money, it seems evident that there is a definite strategy at work on the part of hostile actors. In June 2025, Texas Republican Senator Ted Cruz chaired a committee hearing looking into how the Chinese Communist Party was funding climate advocacy groups in the United States, for the purpose of organizing lawsuits against US energy companies. The session, titled "Climate Lawfare and the Courts: How Foreign Actors Are Undermining American Energy Independence," drew a connection between the Energy Foundation China (EFC), headquartered in San Francisco, and the Chinese Communist Party.

In a previous chapter, we discussed how the EFC was once part of the Energy Foundation, a lefty outfit also headquartered in San Francisco. Witnesses at the hearing included Scott Walter, president of the Capital Research Center, a conservative watchdog group.

Walter told committee members that, regardless of what the motives might be, it is objectively true that "radical climate activists" advocate policies that undermine America and strengthen China. The activists Walter called out are constantly campaigning to block US domestic energy production while also working to make the US dependent on supply chains from China.

He warned policymakers that China has "willing partners" in activist groups such the Rocky Mountain Institute, the California China Climate Institute, and Energy Foundation China.

"The Energy Foundation scheme is not subtle," Walter testified. "It's headed by a former influential Chinese government official and sends money to activists at groups like the Rocky Mountain Institute and the Natural Resources Defense Council. It also sends money to activists in universities like Berkeley, UCLA, and Harvard."[353]

The efforts made by Senator Cruz and others to expose the climate network and its connection to China are helpful, as far as they go. But it's also just as important to take a hard look at how foreign powers can make, and probably have made, use of climate activist groups to advance lawsuits aimed against the US military and energy companies.

One group that stands out from the pack is the Union of Concerned Scientists (UCS). That's an outfit some critics describe as the Union of Left-Wing Lawyers, since it's not clear what percentage of their membership are actual scientists. But some are for sure, and the most famous among them may have been the late Carl Sagan, a very intellectually gifted American astronomer and planetary scientist. I much enjoyed his commentary, his books, and his 1980s TV documentary series *Cosmos*. As much as some of us may have differed with him politically, I always viewed Sagan as a national treasure.

Here's where the knowledge and insight of Paul Kengor, a Grove City College political science professor and Reagan biographer, has special value. As Kengor reminds us, it was Sagan and the members of the Union of Concerned Scientists who were out in front opposing President Reagan's Strategic Defense Initiative (SDI). In the 1980s, UCS claimed that SDI was unworkable and stressed the impossibility of "hitting a bullet with bullet."

"Back in the '80s, the Union of Concerned Scientists argued that there was a consensus you couldn't build SDI and use space-based platforms with lasers to incapacitate an incoming missile," Kengor said. "What really appalled Reagan was the political consensus at the time on behalf of 'mutual assured destruction,' or MAD, which was the idea the world would be better off if it had enough nuclear weapons to annihilate each other many times over. Reagan found it strange that liberals who prided themselves on compassion would support that kind of doctrine."

Someone else worth citing here is Robert Jastrow, a Dartmouth University physics professor who also worked for NASA. Jastrow made a powerful case that the UCS, and other SDI opponents, misled the press and the public by greatly exaggerating the number of orbiting satellites that would be required for a space-based defense.

In retrospect, it becomes more apparent all the time that Reagan was exactly right to pursue a space-based missile defense system, in tandem with other missile defense systems. The US missile defense systems already in place disprove the UCS arguments. These systems include Ground-based Midcourse Defense, for long-range protection; the Aegis Ballistic Missile Defense, for sea-based interception; the Terminal High Altitude Area Defense (THAAD), for higher-altitude terminal defense; and the Patriot Advanced Capability (PAC-3), for lower-altitude terminal-missile threats. And notice how well that "Golden Dome" is working in Israel? Thankfully, following in Reagan's footsteps, President Trump is intent on pursuing a "Golden Dome for America," to protect the homeland from rising threats.

Fast-forward to today and we see the UCS also has been a persistent opponent of hydraulic fracturing—also known as fracking—which makes use of innovative drilling techniques to access oil and gas deposits that were once beyond reach.

"Reagan would have been thrilled with hydraulic fracturing," Kengor said. "In Reagan's 1980 campaign, one of the issues was the energy crisis, and Jimmy Carter telling people if they were cold just wear an extra sweater—and then there was all the talk of 'malaise.' Reagan's response was very much like Donald Trump's. We've got the energy right here, right underneath us, and we ought to be doing everything possible domestically to produce as much energy as we can."

The fact that the same groups and networks opposed to SDI now also oppose fracking is as revealing as it is unsurprising to Kengor.

"Today's environmental movement is loaded with socialists wherever you look, and the Green parties tend to be the ones that are most far left," he said. "Just look at those parties in Europe, and they are all filled with former communists from behind the Iron Curtain."

Here in the United States, green groups—funded through what one researcher calls a "web of dark money," with ties to former President Obama and other Democrats—have been working to thwart President Trump's energy agenda.

In an interview with Fox News Digital, Jason Isaac, CEO of the American Energy Institute, warned that "a whole web of dark-money-funded partisan and foreign-tied organizations" are out to block Trump's plans to expand the use of nuclear energy.

Isaac suggested the groups in question have no interest in sound policy solutions. Instead, he said, "they're about driving the cost of energy up and driving access to energy down, so they can control the narrative and control every aspect of our lives."[354]

What groups are these? Isaac named a few: the Union of Concerned Scientists, the Nuclear Threat Initiative, Greenpeace, Friends of the Earth, and the Sierra Club. Just as the UCS attacked Reagan over SDI and his efforts to make America more secure, the lefty-activist group and its allies are now dead set on opposing Trump's efforts to make America more energy independent.

The Greening of the US Military

This well-funded green network is not exactly new, and it can do great damage to America's economic and military standing when it has friends in government. The Obama and Biden years led to what some critics aptly call a "Greening of the Military."

Doug Truax, a former US Army captain, Ranger, and West Point graduate, is the founder and CEO of Restoration of America. Truax and his group recently launched a project at RestoreTheMilitary.com, designed to "expose the bad actors bogging down the culture of America's fighting forces with woke policies and corporatization, and then work to reshape the military into the fighting force it needs to be." In a series of email messages with me, Truax discussed how green initiatives have worked to undermine the US military.

"Left-wing presidents like Obama and Biden force-fed their radical climate zealotry into official military policy, weakening the lethality of fighting forces and undermining morale," Truax said. "For example, no one in their right mind would rely on unreliable energy sources, like wind and solar, to power crucial military hardware when our brave soldiers' lives are at stake—but that's what was happening. We are one hundred percent behind President Trump's efforts to root out this ideological cancer in our military and to ensure it doesn't return."

But that's not the most concerning issue, Truax pointed out:

> Making the military "green" isn't the only way Obama and Biden weakened our military when it comes to climate. Both liberal presidential administrations worked closely with leftist environmental groups who were collaborating with our enemies—primarily China. Obama and Biden were thus serving as useful idiots on behalf of communist China to weaken our military. China probably was shocked at how easy it was to partner with radical leftists to weaken American institutions. We are now just beginning to unravel the network of leftist organizations—many of them funded by our government—to assess the damage to our national security and to make sure these alliances are permanently broken.

The countermovement against woke policies and climate activism that have burrowed into the US military is already producing some encouraging results. What Truax calls the "re-warriorizing" of America's military culture appears to be underway, and it's a trend that hopefully accelerates in coming years. But while Trump is still in office, there's an additional step he and allies in Congress should take to ensure America's political and economic independence. And it's one aimed right at the heart of the climate industrial complex.

CHAPTER 16

Rediscovering Jefferson's 1776 Declaration as Organic Law, While Rejecting Globalism in 2026

E xaggerated claims about human influences on temperature and climate continue to yield a long list of victims. But the largest and most vulnerable may be the current generation of middle school, high school, and college-aged students. Parental rights groups who are correctly focused on combating the most overt forms of pornography in the classroom have an equally large stake in combating climate porn. Their sons and daughters are being taught that their future is bleak, that humanity is a disease to the planet, and that they should divorce themselves from the relatively high standards of living Americans have enjoyed. The CO_2 Coalition has put into a circulation a compelling blueprint for pushing back against climate porn. After reviewing the National Science Teaching Association's (NSTA) Statement on Climate Change in 2023, the group issued a detailed rebuttal. The CO_2 Coalition found that, true to form, the education establishment emphasized the phony "consensus" on climate rather than prioritizing critical thinking skills and the scientific method. The association is clearly bent on having young students accept the premise of man-made global warming theories despite all their flaws.

As the coalition states in its rejoinder, "Students should be encouraged to review all facts on a subject (in this case climate change) and make up their own minds rather than be indoctrinated into an established political agenda. Unfortunately, the NSTA has taken a strong position that is antithetical to the scientific method, critical thinking and open scientific debate. Its position is one of censorship of any scientist or science that does not support the NSTA-approved 'science.' The NSTA Position Statement on Climate Change fails to delineate between real science and political science."[355]

Take that NSTA! But let's go even further and have a little fun. Climate realists who are willing to challenge what has been described as the "climate industrial complex" seem greatly overmatched. All the money and the organizations are seemingly positioned on the other side of the table. There are the national and international government agencies, the NGOs, and the multibillionaire-dollar foundations. But it is precisely this money trail that puts the lie to what is being peddled to the public in the form of climate porn. Richard Lindzen, the professor emeritus of meteorology at the Massachusetts Institute of Technology (MIT), told the *Daily Mail* that the public seems to be catching on to the unsavory motivations behind climate hysteria.

"I think it's hopeful that people are beginning to at least question this," Lindzen said in the interview. "It's an anomaly, historically, and it'll be an embarrassment to our era," Lindzen said.[356] That is to say, the climate change movement will ultimately be viewed over time as an embarrassment and hopefully an aberration. The meteorologist's central point is that climate alarmism is driven by fear rather than scientific data. That would be fear stoked by political figures who want to bring the energy industry under their control, and globalists who seek new revenue streams. But there is a way out in the form of American exceptionalism. This means going long and throwing deep in places where revolutions seem very unlikely. Only an independent and free United States can put an end to climate policies that live off globalist institutions. Now is a good time to seize on some of the battle cries from our more consequential presidents.

FDR—"The only thing we have to fear is fear itself."[357]

Ronald Reagan—"Someone once said that the difference between an American and any other kind of person is that an American lives in anticipation of the future because he knows it will be a great place. Other people fear the future as just a repetition of past failures. There's a lot of truth in that. If there is one thing we are sure of it is that history need not be relived; that nothing is impossible, and that man is capable of improving his circumstances beyond what we are told is fact."[358]

Remember that part about the precautionary principle? That's the weak-kneed decision-making framework climate activists use to scuddle audacious exercises that advance human freedom and allow for human ingenuity. This is the very concept NASA rejected during the Apollo moon missions, that Dwight Eisenhower dismissed on the eve of D-Day, and that George Washington tossed into the "ash heap of history" before crossing the Delaware River on Christmas night 1776. While it's difficult to imagine today, the American Revolution was essentially dead and dormant before the crossing. In some parts of the country, it may be just as dead now. Take a look at the report the American

Legislative Exchange Council (ALEC) puts out each year titled *Rich States, Poor States,* and that gives a descent overview of where we are. The only way out is to return to the ideals of the American founding. The upcoming celebrations marking the 250th anniversary of the Declaration of Independence is an opportunity for contemporary Americans to rediscover what separates them from European parts of the world. Will there be similar celebrations fifty years from now or one hundred years from now?

American Independence or Bust

Of all the major skirmishes Colonel Edward Hand and the First Pennsylvania Rifle Regiment fought on the way to the Second Battle of Trenton, one stands out.

Hand—an Irish-born American army officer who became an accomplished politician after serving under General Washington—played one of the most pivotal roles during the "Ten Crucial Days" that changed the trajectory of the American Revolution. The delay tactics Hand and his soldiers employed along what is now Route 206 in Lawrence, New Jersey, prevented British and Hessian troops from reaching Trenton until dusk on January 2, 1777.[359]

The Second Battle of Trenton, sometimes called the Battle of Assunpink Creek, ended in something of a standstill. The Americans had positioned themselves on the southern side of a bridge that stretched over the creek in Trenton before Lieutenant General Charles Cornwallis, the British commander, arrived with his forces. As the story is told each year around Christmas by reenactors and historians, Cornwallis had his British and Hessian troops charge the bridge three times, but they were repelled.

Cornwallis then decided to wait till daybreak the following morning, January 3, before trying to finish off Washington (there was no combat at night during that era). But Washington left his campfires lit, giving the impression he was still there, and slipped behind Cornwallis. The "old fox," as Cornwallis called him, then took a back road to Princeton.

That's the short version of events that tends to get overlooked. Talk to some of the reenactors, and they will say the Second Battle of Trenton is properly viewed as the opening act of the Battle of Princeton.

The Ten Crucial Days had begun with Washington's famous Christmas night crossing of the Delaware, which led to his victory over the Hessians quartered in Trenton the following day. No, the Hessians were not drunk, despite popular legend. But they were back on their heels right from the beginning and were not expecting the full force of Washington's Continental Army to come crashing down on them.

The Ten Crucial Days ended with Washington's victory over the British in Princeton on January 3, 1777. Divine intervention is widely viewed as a factor in both events. The harsh winter conditions had made Washington's Christmas night river crossing seem inconceivable in the eyes of the enemy. Then again, on the night Washington slipped behind Cornwallis in Trenton after the second battle, the weather turned, the ground froze, and what were muddy roads became rock solid and perfectly suited for the Continentals to move out with their horses and cannons.

The Battle of Princeton resulted in a major victory over the British. Princeton is what brought France back into the war and reignited the American Revolution after it appeared to be dead. Reenactors I've spoken with are insistent on this point. After a series of crushing victories over the Continentals, the British generals all had good reason to believe the war was over. But

Washington's stunning Christmas crossing permanently altered the trajectory of the American War of Independence.

The Ten Crucial Days are replete with turning points that historians rightly credit for saving the American Revolution. They point to the counterattack Washington himself led against the British garrison in Princeton as the pivotal moment that reinvigorated the American cause. That's a fair argument to make since the battle demonstrated that Americans could go toe-to-toe with British regulars. Then again, there would not have been a Battle of Princeton without the prior victory over the Hessians in Trenton. And there may not have been anything left of Washington's army if Cornwallis had made it across that bridge before dark.

So, there's a case to be made that American independence was saved somewhere along present-day Route 206, between Rider University and Notre Dame High School in Lawrence, New Jersey. Because Colonel Hand and his riflemen were able to delay the British march to Trenton, Washington was able to avoid a full-scale battle with a superior force.

The largest skirmish between Hand's riflemen and the British took place in and around what is now the parking lot of Notre Dame High School, where those overprivileged little punks park their expensive cars. (Okay, I'm an alumnus and a donor, so I can call them whatever I want.) Those cars now occupy the space where the Revolution very well may have been saved.

Hey Kids! Open Those Founding Documents

With the 250th anniversary of American independence just a few months away from the publication date of this book, now would be a good time for high schools and colleges to double down on the Declaration of Independence, most especially its emphasis on natural, God-given rights. Instructors should explain why the Declaration is the organic (fundamental) law of the United States and how it's connected to the US Constitution.

That might sound like a pipe dream in some public schools, where revisionist history, radicalized curriculum, and woke ideology run wild. But I sense positive changes in the national mood that are beginning to affect education too. Alternative institutions, along with the home-schooling movement, have made serious inroads in the educational establishment, and there's also the growing availability of scholarships to cover private school tuition.

Consider, for instance, Hillsdale College—a thriving, private liberal arts institution in Hillsdale, Michigan, devoted to teaching its students the ideals of the founding period. Hillsdale even offers online courses for the benefit of the general public that touch on a range of economic, historical, and literary topics. Grove City College in Pennsylvania is another example of an educational institution that celebrates the ideals of the American founding. My goal here is not to provide an exhaustive list, but I will also add in my own Regent University in Virginia Beach. (Full disclosure: I'm an alumnus.) Pat Robertson—the televangelist who founded the university, along with the Christian Broadcasting Network—made important contributions to the cause of climate realism in his final years. Robertson had previously embraced alarmist views on climate, but to his everlasting credit, he followed the evidence. The Regent Law School is also among the handful of legal-education institutions that acquaint their students with "originalist" views of the Constitution, as opposed to the secular, left-wing conception of a "living

Constitution" that can be as malleable as leftists want it to be in order to achieve their policy goals.

As a further measure of our *cultural* "climate change," even in more established, elite institutions like Princeton University, proponents of American exceptionalism are not just surviving but thriving.

The James Madison Program in American Ideals and Institutions within the Department of Politics at Princeton has made its mission to explore the conditions essential to preserving America's experiment in ordered liberty. Under the leadership of Professor Robert George, the program's director, Princeton students and interested members of the community are exposed to the thoughts of America's founders and leading statesmen.

The role of private, nonprofit educational organizations is also important. One that deserves special mention is the Young America's Foundation (YAF), a Reston, Virginia–based nonprofit known for its student-oriented programming. YAF has gained media attention over the past few decades for bringing conservative speakers onto college campuses. The foundation's educational programming has expanded to include high school and middle school students.

The many instances of climate pornography featured on campus and in the classroom provide YAF with ample targets to expose to public scrutiny. Here are just a few examples that came to light, thanks to YAF's "Campus Bias Tip Line."

Campaign organizers for an organization called "Queers for Climate Justice," Natalis Villarán-Quiñones and Deseree Fontenot, were invited to speak at San Francisco State University in February 2024. Students were invited to watch a film called *Can't Stop Change: Queer Climate Stories from the Florida Frontline*, and then participate in a question-and-answer session with Villarán-Quiñones, who was one of the filmmakers.

Several leftist organizations—including the Environment Resource Center, Race and Resistance Studies Department, Climate HQ, and Queer Trans Resource Center—were responsible for organizing the event. The film itself tells stories "of queer and trans resistance, resilience, and brilliance in the face of rising seas, stronger storms and escalating state violence."[360] They're not leaving much out, are they? Apparently, climate porn has its own special niche even in the campus Left's LGBTQ agenda.

YAF also discovered the University of Colorado Boulder's Office of Health & Wellness Services has been providing students with strategies for "coping with climate anxiety."[361] As part of this effort, a university resource page declares "more than two-thirds of Americans experience some form of climate anxiety," and then proceeds to list strategies students can use when feelings of "ecological distress" become evident. Students are advised to contact legislators demanding action, reduce the amount of meat they eat, have conversations with family and friends about "climate change," and donate money, among other suggestions.[362]

At the same time, the university warns that "working on too many climate projects or advocating for too many causes can be unwieldy," and advises that students take occasional breaks from climate news and speak with friends, family members, and counselors to develop coping skills. There are also support resources, including a "Climate Café," which is described as a "confidential space" for students to explore their various responses to the "climate crisis."[363]

What, exactly, is "climate anxiety"? The university defines it as "distressing feelings related to the impact of climate change." Such distress, according to the university definition, "is often rooted in feelings of uncertainty, lack of control and concerns over well-being or safety." The university website links back to a survey from the American Psychological Association that says more than two-thirds of Americans experience some form of climate anxiety.[364]

Not to be outdone, a student organization at the University of California, Berkeley held a "Rally to Ban Cars" in July 2023, while pointing to the need for "climate action in the streetscape." Some of the students even illegally closed down a street near campus, allowing only pedestrians, cyclists, and buses to pass.[365]

Leaving aside the fact that a car ban on one street is not going to impact the climate, it's quite clear that "climate action" is little more than a proxy for a long list of leftist causes. The students themselves acknowledge as much. But there is a special utility to the climate cause that anti-constitutional progressives on and off campus have seized upon. There have been efforts to ban textbooks that express any degree of skepticism toward man-made global warming and to silence climate skeptics. As we saw in previous chapters, there has been an all-too-successful assault on free speech and scientific inquiry in the name of climate.

The Organic Law in the Twenty-First Century

Which brings us back to the legacy of our nation's founders. Here in America, we can always call attention to the Declaration of Independence. An aroused and informed public will be less inclined to surrender their God-given rights and more motivated to reacquire what's been lost. That's an optimistic scenario, but achievable, so long as current and future generations of Americans come back to an understanding that the Declaration is indisputably the organic law of the United States.

For guidance about this, I turn my thoughts back to my late friend Louis Ingram—bless his heart. He was an attorney but so much more than that. Ingram was the national chairman of the Carpe Diem Project to limit the appellate jurisdiction of the US Supreme Court. He was also managing director of the Parents' National Coalition for Independent Academic Accreditation. The latter was a project devoted to introducing cultural education and more discipline in government schools, in order to educate the "good person" rather than indoctrinate the "good citizen." Very relevant today.

In addition, Ingram served as assistant to the secretary of the Interstate Commerce Commission, and he spent time on Capitol Hill as the legislative director of the Republican Study Committee in the House of Representatives. He served on President-elect Reagan's transition team for interstate commerce. Beyond all this, he also had theatrical experience.

Yes, Louis Ingram was a character, and I'm sorry to say I lost track of him in his later years—he passed away some time ago. But at the time we were in touch during the spring and summer of 2004, he passed along a copy of his essay "Treason to the Constitution: Usurpation of Jurisdiction and Subversion of the People's Charter by the Supremes in Violation of Their Oaths." This ought to be required reading, beginning some time in high school. I suspect Ingram would have a more congenial view of the Supreme Court that has emerged here in the early twenty-first century. But I'm sure he would still like to see the third branch put back into a more constitutional box, if you will.

That part of Ingram's essay devoted to his analysis of the Declaration as the organic law of the United States is what's most relevant here. The only way to break free from the globalist climate movement is to restore the Declaration to its proper station as the motivating rationale for self-government. This native source for American renewal is unfortunately not available in Europe and other parts of the world, which have succumbed to the anti-capitalist and anti-population zealots.

In true Ingram fashion, at least the version I remember, he insisted that "We the People" are nicely positioned to tell the globalists at the UN and the EU to "go shove it." He meant specifically their incessant efforts to bypass democratic chambers with top-down directives crafted to expand government control. "No Climate Taxation Without Representation" could be resurrected as the new battle cry.

But first let's be clear that it's the Good Lord who endows us with unalienable rights. The Jeffersonian language in the Declaration invoking the "Creator" and "the Laws of Nature and of Nature's God" demonstrates that the US Constitution was later established to "secure" preexisting natural rights. The alternative view, which has predominated throughout human history, says it's government that grants rights—which is problematic, since whatever the government grants, the government can promptly withdraw, and often does.

Here's how my old friend Ingram put it, and I don't think anyone has put it better:

> What one thinks about the source of human rights inexorably controls what one thinks about government power. If one thinks government is the source of rights, that is, if one is a secularist, then one must long for the embrace of government power. It is the political world of trendy, designer rights, such as the right of privacy, which pop in and out of elite fashion.

On the other hand, if one thinks God is the source of those Rights, then one must fear government power because it will, unchecked as we have experienced, re-define those rights to the detriment of we the people.

Those efforts to redefine rights began in earnest at the national level under President Woodrow Wilson. They accelerated under Franklin Delano Roosevelt and later Lyndon Baines Johnson. The federal beast, with all its unaccountable agencies, is what has given life to the extra-constitutional and anti-scientific cause of climate activism.

That's why in no less of a location than Washington Crossing Park could an unhinged government deny its citizens access to a lush, historically significant space that those same citizens paid to preserve. At the time, COVID policies stood in for what climate activists have always sought to achieve: controlling human activity and abolishing human freedom.

As much as contemporary Americans might celebrate the ideals of the American Revolution, they live in a world where Wilsonian, unelected bureaucrats call the shots. In my home state of New Jersey, the American Revolution is every bit as dead now as it was before Washington crossed the Delaware and won the First Battle of Trenton over the Hessians.

A key culprit in this state is the New Jersey Supreme Court, which has usurped legislative and executive authority. This process began with the *Mount Laurel* decision in the 1970s, which led to suburban sprawl, and the *Abbott v. Burke* ruling in the 1980s on school funding, which hiked property taxes across the state. In the former, the public and its elected officials were cut out of any decisions on "affordable housing," and in the latter, unelected judges raised taxes. Go back to Jefferson's Declaration, substitute the pronoun "they" for "he," and many of those complaints against King George III can easily be turned back on today's judiciary—especially the one in my home state.

But with the Declaration coming back into vogue, abuses of government power done under euphemistic-sounding terms like "climate action" are running up against the rediscovery of natural rights.

As my friend Ingram informs us, "Restraint of power is the common thread running through the U.S. Constitution, a thread which distinguishes it from every other constitution from around the world. As we have already seen, The Signers of the Declaration articulated their complaints about experienced abuse of power. The Framers of the Constitution responded to those particulars so precisely that it is impossible to disconnect the two documents. The connection was no accident."

There are many specific examples where the Declaration and its complaints against King George III led to responses in the Constitution.

The Declaration points to the king's refusal to assent to laws, and the Constitution answers with the presidential veto override. Another complaint in the Declaration involves the king forbidding governors to pass laws—and the Constitution answers with the Tenth Amendment, reserving powers to the states. The king also repeatedly dissolved representative bodies, and the Constitution answers by vesting control over legislative meetings in Congress. The list goes on.

With the Declaration firmly established as the organic law of these United States, there's another step either the Trump administration, or another future administration, should take that would build on the incremental steps that have been taken recently to restore American independence.

Withdrawing from the Paris Climate Agreement was a major victory for the cause of constitutional government and a major setback for climate activists across the globe. But remember, President Trump could still seize the opportunity to label the agreement as a treaty, and then submit it to the US Senate, where it will surely be voted down. This would set a powerful precedent to prevent a future executive from working in cahoots with UN or EU entities to bypass our elected branches.

The problem is that most elected officials will almost certainly try and sidestep any effort to make them accountable before the voters. The operative word here is "most." The handful willing to stand up and be counted can move mountains—if they have enough popular support.

The victories for American independence and sovereignty the second Trump administration has recorded are meaningful and real. The fact that they coincide with the 250th anniversary of the Declaration of Independence can be viewed as providential. The question is, are they temporal or permanent? Unfortunately, because this movement is in its inchoate phase, some of Trump's key accomplishments could be reversed if globalists recapture the presidency.

That's why it's essential to build on what has been won. For example, there could be no better way to celebrate American independence than to completely withdraw from the United Nations, the great incubator of climate activism perpetually targeting human freedom and the American constitutional structure.

Up and down that route where the Second Battle of Trenton and the Battle of Princeton raged, each of the schools and educational institutions could spend some time discussing how incompatible the UN's view of "collective rights" is with the Declaration's view of individual rights. Professor Robert George's James Madison Program at Princeton University has already performed this function in multiple venues, and I say: Keep going. As an alumnus of Rider University and Notre Dame High School, I'm going to insist they both mark America's 250th anniversary by comparing and contrasting our nation's founding with what the United Nations has wrought.

Dr. Dan Eichenbaum, you may recall, is the chap who wants to take down the Clinton-era executive order that enabled the UN' s "Agenda 21" to take root nationally and locally. On his popular radio program, Eichenbaum provides a vital platform for scholars who understand and promote the importance of private property and the liberty it generates.

In our exchanges, Dr. Dan has frequently driven home how "our founders considered the totality of a person's property to include not only his land, his home, and his physical possessions, but also the work of his hands, the inventions of his brain, and ultimately his life itself." Karl Marx, the architect of socialist theory, made it clear from the outset of his *Communist Manifesto* that the elimination of private property was preeminent in his plan.

Please note: The ranchers in Arizona, who successfully beat back the Center for Biological Diversity; the elderly navy vet in Montana, who spent time in jail; Martha Boneta Fain, who fought against environmental trespassers in Virginia; and the homeowners in North Carolina, who were bedeviled with "climate risk assessments"—all of their cases track back to efforts to dislodge them from private property.

The ideology at work here is not new. Drill down a bit into the UN's many climate campaigns, and they are invariably directed against capitalism, free enterprise, private property, and self-government.

New generations of Americans will either rediscover and recommit themselves to the natural rights philosophy of the Declaration, or they can watch this once-great republic absorbed into a larger, globalist framework, where a small group of unaccountable elites set policies without the consent of the governed.

Our US Constitution and the Declaration of Independence are built upon the foundation of individual rights, where the natural law is operative. By contrast, the UN and its Declaration of Human Rights are built upon the notion of collective rights, where the arbitrary will of politicians is operative. Our nation's Declaration states "that all Men are created equal, that they are endowed by their Creator with certain unalienable rights...." The UN Declaration says: "Rights and freedoms may in no case be exercised contrary to the purposes and principles of the United Nations."

Let that sink in for a minute. Under the US system, you are born with rights, and the government exists to protect them. Among those rights, you and the product of your labor belong to you. Not so with the UN, where government grants, restricts, or withdraws your rights according to its needs or whims. Under the UN, and in true Karl Marx fashion, you and the products of your labor belong to the community.[366]

So, in the spirit of the 1776 revolutionaries, perhaps we can make our own kind of revolution in 2026.

Washington did not sit on his victory over the Hessians in Trenton. Instead, he recrossed the Delaware at great peril and found a way to outmaneuver the British. In similar fashion, Trump, or his successor, should build on the "America First" agenda by getting behind a proposal from Senator Mike Lee, a

Utah Republican, who advanced legislation in February 2025 to pull the US out of the United Nations.

Hey, UN, Get Out of the US

Lee's proposed Disengaging Entirely from the United Nations Debacle (DEFUND) Act is heavily focused on cutting financial ties between the US and the UN.[367] While the United States is just one of 193 member nations, it finances one-fifth of the UN system, with most of the contributions being voluntary. The Council on Foreign Relations, a US foreign policy think tank, reports that the United States donated more than $18 billion to the UN in 2022.[368]

Lee has also made the point that with these contributions, "U.S. dollars are being used to make a mockery of [America's] values." He cites several examples, including contributions that have given refuge to terrorists through the United Nations Relief and Works Agency (UNRWA); promoted coercive abortions under the phony label of "reproductive rights"; provided political cover for China's human rights abuses; and supplied UN support to the International Criminal Court for prosecuting Israeli Prime Minister Benjamin Netanyahu. Lee has also balked at the organization's "bloated, bureaucratic, supranational framework," which is precisely the sort of arrangement America's founders sought to avoid.

On the Senate side, the DEFUND Act is cosponsored by Republican Senators Marsha Blackburn and Rick Scott. House Armed Services Committee Chairman Mike Rogers and Representative Chip Roy have introduced a companion bill in the House of Representatives.

When he unveiled his proposal, Lee made it clear he didn't want US taxpayers footing the bill any longer for policies that are diametrically opposed to American values.

"No more blank checks for the United Nations," Lee said in a press release. "Americans' hard-earned dollars have been funneled into initiatives that fly in the face of our values, enabling tyrants, betraying allies, and spreading bigotry. With the DEFUND Act, we're stepping away from this debacle. If we engage with the U.N. in the future, it will be on our terms, with the full backing of the Senate and an ironclad escape clause."

This is not the first time a legislative proposal to withdraw from the UN has been put on the table. But it might be the first time events are converging in a way that makes it possible to give the proposal a real go.

There's an administration in place devoted to American sovereignty that can back up some of the lonely voices in Congress. There's also the anniversary date of July 4, 2026, and the celebrations leading up to that moment marking American independence. What better way to celebrate American independence than by withdrawing from the United Nations—the major international publisher and purveyor of climate porn?

But, as it always does, taking that step comes down to "We the People." By reestablishing in our hearts, minds, and memories the connection between the Declaration of Independence and the US Constitution, membership in the UN becomes untenable.

Donald Trump's comment in a rebuke to international climate activists—"I represent Pittsburgh, not Paris"—is very much in that spirit. The revolutionary antecedent to that statement would be "No Taxation without Representation." The political class can be pushed and even defeated, but time is a factor.

Either the current generation of Americans will rediscover the Declaration and drive a stake through the heart of the climate movement, or America's tricentennial of July 4, 2076, may come and go without recognition or fanfare...because there won't be a tricentennial to celebrate.

AFTERWORD

The year 2026 began with a huge leap back in the direction of American independence, very much in step with the Spirit of 1776. Those of us who feared the US could be pulled back into UN climate agreements in a future administration have good cause to celebrate. In early January, Donald Trump hit the ground running with one of the most significant and far-reaching moves of his presidency. That was when he pulled the US out of sixty-six international organizations, conventions, and treaties that operate—as a White House memo aptly puts it—"contrary to the interests of the United States."

Included here is a long and copious list of raw deals that have fleeced the American taxpayer for decades. The 1992 UN Framework Convention on Climate Change (UNFCCC) and the Intergovernmental Panel on Climate Change (IPCC) established in 1988 are among the most offensive.

By freeing the US from both UN initiatives, Trump has made certain a future President Gavin Newsom, Alexandria Ocasio-Cortez, or whatever other anti-constitutional, progressive cartoon character steps up in 2028, cannot simply reinsert the US back into Paris-type schemes.

There is no way to separate affordable and reliable energy from economic growth and prosperity. That's one of the key lessons to draw from the very unfortunate examples around the world where anti-energy climate policies have taken hold. It's one that's now resonating. Delegates from the nearly two hundred countries that attended the UN's 30th climate summit in Brazil held in November and December of 2025 declined to set any specific limits on their greenhouse gas emissions. The movement that began with the Rio De Janeiro summit in 1992 appears to have passed its peak. One delegate from Nigeria was particularly outspoken telling attendees:

"We will not be in support of any climate change implementation that would lead to our sudden economic contraction and heighten social instability." And why should they? Nigeria is an oil rich nation.

But globalist designs do not end with the UN. The EU continues to peddle its own version of net zero boondoggles in the form of compliance regulations impacting larger companies. We are not just talking about European companies but also UK and US companies. America will continuously need to declare its independence at every turn.

The good news is Trump's audacious break from international climate treaties and agreements has given added impetus to America's great "laboratories of democracy" in the best traditions of federalism. Policies implemented on a smaller, state-level scale that meet with success can sometimes go national.

That process could now be underway in the New England region of all places. That's where a coalition of free market think tanks, along with the Americans for Prosperity Foundation, released a monumental report measuring the impact of meeting future energy needs with nuclear and natural gas plants as opposed to wind and solar power. The coalition finds that New Englanders would save hundreds of billions of dollars while also avoiding power blackouts by way of replacing state-mandated renewable energy projects with nuclear and natural gas power.

Mike Stenhouse, the CEO of the Rhode Island Center for Freedom and Prosperity, sees an opportunity for local elected officials to take a hard look at the staggering costs associated with net zero and reverse course. He points to figures from the study that show the current "renewable scenario" would increase costs by an additional $815 billion through 2050 in comparison to the current grid causing New England families to see their electricity bills increase from $175 per month in 2024 to $384 per month by 2050. Wouldn't it be something if the smallest state in the union became a nationwide trend setter by shifting over to nuclear and natural gas? This move would also result in dramatically lower emissions. Remember, higher emissions rates are what climate activists are supposedly so concerned about. So, what's not to like about natural gas and nuclear?

Another factor for policymakers in coastal regions to consider involves the uncertain future of offshore wind. Not only do they not make sense economically and environmentally, but as discussed, they are also detrimental to national security and to military operations.

In another blow to climate activism, Trump's Interior Department announced in December 2025 that it would halt "all large-scale offshore wind projects under construction" citing national security concerns from within classified reports. This pause impacts the Vineyard Wind project underway in Massachusetts, the Revolution Wind project in Rhode Island and Connecticut, and the Sunrise Wind and Empire Wind projects covering New York.

Since then, there has been the expected legal back and forth. A federal judge has ruled in favor of allowing the Revolution Wind project to continue providing the wind industry with at least a temporary win. Proponents of the project point out that Revolution Wind has received all its federal permits and is about 90 percent complete. The Trump administration could possibly offer up more specifics about its national security concerns depending upon what can be declassified. Even if it doesn't, Save LBI, has the wind industry dead to rights. The conservation group has circulated press material challenging the notion that wind companies were unaware of how their projects interfere with onshore military radars. As Save LBI notes, this problem has been made public several times by the Department of War and the BOEM agency. As Save LBI explains in a press release,

> The problem stems from, "The immense size of turbine structures arranged in dense rows creates a radar cross-section thousands of times larger than that of the smaller aircraft or objects these systems are designed to detect. This results in significant blind spots behind wind complexes that are invisible to radar coverage."

Couldn't this problem simply be fixed?

Save LBI makes the argument that shoreline and ocean geometry makes a solution impractical. That's because radars would need to be placed in an area sufficiently distant from the blind spots so they could be seen. But this approach comes with its own problems with coverage gaps because of the curvature of the earth.

Let's also not forget that in many cases we are dealing with offshore wind farms that are foreign owned and connected with foreign governments that could exploit points of vulnerability.

For all these reasons, there is good reason to believe the national security arguments against offshore wind will carry the day. So could climate realism.

Even with the US pulling out, the IPCC gets another bite at the apple with what's known as "Seventh Assessment Report," which is already a work in progress. The full report is due out in 2029. That's one reason why the Heritage Foundation study done in partnership with the CERES group of scientists comes at an opportune moment. Recall that the report highlighted the problems with the Urban Heat Island effect and the changes in solar activity that influence climate. The CERES group identified twenty-seven different estimates of changes in Total Solar Irradiance that have occurred since 1850. That's a sizable sample. Some of those estimates show global warming is mostly natural while others suggest there may be a mix of natural and human influences. The IPCC could do a great service by acknowledging these natural contributions rather than rushing toward premature, politically motivated judgments. Anyway, that's just a suggestion.

For decades, globalists pushing the climate agenda have had the upper hand over Americans who cherish political and economic independence. But there are emerging trendlines that give cause for optimism. Trump has not yet made any moves to pull out of UN entirely, but he has taken a huge leap in that direction. At the state level, even blue states are eyeballing policies that elevate energy abundance over energy poverty. The unelected, unconstitutional administrative state is being challenged in a way it never has before. And finally, scientists willing to challenge the "climate industrial complex" are finding new platforms for expression.

This all suggests there may yet be much to celebrate not just on July 4, 2026, but in another fifty years during the tricentennial, marking an independent, free United States of America. At least, I hope so.

ENDNOTES

1   Associated Press, "'No Known Connections' Between Wind Power
     and Whale Deaths: Feds," CBS News/Philadelphia, January 19, 2023,
     accessed October 11, 2024, https://www.cbsnews.com/philadelphia/
     news/no-known-connections-between-wind-power-and-whale-
     deaths-feds/.

2   Steven Rodas, "Citing 'Disinformation,' Murphy Will Not Stop
     Offshore Wind Work After Whale Deaths," NJ.Com, February 21,
     2023, updated May 3, 2023, accessed October 3, 2024. https://www.
     nj.com/news/2023/02/citing-disinformation-murphy-will-not-stop-
     nj-offshore-wind-work-after-whale-deaths.html.

3   Jim Murphy and Lauren Anderson, "Responsible Wind Power and
     Wildlife," National Wildlife Federation, January 28, 2019, accessed
     November 28, 2024, https://www.nwf.org/Educational-Resources/
     Reports/2019/01-28-19-Responsible-Wind-Power-Wildlife.

4   "Climate Change," Natural Resources Defense Council, https://www.
     nrdc.org/issues/climate-change.

5   Michal Privara and Petr Bob, "Pornography Consumption and
     Cognitive-Affective Distress," *Journal of Nervous and Mental Disease*
     211, no. 8 (August 1, 2023): 641-646, doi: 10.1097/NMD.
     0000000000001669, PMID: 37505898; PMCID: PMC10399954,
     https://pubmed.ncbi.nlm.nih.gov/37505898/.

6   "Biden-Harris Administration Approves Ninth Offshore Wind Project," US Interior Department, July 2, 2024, accessed November 8, 2024, https://www.doi.gov/pressreleases/biden-harris-administration-approves-ninth-offshore-wind-project.

7   "About" page, Save Long Beach Island Inc., https://www.savelbi.org/about.

8   "Overview" page, Save Long Beach Island Inc., https://www.savelbi.org/offshore-wind-overview.

9   "Presentations" page, Save Long Beach Island Inc., https://www.savelbi.org/_files/ugd/a85a2b_e0e830a618d446729c42a485466bea1e.pdf.

10 "Economic Impacts" page, Save Long Beach Island Inc., https://www.savelbi.org/economic-impacts.

11 Save Long Beach Island, "Save LBI Sues U.S. Agencies and Atlantic Shores Offshore Wind, Challenging Federal Approvals Greenlighting Marine Ecosystem Devastation, Including Risks to Critically Endangered Whales," press release, January 13, 2025, https://www.savelbi.org/_files/ugd/a85a2b_ea578a317854424389201d397b96325e.pdf.

12 Interview with Bob Stern, January 16 2025.

13 Ibid.

14 Rachel Rodman and Alec Albright, "U.S. Supreme Court Strikes Down Chevron Doctrine—What Else You Need to Know," White & Case, July 8, 2024, accessed February 12, 2025, https://www.whitecase.com/insight-alert/us-supreme-court-strikes-down-chevron-doctrine-what-you-need-know.

15 Interview with Bob Stern, December 8, 2024.

16 Ibid.

17 Travis Fisher and Kevin Dayaratna, "New Jersey's $8,000-per-resident Wind Energy Scheme Won't Reduce Climate Change," Heritage Foundation, March 22, 2023, accessed September 8, 2024, https://www.heritage.org/renewable-energy/commentary/new-jerseys-8000-resident-wind-energy-scheme-wont-reduce-climate-change.

18 "Climate Change Reconsidered II: Fossil Fuels," Nongovernmental International Panel on Climate Change, April 9, 2014, accessed October 14, 2024, updated December 4, 2018, http://climatechangereconsidered.org/climate-change-reconsidered-ii-fossil-fuels/.

19 "Fact Sheet: President Biden Sets 2035 Climate Target Aimed at Creating Good-Paying Union Jobs, Reducing Costs for All Americans, and Securing U.S. Leadership in the Clean Energy Economy of the Future," Biden White House, December 19, 2024, accessed March 12, 2025, https://bidenwhitehouse.archives.gov/briefing-room/statements-releases/2024/12/19/fact-sheet-president-biden-sets-2035-climate-target-aimed-at-creating-good-paying-union-jobs-reducing-costs-for-all-americans-and-securing-u-s-leadership-in-the-clean-energy.

20 "California Releases World's First Plan to Achieve Net Zero Carbon Pollution," Office of California Governor Gavin Newsom, November 16, 2022, accessed March 15, 2025, https://www.gov.ca.gov/2022/11/16/california-releases-worlds-first-plan-to-achieve-net-zero-carbon-pollution/.

21 "Fact Sheet: President Biden Signs Executive Order to Revitalize Our Nation's Commitment to Environmental Justice for All," Biden White House, April 21, 2023, accessed March 8, 2025, https://bidenwhitehouse.archives.gov/briefing-room/statements-releases/2023/04/21/fact-sheet-president-biden-signs-executive-order-to-revitalize-our-nations-commitment-to-environmental-justice-for-all/.

22 "FERC Transparency Project," Institute for Energy Research, https://www.instituteforenergyresearch.org/type/ferc/.

23 Charles Schmidt, "Climate Anxiety: The Existential Threat Posed by Climate Change is Deeply Troubling to Many Young People," *Harvard Medicine,* Spring 2023, accessed March 9, 2025, https://magazine.hms.harvard.edu/articles/climate-anxiety.

24 Hannes Sarv, "Exclusive: Interview with Professor William Happer—Climate Scare Is Based on Lies," *Freedom Research,* February 26, 2025, accessed March 2, 2025, https://www.freedom-research.org/p/exclusive-interview-with-prof-william.

25 David Kreutzer, Nicolas Loris, Katie Tubb, and Kevin Dayaratna, "The State of Climate Science: No Justification for Extreme Policies," Heritage Foundation, April 22, 2016, accessed March 12, 2025, https://www.heritage.org/environment/report/the-state-climate-science-no-justification-extreme-policies/#_ftn6.

26 Ibid.

27 "97% Consensus? No! Global Warming Math Myths and Social Proofs," Friends of Science, February 17, 2014, accessed March 12, 2025, https://friendsofscience.org/assets/documents/97_Consensus_Myth.pdf.

28 Ibid.

29 Ibid.

30 Richard Lindzen, "Manufacturing Consensus on Climate Change," *The American Mind,* November 21, 2024, accessed March 8, 2025, https://americanmind.org/salvo/manufacturing-consensus-on-climate-change/.

31 Ibid.

32 Kevin Mooney, "Climategate's 15 Year Anniversary Could Give Momentum to Team Trump," *Restoration News,* November 22, 2024, accessed March 2, 2025, https://restoration-news.com/climategate-15-year-anniversary-could-give-momentum-to-team-trump.

33 Ibid.

34 Ibid.

35 Ibid.

36 Ibid.

37 Ibid.

38 Save Long Beach Island, "A Letter from Save LBI President Bob Stern. Facebook. March 15, 2025. https://www.facebook.com/savelbi/

posts/a-letter-from-savelbi-president-bob-stern-regarding-the-remanding-of-the-atlanti/643500445110485/

39 Kevin Dayaratna, Diana Furchtgott-Roth, et al., "Powering Human Advancement: Why the World Needs Affordable and Reliable Energy," Heritage Foundation, December 14, 2023, accessed March 12, 2025, https://www.heritage.org/energy/report/powering-human-advancement-why-the-world-needs-affordable-and-reliable-energy.

40 Charles C. W. Cooke, "Moon Landing Deniers Express Global Warming Skepticism," *National Review*, April 11, 2012, accessed March 11, 2025, https://www.nationalreview.com/corner/moon-landing-deniers-express-global-warming-skepticism-charles-c-w-cooke/.

41 The Right Climate Stuff Research Team, *Anthropogenic Global Warming Science Assessment Report, The Right Climate Stuff*, April 2013, https://www.therightclimatestuff.com/wp-content/uploads/2021/12/685693aba9ce357ada1d7006c9792308.pdf.

42 Ibid.

43 Adam R. H. Stevens, Sabine Bellstedt, et al., "The Imperative to Reduce Carbon Emissions in Astronomy," Nature Astronomy 4, 843–851 (2020), accessed December 12, 2024, https://doi.org/10.1038/s41550-020-1169-1.

44 Ibid.

45 "Webb Telescope Latest News," NASA, accessed December 15, 2024, https://science.nasa.gov/mission/webb/latestnews/.

46 Jürgen Knödlseder, Sylvie Brau-Nogué, et al., "Estimate of the Carbon Footprint of Astronomical Research Infrastructures," *Nature Astronomy* 6, 503–513 (2022), https://doi.org/10.1038/s41550-022-01612-3.

47 Astronomers for Planet Earth, accessed December 17, 2024, https://a4e.org/.

48 Ibid.

49 Ibid.

[50] Ibid.

[51] Roxana Bardan, "NASA Confirms DART Mission Impact Changed Asteroid's Motion in Space," NASA, October 11, 2022, accessed December 23, 2024, https://www.nasa.gov/news-release/nasa-confirms-dart-mission-impact-changed-asteroids-motion-in-space/.

[52] Marc Morano, "Global Warming on Mars and Cosmic Ray Research Are Shattering Media-Driven 'Consensus,'" press release, US Senate Committee on Environment and Public Works, March 1, 2007, accessed December 26, 2024, https://www.epw.senate.gov/public/index.cfm/press-releases-all?ID=0DF9B3CD-802A-23AD-4984-5AC0C6D42605.

[53] Sharmila Kuthunur, "The Major Surface Features of Mars," Love the Night Sky, accessed December 23, 2024, https://lovethenightsky.com/mars-major-surface-features/.

[54] Ibid.

[55] Ibid.

[56] Ibid.

[57] American Geophysical Union, "Cosmic Rays Are Not the Cause of Climate Change, Scientists Say," *ScienceDaily*, January 23, 2004, https://www.sciencedaily.com/releases/2004/01/040123001629.htm.

[58] Willie Soon, Ronan Connolly, and Michael Connolly, "New CERES Report for Heritage Foundation Summarizing the UHI and TSI Problems in the IPCC Reports," CERES-Science, December 12 2024, accessed January 4, 2025, https://www.ceres-science.com/post/ceres-report-for-the-heritage-foundation.

[59] CERES Team, "The Orchestrated Disinformation Campaign by RealClimate.org to Falsely Discredit and Censor Our Work," CERES-Science, September 18, 2023, accessed January 4, 2025, https://www.ceres-science.com/post/the-orchestrated-disinformation-campaign-by-realclimate-org-to-falsely-discredit-and-censor-our-work.

[60] Ibid.

[61] Willie Soon, Ronan Connolly, and Michael Connolly, "The Unreliability of Current Global Temperature and Solar Activity Estimates and Its Implications for the Attribution of Global Warming," Heritage Foundation, December 11, 2024, accessed January 4, 2025, https://www.heritage.org/climate/report/the-unreliability-current-global-temperature-and-solar-activity-estimates-and-its.

[62] Kevin Mooney, "Natural Influences Driving Sea Level Rise Overlooked in Media's Climate Coverage, Heritage Report Says," *Daily Signal,* March 13, 2024, accessed February 14, 2025, https://www.dailysignal.com/2024/03/13/natural-influences-driving-sea-level-rise-overlooked-in-medias-climate-coverage-heritage-report-says/.

[63] Ibid.

[64] Ibid.

[65] Ibid.

[66] Ibid.

[67] Caroline Fassett, "What N.J. Parks Are Closed? A Full List of Parks Gov. Murphy Just Closed in Response to Coronavirus," *NJ Advance Media for NJ.com,* April 7, 2020, accessed January 4, 2025, https://www.nj.com/coronavirus/2020/04/is-my-local-park-closed-a-full-list-of-parks-gov-murphy-just-closed-in-response-to-coronavirus.html.

[68] Zoe Read, "N.J. Gov. Phil Murphy Pledges Commitment to Fighting Climate Change amid Trump Presidency," WHYY, November 14, 2024, accessed January 18, 2025, https://whyy.org/articles/new-jersey-phil-murphy-trump-climate-change/.

[69] "Precautionary Principle: The Wingspread Statement," Collaborative for Health & Environment, https://www.healthandenvironment.org/resources/resource-library/eh-history/precautionary-principle-the-wingspread-statement.

[70] Roger Pielke Jr., "I Am Under 'Investigation,'" *The Climate Fix,* February 25, 2015, accessed February 16, 2025, https://theclimatefix.wordpress.com/2015/02/25/i-am-under-investigation/.

71 Roger Pielke Jr., "My Unhappy Life as a Climate Heretic," *Wall Street Journal*, December 2, 2016, https://www.wsj.com/articles/my-unhappy-life-as-a-climate-heretic-1480723518.

72 Ibid.

73 Roger Pielke Jr., "I Am Under 'Investigation,'" *The Climate Fix*, February 25, 2015, accessed February 16, 2025, https://theclimatefix.wordpress.com/2015/02/25/i-am-under-investigation/.

74 Marc Morano, "Dr. Roger Pielke Jr. on Climate 'Witch Hunt': 'My 11-Year Old Asked Me if I Was Going to Jail,'" *Climate Depot*, March 2, 2015, accessed February 16, 2025, https://www.climatedepot.com/2015/03/02/dr-roger-pielke-jr-s-on-the-witch-hunt/.

75 Marc Morano and Mick Curran, interview of William "Bill" Gray, *Climate Hustle* (documentary film, 2017), https://www.imdb.com/title/tt5354362/.

76 Juliet Eilperin and David A. Fahrenthold, "Climatologist Draws Heat from Critics," *Washington Post*, September 17, 2006, accessed February 18, 2025, http://www.washingtonpost.com/wp-dyn/content/article/2006/09/16/AR2006091600644.html.

77 Ibid.

78 Juliet Eilperin and David A. Fahrenthold, "Climatologist Draws Heat from Critics," *Washington Post*, September 17, 2006, accessed February 18, 2025, http://www.washingtonpost.com/wp-dyn/content/article/2006/09/16/AR2006091600644.html.

79 Marianne Lavelle, "War on NOAA? A Climate Denier's Arrival Raises Fears the Agency's Climate Mission Is Under Attack," October 25, 2020, accessed November 15, 2025, https://insideclimatenews.org/news/25102020/noaa-climate-denial-david-legates/#:~:text=That%20led%20to%20a%20dust%2Dup%20with%20Delaware's,in%20making%20public%20statements%20on%20climate%20change.

80 Glenn Beck, "Exposed: The Climate of Fear," CNN, May 2, 2007, http://transcripts.cnn.com/TRANSCRIPTS/0705/02/gb.01.html.

81 "Denier David Legates Asked to Step Down as Delaware State Climatologist," *ThinkProgress*, July 18, 2011, accessed February 18,

2025, https://archive.thinkprogress.org/denier-david-legates-asked-to-step-down-as-delaware-state-climatologist-16b9508c26dc/.

[82] Paul Koberstein, "Hot or Not," *Willamette Week*, August 24, 2005, accessed November 17, 2025, https://www.wweek.com/portland/article-4738-hot-or-not.html.

[83] Lubos Motl, "Totalitarianism vs. State Climatologist in Virginia," *The Reference Frame*, September 28, 2007, accessed February 18, 2025, https://www.climatescience.org.nz/blog/20071002%20marc%20moranos%20round-up/

[84] Judith Curry, "JC in Transition," *Climate Etc.*, January 3, 2017, https://judithcurry.com/2017/01/03/jc-in-transition/.

[85] Ibid.

[86] Ibid.

[87] Doug McKelway, "Climategate II? Scientific Community Accused of Muzzling Dissent on Global Warming," Fox News, May 16, 2014, accessed February 18, 2025, https://www.foxnews.com/politics/climategate-ii-scientific-community-accused-of-muzzling-dissent-on-global-warming

[88] Ben Webster, "'Witch Hunt' Forces Out Climate Scientist," *Times* (UK), May 15, 2014, https://www.thetimes.com/uk/environment/article/witch-hunt-forces-out-climate-scientist-6bswv8sd82m.

[89] Marc Morano, "'Science as McCarthyism: Lennart Bengtsson Blames U.S. Climate Scientists for McCarthy-Style Witch-hunt," *Climate Depot*, May 15, 2014, https://www.climatedepot.com/2014/05/15/science-as-mccarthyism-lennart-bengtsson-blames-u-s-climate-scientists-for-mccarthy-style-witch-hunt-worried-for-his-safety-his-joining-skeptic-group-compared-to-joining-the-ku-klux-kl/.

[90] Richard Tol, "Examining the UN Intergovernmental Panel on Climate Change Process," Full U.S House of Representatives Science Committee Hearing—May 29, 2014, https://www.govinfo.gov/content/pkg/CHRG-113hhrg88147/pdf/CHRG-113hhrg88147.pdf. (Testimony by Tol is in the linked hearing transcript at pp. 14–23.)

91 Marc Morano and Mick Curran, interview of William "Bill" Gray, *Climate Hustle* (documentary film, 2017), https://www.imdb.com/title/tt5354362/.

92 Vadim J. Birstein, *The Perversion of Knowledge: The True Story of Soviet Science* (New York: Basic Books, 2004, accessed February 22, 2025, https://www.amazon.com/Perversion-Knowledge-Story-Soviet-Science/dp/0813342805. Academician Schmalhausen, professors Formozov and Sabinin, and three thousand other biologists, victims of the August 1948 Session, lost their professional jobs because of their integrity and moral principles.

93 Leo Hickman, "Climate Scientists Back Call for Sceptic Thinktank to Reveal Backers," *The Guardian*, January 22, 2012, accessed February 22, 2025, https://www.theguardian.com/environment/2012/jan/23/climate-sceptic-lawson-thinktank-funding.

94 Clip of James Hansen from ABC World News in Marc Morano and Mick Curran's *Climate Hustle* (documentary film, 2017), https://www.imdb.com/title/tt5354362/.

95 Adam Weinstein, "Arrest Climate-Change Deniers," *Gawker*, March 28,2014.https://www.gawkerarchives.com/arrest-climate-change-deniers-1553719888

96 Jesse Ferreras, "David Suzuki Says Harper Should Be Jailed over His Climate Positions," *Huffington Post Canada*, February 2, 2016, accessed February 22, 2025, http://www.huffingtonpost.ca/2016/02/02/ david-suzuki-stephen-harper-jailed-climate_n_9143278.html.

97 Marc Morano, "Climate Depot's Morano & Other Skeptics 'Sentenced to Death' for 'Crimes Against Humanity,'" *Climate Depot*, August 8, 2017, accessed February 22, 2025, http://www.climatedepot.com/2017/08/08/climate-depots-morano-other-skeptics-sentenced-to-death-for-crimes-against-humanity/.

98 Marc Morano, "'Execute' Skeptics! Shock Call to Action: At What Point Do We Jail or Execute Global Warming Deniers'—'Shouldn't We Start Punishing Them Now?'" *Climate Depot*, June 3, 2009, https://www.climatedepot.com/2009/06/03/

execute-skeptics-shock-call-to-action-at-what-point-do-we-jail-or-
execute-global-warming-deniers-shouldnt-we-start-punishing-them-
now/.

99 Ibid.

100 Peter Sinclair, "Scientist's Letter Asks Obama to Prosecute Climate
Deniers," *This Is Not Cool*, September 19, 2015, accessed November
15, 2025, https://thinc.blog/2015/09/19/scientists-letter-asks-obama-
to-prosecute-climate-deniers/#:~:text=I%20fear%20this%20
approach%20plays%20into%20the,gay%20mosques%2C%20so%20
they've%20been%20looking%20for.

101 Marc Morano, "Update: Romm Defends Remarks as 'Not a Threat,
but a Prediction'—Strangle Skeptics in Bed! 'An Entire Generation
Will Soon Be Ready to Strangle You and Your Kind While You Sleep
in Your Beds,'" *Climate Depot*, June 5, 2009, https://www.
climatedepot.com/2009/06/05/update-romm-defends-remarks-as-not-
a-threat-but-a-prediction-strangle-skeptics-in-bed-an-entire-
generation-will-soon-be-ready-to-strangle-you-and-your-kind-while-
you-sleep-in-your-beds/.

102 Arianna Skibell, "Trump's 30-Day Climate Assault," *Politico*, February
20, 2025, accessed February 23, 2025, https://www.politico.com/
newsletters/power-switch/2025/02/20/trumps-30-day-climate-
assault-00205201.

103 "Former Vice President Al Gore and a Coalition of Attorneys General
from Across the Country Announce Historic State-Based Effort to
Combat Climate Change," Office of New York State Attorney
General, March 29, 2016, accessed January 18, 2025, https://algore.
com/news/former-vice-president-al-gore-and-a-coalition-of-attorneys-
general-from-across-the-country-announce-historic-state-based-effort-
to-combat-climate-change.

104 Ibid.

105 Valerie Richardson, "Virgin Islands AG Raises Free-Speech Fears with
Subpoena for Climate Dissenters," *Washington Times*, April 7, 2016,

accessed January 18, 2025, https://www.washingtontimes.com/
news/2016/apr/7/virgin-islands-ag-raises-free-speech-fears-subpoen/.

106 Hans A. von Spakovsky, "Prosecuting Climate Change 'Deniers' Is an
Abuse of Power," Heritage Foundation, April 22, 2016, accessed
January 22, 2025, https://www.heritage.org/environment/
commentary/prosecuting-climate-change-deniers-abuse-power.

107 Mark Hemingway, "Senator: Use RICO Laws to Prosecute Global
Warming Skeptics," *Washington Examiner*, June 2, 2015, accessed
January 25, 2025, https://www.washingtonexaminer.com/
news/1279449/senator-use-rico-laws-to-prosecute-global-
warming-skeptics/.

108 Kevin Mooney, "The California Gathering that Hatched Plan to
Prosecute Skeptics of Climate Change," *Daily Signal*, December 28,
2016, accessed January 21, 2025. https://www.dailysignal.
com/2016/12/28/the-california-gathering-that-hatched-plan-to-
prosecute-skeptics-of-climate-change/

109 Kevin Mooney, "Democrat AGs, Green Groups Defy Subpoenas on
'Coordinated' Climate Efforts," *Daily Signal*, August 2, 2016,
accessed January 29, 2025, https://www.dailysignal.com/2016/08/02/
democrat-ags-green-groups-defy-subpoena-on-coordinated-climate-
efforts/.

110 "Big Green Inc.," Institute for Energy Research, accessed October 4,
2024, https://www.instituteforenergyresearch.org/big-green-inc/.

111 Kevin Mooney, "Secret Deal Among AGs to Prosecute Climate
Change 'Deniers' Challenged in Court," *Daily Signal*, August 8,
2016, accessed January 27, 2025, https://www.dailysignal.
com/2016/08/08/secret-deal-among-ags-to-prosecute-climate-
change-deniers-challenged-in-court/.

112 Ibid.

113 Timothy Cama, "State AGs Sought to Keep Climate Probe Details
Secret," *The Hill*, August 4, 2016, accessed January 25, 2025, https://
thehill.com/policy/energy-environment/290376-state-ags-sought-to-
keep-climate-probe-details-secret/.

[114] Ian Tuttle, "Getting Rich Off Climate Extremism," *National Review*, October 1, 2015, accessed February 4, 2025, https://www.nationalreview.com/2015/10/climate-extremist-taxpayer-funded-ian-tuttle/.

[115] Kevin Mooney, "House Probe Reveals Audit Detailing Climate Change Researcher's 'Double Dipping,'" *Daily Signal*, March 2, 2016, accessed February 6, 2025, https://www.dailysignal.com/2016/03/02/house-probe-reveals-audit-detailing-climate-change-researchers-double-dipping-with-taxpayer-funds/.

[116] Lachlan Markay, "Scientist Demands Federal Investigation of Climate Change Skeptics," *Washington Free Beacon*, September 22, 2015, http://freebeacon.com/issues/scientist-demandscriminal-investigation-of-climate-change-skeptics/.

[117] Kevin Mooney, "House Probe Reveals Audit Detailing Climate Change Researcher's 'Double Dipping,'" *Daily Signal* March 2, 2016, accessed February 6, 2025, https://www.dailysignal.com/2016/03/02/house-probe-reveals-audit-detailing-climate-change-researchers-double-dipping-with-taxpayer-funds/.

[118] Ibid.

[119] Ibid.

[120] Hannes Sarv, "INTERVIEW. Professor William Happer on Climate Crisis: It's All a Made-Up Scare Story," *Freedom Research*, April 1, 2025, accessed April 4, 2025, https://www.freedom-research.org/p/interview-professor-william-happer.

[121] Ibid.

[122] "Ending Cooperative Agreements' Funding to Princeton University," US Department of Commerce, April 8, 2025, accessed April 12, 2025, https://www.commerce.gov/news/press-releases/2025/04/ending-cooperative-agreements-funding-princeton-university.

[123] Ibid.

[124] Richard Luscombe, "Trump Administration Cuts $4 million to Princeton's Climate Research Funding," *The Guardian*, April 10, 2025, accessed April 11, 2025, https://www.theguardian.com/

us-news/2025/apr/10/trump-administration-cuts-princeton-climate-research-funding.

125 Austin Gae and Kevin Dayaratna, "Social Cost of Carbon: DSCIM's Unreliable Foundations," Heritage Foundation, May 16, 2025, accessed August 14, 2025, https://www.heritage.org/energy/report/social-cost-carbon-dscims-unreliable-foundations.

126 Brent Scher, "Trump Admin Moves to Shut Down Government's Climate Doom Factory," *Daily Wire*, April 9, 2025, accessed April 11, 2025, https://www.dailywire.com/news/trump-admin-moves-to-shut-down-governments-climate-doom-factory.

127 Ibid.

128 "Canadians Are Suffering from Trudeau's Carbon Tax," Institute for Energy Research, February 20, 2025, accessed April 2, 2025, https://www.instituteforenergyresearch.org/international-issues/canadians-are-suffering-from-trudeaus-carbon-tax.

129 Ibid.

130 Ibid.

131 Ibid.

132 Julio Mejia and Elmira Aliakbari, "Federal Government Should Acknowledge Impact of Carbon Tax Hike," *Ottawa Sun*, March 27, 2024, accessed via Fraser Institute, April 4, 2025, https://www.fraserinstitute.org/commentary/federal-government-should-acknowledge-impact-carbon-tax-hike.

133 Ibid.

134 "A Distributional Analysis of the Federal Fuel Charge—Update," Office of the Parliamentary Budget Officer, October 10, 2024, accessed April 8, 2025, https://distribution-a6172746566661637473.pbo-dpb.ca/a019e3958622ad6063532c48ff972c24bbc9477b82af73e6ec5d93d208262b88.

135 Franco Terrazzano, "PBO Confirms Carbon Taxes Costs More Than Rebates," Canadian Taxpayers Federation, October 10, 2024, accessed April 9, 2025, https://www.taxpayer.com/newsroom/pbo-confirms-carbon-tax-costs-more-than-rebates.

136 "A Distributional Analysis of the Federal Fuel Charge," Office of the Parliamentary Budget Officer, October 10, 2024, accessed April 8, 2025, https://distribution-a617274656661637473.pbo-dpb.ca/a019 e3958622ad6063532c48ff972c24bbc9477b82af73e6ec5d93d20826 2b88.

137 Ryan Thorpe, "Carbon Tax Bureaucracy Costs Taxpayers $800 Million," Carbon Taxpayers Federation, November 19, 2024, accessed April 2, 2025, https://www.taxpayer.com/newsroom/carbon-tax-bureaucracy-costs-taxpayers-800-million.

138 Ibid.

139 Franco Terrazzano and Kris Sims, "Carbon Tax on Trucking Is a Tax on Everything," *Toronto Sun,* September 11, 2024, accessed April 8,2025, https://torontosun.com/opinion/columnists/opinion-carbon-tax-on-trucking-is-a-tax-on-everything.

140 Ibid.

141 Sam Cooper, "Conservative Candidate Joe Tay Paused Public Campaigning After Chinese Threat Warning," *The Bureau,* April 22, 2025, accessed April 25, 2025, https://www.thebureau.news/p/conservative-candidate-joe-tay-paused.

142 Andy Lee, *Real Andy Lee Show,* April 7, 2025, accessed April 25, 2025, https://x.com/RealAndyLeeShow/status/1909273718041231621

143 David Ljunggren, "Canada Spies Found China Interfered in Last Two Elections, Probe Hears," Reuters, April 8, 2024, accessed April 12, 2025, https://www.reuters.com/world/americas/canada-spies-found-china-interfered-last-two-elections-probe-hears-2024-04-08/.

144 Ibid.

145 Wa Lone, "Carney Says China Is a Foreign Interference, Geopolitical Threat for China," Reuters, April 18, 2025, accessed April 11, 2025, https://www.reuters.com/world/carney-says-china-is-foreign-interference-geopolitical-threat-canada-2025-04-18/.

146 Debbie Lesko, "Trump's Stand Against States' Climate Overreach Is Long Overdue," *The Hill,* April 27, 2025, accessed April 29, 2025, https://thehill.com/opinion/5267953-trump-executive-order-energy/.

147 Ibid.

148 Kevin Mooney, "Climate Change Alarmism Is 'Garbage In, Garbage Out,' Retired NASA Physicist Says," *Daily Signal*, November 22, 2017, accessed January 2, 2025, https://www.dailysignal. com/2017/11/22/climate-change-alarmism-is-garbage-in-garbage-out-retired-nasa-physicist-says/.

149 Ibid.

150 Ibid.

151 Ibid.

152 The Right Climate Stuff, accessed Jan 2, 2025, https://www. therightclimatestuff.com/.

153 Steve Goreham, "Time to Defund Climate Models?" *MasterResource*, April 29, 2025, accessed May 14, 2025, https://www.masterresource. org/climate-models-climate-change/climate-models-defund/.

154 Diana Furchtgott-Roth, "China Abandons Paris Agreement, Making U.S. Efforts Painful and Pointless," Heritage Foundation, July 21, 2023, accessed January 1, 2025, https://www.heritage.org/global-politics/commentary/china-abandons-paris-agreement-making-us-efforts-painful-and-pointless.

155 S. Fred Singer et al., *Hot Talk, Cold Science: Global Warming's Unfinished Debate* (Oakland, CA: Independent Institute, 2021).

156 Diana Furchtgott-Roth, "China Abandons Paris Agreement, Making U.S. Efforts Painful and Pointless," Heritage Foundation, July 21, 2023, accessed January 1, 2025, https://www.heritage.org/global-politics/commentary/china-abandons-paris-agreement-making-us-efforts-painful-and-pointless.

157 Kevin Killough, "New Study Finds That CO2 Is Increasing the Rate by Which the Globe Is Greening, Even Under Drought," CO_2 Coalition, February 16, 2024, accessed August 22, 2025, https:// co2coalition.org/news/new-study-finds-that-co2-is-increasing-the-rate-by-which-the-globe-is-greening-even-under-drought/.

158 Xin Chen, Tiexi Chen, et al., "The Global Greening Continues Despite Increased Drought Stress Since 2000," *Global Ecology and*

Conservation 49 (January 2024), e0279, https://doi.org/10.1016/j.gecco.2023.e02791.

159 Ibid.

160 "Key Aspects of the Paris Agreement," United Nations Climate Change, accessed January 4, 2015, https://unfccc.int/most-requested/key-aspects-of-the-paris-agreement.

161 Nationally Determined Contributions Registry, United Nations Climate Change, accessed January 4, 2015, https://unfccc.int/NDCREG.

162 Marlo Lewis Jr., "The Paris Climate Agreement Is a Treaty Requiring Senate Review," Competitive Enterprise Institute, February 24, 2016, accessed January 4, 2025, https://www.cei.org/wp-content/uploads/2016/04/Marlo-Lewis-The-Paris-Agreement-Is-a-Treaty-Requiring-Senate-Review.pdf.

163 Joe Thwaites et al., "What Does the Paris Agreement Do for Finance?" World Resources Institute, December 18, 2015, accessed January 4, 2025, https://www.wri.org/insights/what-does-paris-agreement-do-finance.

164 "Presidential Actions: Putting America First in International Environmental Agreements," Trump White House, January 20, 2025, accessed February 2, 2025, https://www.whitehouse.gov/presidential-actions/2025/01/putting-america-first-in-international-environmental-agreements/.

165 Interview with Chris Horner, July 2019.

166 "Treaty Affairs: Circular 175 Procedure," US State Department, https://2009-2017.state.gov/s/l/treaty/c175/index.htm.

167 Erin Amsberry, "IER Sues State Department for Public Records," Institute for Energy Research, August 1, 2018, accessed January 8, 2025, https://www.instituteforenergyresearch.org/uncategorized/ier-sues-state-department-for-public-records/.

168 Ibid.

169 "'China's Green Offensive': GAO FOIA Suit Featured in Series," Government Accountability & Oversight, November 2, 2020,

accessed January 8, 2025, https://govoversight.org/
chinas-green-offensive-gao-foia-suit-featured-in-series/.

[170] Rob Bishop and Bruce Westermann, "Letter to Rhea Suh, Natural
Resources Defense Council," Committee on Natural Resources, US
House of Representatives, June 5, 2018, https://republicans-
naturalresources.house.gov/uploadedfiles/bishop-westerman_to_
nrdc_06.05.18.pdf.

[171] *Winter v. Natural Resources Defense Council, Inc.*, 55 U.S. 7 (2008),
Justia, US Supreme Court, https://supreme.justia.com/cases/federal/
us/555/7/.

[172] James Taylor, "Policy Brief: Global Warming Energy Restrictions
Threaten U.S. National Security," Heartland Institute, March 5,
2019, accessed January 18, 2025, https://heartland.org/publications/
global-warming-energy-restrictions-threaten-us-national-security/.

[173] Ken Stiles phone interview, July 31, 2025.

[174] Lauren Leffer, "The Military Could Throw a Big Wrench in Biden's
Offshore Wind Plans," *Gizmodo*, April 17, 2023, accessed August 22,
2025, https://gizmodo.com/the-military-could-throw-a-big-wrench-
in-bidens-offshor-1850344176.

[175] Ibid.

[176] Adam Wanger, "Why the Military Is Blocking the Development of
Potential New NC Offshore Wind Leases," *News & Observer*, August
9, 2023, accessed August 22, 2025, https://www.newsobserver.com/
news/politics-government/article278029168.html.

[177] Kevin Mooney, "Virginia Democrat Poised to Impose Carbon Taxes
as Governor," *Restoration News*, June 3, 2025, accessed July 8, 2025.
https://restoration-news.com/virginia-democrat-poised-to-impose-
carbon-taxes-as-governor

[178] André Béliveau, "State of RGGI: Past, Present, and Future,"
Commonwealth Foundation, December 5, 2024, accessed August 12,
2025, https://commonwealthfoundation.org/research/rggi-pa-
backgrounder/.

179 Commonwealth Foundation, "Pennsylvania Energy Returns to the National Spotlight—No Thanks to Governor Shapiro," July 16, 2025, accessed August 12, 2025, https://commonwealthfoundation. org/blog/pennsylvania-energy-national-spotlight-despite-josh-shapiro/.

180 Interview with Erik Telford at Commonwealth Foundation, February 2025.

181 Rachel Frazin, "Pennsylvania Abandons Northeast Climate Pact," *The Hill*, November 13, 2025, accessed November 18, 2025, https:// thehill.com/policy/energy-environment/5605079-pennsylvania-rggi-northeast-climate-pact-shapiro/.

182 "EPA Grants Waiver for California's Advanced Clean Cars II Regulations," Press Office, US Environmental Protection Agency, December 18, 2024, accessed May 3, 2025, https://www.epa.gov/ newsreleases/epa-grants-waiver-californias-advanced-clean-cars-ii-regulations.

183 "Gov. Gavin Newsom Will Phase Out Gasoline-Powered Cars & Drastically Reduce Demand for Fossil Fuel in California's Fight Against Climate Change," Governor's Office, State of California, September 23, 2020, accessed February 3, 2025, https://www.gov. ca.gov/2020/09/23/governor-newsom-announces-california-will-phase-out-gasoline-powered-cars-drastically-reduce-demand-for-fossil-fuel-in-californias-fight-against-climate-change/.

184 "Murphy Administration Adopts Zero-Emission Vehicle Standards to Improve Air Quality, Fight Climate Change, and Promote Clean Vehicle Choice," Governor's Office, State of New Jersey, November 21 2023, accessed April 24, 2025, https://www.nj.gov/governor/news/ news/562023/20231121a.shtml.

185 "When Government Chooses Your Car," Institute for Energy Research, December 12, 2024, accessed February 2, 2025, https:// www.instituteforenergyresearch.org/regulation/when-government-chooses-your-car/.

[186] Samuel Peterson, "Policy Brief: When Government Chooses Your Car," Institute for Energy Research, December 12, 2024, accessed March 11, 2025, https://www.instituteforenergyresearch.org/regulation/policy-brief-when-government-chooses-your-car/.

[187] "When Government Chooses Your Car," Institute for Energy Research, December 2024, accessed February 2, 2025, https://www.instituteforenergyresearch.org/wp-content/uploads/2024/12/WHEN-GOVERNMENT-CHOOSES-YOUR-CAR.IER_.pdf.

[188] John Hugh DeMastri, "'Incredibly Deadly': E-Bike Blaze Kills Four Amid Surge of Lethal Battery Fires In New York City," *Daily Caller*, June 20, 2023, accessed January 12, 2024, https://dailycaller.com/2023/06/20/e-bike-blaze-kills-four-lethal-batteries-nyc/.

[189] "Some Residential Underground Carparks in Seoul Ban EVs After Explosion Case," *Straits Times* (Singapore), August 8, 2024, accessed March 12, 2025, https://www.straitstimes.com/asia/east-asia/some-residential-underground-carparks-in-seoul-ban-evs-after-explosion-case.

[190] Ibid.

[191] Kevin Mooney, "Infrastructure Bill Boosts China, While Reconciliation Proposals Pummel American Consumers," *RealClear Energy*, August 16, 2021, accessed April 4, 2025, https://www.realclearenergy.org/articles/2021/08/16/infrastructure_bill_boosts_china_while_reconciliation_proposals_pummel_american_consumers_790209.html.

[192] "When Government Chooses Your Car," Institute for Energy Research, December 2024, accessed February 2, 2025, https://www.instituteforenergyresearch.org/wp-content/uploads/2024/12/WHEN-GOVERNMENT-CHOOSES-YOUR-CAR.IER_.pdf.

[193] Kenneth Schrupp, "Newsom Strengthens Chinese Relations as Scrutiny Grows Over Walz' China Ties," *Center Square*, August 7, 2024, accessed January 8, 2025, https://www.thecentersquare.com/california/article_33caa3f6-5503-11ef-8df2-d3b1563fd1fd.html.

[194] Ibid.

[195] Ibid.

196 Sarah Mcfarlane, "Rogue Communication Devices Found in Chinese Solar Power Inverters," Reuters, May 14, 2025, accessed May 16, 2025, https://www.reuters.com/sustainability/climate-energy/ghost-machine-rogue-communication-devices-found-chinese-inverters-2025-05-14/.

197 Dan Milmo, "'Source of Data': Are Electric Cars Vulnerable to Cyber Spies and Hackers?" *The Guardian*, April 29, 2025, accessed May 16, 2025, https://www.theguardian.com/environment/2025/apr/29/source-of-data-are-electric-cars-vulnerable-to-cyber-spies-and-hackers.

198 "What Governor Newsom's Trip to China Accomplished," Office of California Governor Gavin Newsom, October 30, 2023, accessed May 16, 2023, https://www.gov.ca.gov/2023/10/30/what-governor-newsoms-trip-to-china-accomplished/.

199 Alejandro Lazo, "Newsom's Visit Underscores Electric Car Reality: China Hold the Keys to Battery Industry," *CalMatters*, October 26, 2023, accessed May 16, 2025, https://calmatters.org/environment/2023/10/gavin-newsom-china-trip-electric-cars/.

200 Director's Order, Bureau of Ocean Energy Management, US Department of Interior, August 22, 2025, accessed August 29, 2025, https://www.boem.gov/sites/default/files/documents/renewable-energy/Director%26%23039%3BsOrder-20250822.pdf.

201 Craig Rucker, "CFACT Helps Light UP Cape May Beach to Save Whales," CFACT, October 2, 2024, accessed April 4, 2025, https://www.cfact.org/2024/10/02/cfact-helps-light-up-cape-may-beach-to-save-whales/.

202 Interview with Craig Rucker, March 12, 2025.

203 Ibid.

204 "The Evidence That the Offshore Wind Energy Vessel Surveys Are the Cause of the Recent New Jersey Whale & Dolphin Deaths," Save LBI, November 2, 2023, accessed December 8, 2024, https://www.savelbi.org/_files/ugd/a85a2b_bf7fe79f48e84f00b44c5e056c0dadfc.pdf.

205 Ibid.

206 "Is the Sky Falling? Reconsidering the Endangerment Finding," Heritage Foundation, May 13, 2025, https://www.heritage.org/climate/event/the-sky-falling-reconsidering-the-endangerment-finding.

207 David Kreutzer, "Little Women and the Price of Gasoline," Institute for Energy Research, March 12, 2021, accessed November 17, 2025, https://www.instituteforenergyresearch.org/climate-change/little-women-and-the-price-of-gasoline/.

208 Ibid.

209 Interview with Kevin Dayaratna, May 15, 2025.

210 Ibid.

211 Ibid.

212 Ibid.

213 Willie Soon, Ronan Connolly, and Michael Connolly, "The Unreliability of Current Global Temperature and Solar Activity Estimates and Its Implications for the Attribution of Global Warming," December 11, 2024, accessed May 14, 2025, https://www.heritage.org/climate/report/the-unreliability-current-global-temperature-and-solar-activity-estimates-and-its.

214 Ibid.

215 Ibid.

216 Ibid.

217 Ibid.

218 Ibid.

219 Ibid.

220 Interview with Kevin Dayaratna, May 15, 2025.

221 Ibid.

222 Interview with Dan Eichenbaum, April 9, 2025.

223 Ibid.

224 Ibid.

225 Ibid.

226 Arianna Skibell, "Quitting Paris Was Just the Start," *Politico*, May 14, 2025, accessed May 28, 2025, https://www.politico.com/newsletters/

power-switch/2025/05/14/quitting-paris-was-just-the-start-00349 787.

[227] Kevin Mooney, "How Big Money Impacts Environmental Policy," *Daily Signal*, April 29, 2015, accessed April 2, 2025, https://www. dailysignal.com/2015/04/29/ how-big-money-impacts-environmental-policy-2/.

[228] H. Sterling Burnett, "Investigation of Dr. Willie Soon: Smoke, No Fire," Heartland Institute, March 6, 2015, accessed April 29, 2025, https://heartland.org/opinion/investigation-of-dr-willie-soon-smoke-no-fire/.

[229] Interview with Ken Stiles, August 2017.

[230] Kevin Mooney, "CIA Veteran Sees Russian Connection to 2 Groups Opposing Fracking, Pipelines," *Daily Signal*, August 25, 2017, accessed May 24, 2025, https://www.dailysignal.com/2017/08/25/ cia-veteran-sees-russian-connection-to-2-groups-opposing-fracking-pipelines/.

[231] Ibid.

[232] Interview with Ken Stiles, August 2017.

[233] Ibid.

[234] Matt Busse, "Mountain Valley Pipeline, Critics Clash over Southgate Extension Plan," *Cardinal News*, April 2, 2025, accessed April 4, 2025, https://cardinalnews.org/2025/04/02/mountain-valley-pipeline-critics-clash-over-southgate-extension-plan/.

[235] Interview with Ken Stiles, August 2017.

[236] Kevin Mooney, "Va. Farmer Says Green Group Urged County to Harass Her with Zoning Citations," *Daily Signal*, July 17, 2014, accessed May 8, 2025, https://www.dailysignal.com/2014/07/17/ va-farmer-says-green-group-urged-county-harass-zoning-citations/.

[237] Ibid.

[238] Kevin Mooney, "High-Profile Dispute Between Farm, Green Group Yields Property Rights Bill," *Daily Signal*, July 17, 2014, accessed May 8, 2025. https://www.dailysignal.com/2015/02/23/ high-profile-dispute-farm-green-group-yields-property-rights-bill/

239 Kevin Mooney, "Va. Farmer Says Green Group Urged County to Harass Her with Zoning Citations," *Daily Signal*, July 17, 2014, accessed May 8, 2025, https://www.dailysignal.com/2014/07/17/va-farmer-says-green-group-urged-county-harass-zoning-citations/.

240 "The Facts: *Chilton v. Center for Biological Diversity*," Southwest Communities Coalition, November 6, 2019, accessed August 14, 2025, https://southwesterncommunitiescoalition.org/2019/11/the-facts-chilton-v-center-for-biological-diversity/.

241 Ibid.

242 Mitch Tobin, "Rancher Wins Big in Libel Suit Against Enviros," *High Country News*, February 21, 2005, accessed August 14, 2025, https://www.hcn.org/issues/issue-292/rancher-wins-big-in-libel-suit-against-enviros/.

243 J. P. S. Brown, *Chilton vs. Center for Biological Diversity: Truth Rides a Cowhorse* (Make a Hand Publishing, 2015), 7–8.

244 Kevin Mooney, "This Veteran, Who Supplied Water to Firefighters, Went to Prison for Digging Ponds," *Daily Signal*, March 28, 2019, accessed June 4, 2025, https://www.dailysignal.com/2019/03/28/clean-water/.

245 Ibid.

246 Ibid.

247 Ibid.

248 Ibid.

249 Ibid.

250 US Environmental Protection Agency, "Administrator Zeldin Announces EPA Will Revise Waters of the United States Rule," press release, March 12, 2025, accessed May 22, 2025, https://www.epa.gov/newsreleases/administrator-zeldin-announces-epa-will-revise-waters-united-states-rule.

251 Kevin Mooney, "Deceased Navy Veteran's Name Cleared in 'Clean Water' Case," *Daily Signal*, July 16, 2019, accessed June 2, 2025, https://www.dailysignal.com/2019/07/16/deceased-navy-veterans-name-cleared-in-clean-water-case.

252 Bonner Russell Cohen, "Badlands Nightmare Ends for Ranching Couple Charles and Heather Maude," *Washington Times*, May 1, 2025, accessed June 12, 2025, https://www.washingtontimes.com/news/2025/may/1/badlands-nightmare-ends-ranching-couple-charles-heather-maude/#google_vignette.

253 Ibid.

254 Ibid.

255 Ibid.

256 Ibid.

257 Jerome Corsi, *The Truth About Energy, Global Warming, and Climate Change: Exposing Climate Lies in an Age of Disinformation* (Nashville, TN: Post Hill Press, 2022), 19–44.

258 Ibid.

259 Ibid.

260 Southern Environmental Law Center, "MVP Resurrects Controversial Southgate Pipeline," press release, February, 3, 2025, accessed March 8, 2025, https://www.selc.org/press-release/mvp-resurrects-controversial-southgate-pipeline/.

261 Matt Busse, "Mountain Valley Pipeline, Critics Clash Over Southgate Extension Plan," *Cardinal News*, April 2, 2025, accessed April 12, 2025, https://cardinalnews.org/2025/04/02/mountain-valley-pipeline-critics-clash-over-southgate-extension-plan/.

262 Ibid.

263 "Our Commitment to Safety," Mountain Valley Pipeline, accessed July 8, 2025, https://www.mountainvalleypipeline.info/safety-environmental-commitment

264 "Southern Environmental Law Center," *Influence Watch*, Capital Research Center, accessed July 8, 2025, https://www.influencewatch.org/non-profit/southern-environmental-law-center/.

265 Hayden Ludwig, "Planned Parenthood: The Biggest Bastion of Eugenics and White Supremacy in America," *Organization Trends*, Capital Research Center, December 4, 2019, accessed July 2, 2025,

https://capitalresearch.org/article/planned-parenthood-the-biggest-bastion-of-eugenics-and-white-supremacy-in-america/.

266 Ibid.

267 Hayden Ludwig interview, August 28, 2025.

268 Ibid.

269 Hayden Ludwig, "Big Abortion Brought in $4.3 Billion in 2023 Alone," *Restoration News*, May 27, 2025, accessed July 2, 2025, https://restoration-news.com/big-abortion-brought-in-4-3-billion-in-2023-alone.

270 "Planned Parenthood Federation of America," *Influence Watch*, Capital Research Center, accessed July 9, 2025, https://www.influencewatch.org/non-profit/planned-parenthood-federation-of-america/.

271 "Climate Justice," Planned Parenthood of California Central Coast, accessed July 10, 2025, https://www.plannedparenthood.org/planned-parenthood-california-central-coast/about20us/climate-justice.

272 Joanne Kenen, "Can Hospitals Turn into Climate Change Fighting Machines?" *Politico*, June 6, 2023, accessed July 2, 2025, https://www.politico.com/news/magazine/2023/06/06/hospital-climate-change-waste-00098612.

273 Ibid.

274 Ibid.

275 Ibid.

276 Ibid.

277 Marc Morano, "Flashback 2020 Study in American Cancer Society Journal in 2020 Fretted over 'Carbon Footprint of Cancer Care,'" *Climate Depot*, June 19, 2023, accessed July 2, 2025, https://www.climatedepot.com/2023/06/19/politco-hospitals-turning-into-climate-change-fighting-machines-limiting-water-with-timers-for-operating-room-sinks-more-earth-friendly-drugs-reducing-anesthetic-gas-decarbo/.

278 Sabrina R. Hu and Jeffery Q. Yang, "Harvard Medical School Will Integrate Climate Change into M.D. Curriculum," *Harvard Crimson,* February 3, 2023, accessed June 8, 2025, https://www.thecrimson. com/article/2023/2/3/hms-climate-curriculum/.

279 Stefan Labbe, "B.C. Doctor Clinically Diagnoses Patient as Suffering from 'Climate Change': The Head of a Nelson, B.C., Emergency Department Says It's Time Doctors Start Looking at the Underlying Cause of Medical Conditions Triggered by Smoke and Heat," *Times Colonist,* November 4, 2021, accessed June 12, 2025, https://www. timescolonist.com/bc-news/bc-doctor-clinically-diagnoses-patient-as-suffering-from-climate-change-4723540.

280 Ibid.

281 Marc Morano, "Watch: Hospital Staff Sing & Protest by Featuring Death Certificates Citing 'Climate Change' as Cause oof Death," *Climate Depot,* October 25, 2022, accessed July 10, 2025, https:// www.climatedepot.com/2022/10/25/watch-doctors-hospital-staff-sing-about-climate-change-feature-death-certificates-citing-climate-change-as-cause-of-death-cutting-down-on-carbon-will-stop-our-bodies-droppin-leaders/.

282 I. E. Blanchard and L. H. Brown (North American EMS Emissions Study Group), "Carbon Footprinting of North American Emergency Medical Services Systems," *Prehospital Emergency Care* 15, no. 1 (January–March 2011): 23–29, https://pubmed.ncbi.nlm.nih. gov/20874502/.

283 "Population Connection (Zero Population Growth)," *Influence Watch,* Capital Research Center, accessed July 12, 2025, https://www. influencewatch.org/non-profit/population-connection-zero-population-growth/.

284 "Population and Climate Change," Population Connection, accessed July 12, 2025, https://populationconnection.org/why-population/climate-change/.

285 Ibid.

[286] Marc Morano, "Climate Lockdowns: New CO_2 Monitoring Credit Card Enables Tracking of 'Carbon Footprint on Every Purchase'— 'Monitors & Cuts Off Spending When We Hit Our Carbon Max'— Mastercard & UN Join Forces," *Climate Depot*, September 13, 2021, accessed July 2, 2025, https://www.climatedepot.com/2021/09/13/new-co2-monitoring-credit-card-enables-tracking-of-carbon-footprint-on-every-purchase-monitors-cuts-off-spending-when-we-hit-our-carbon-max-mastercard-un-join-forces/.

[287] Francesco Fuso Nerini, Tina Fawcett, et al., "Personal Carbon Allowances Revisited," *Nature Sustainability* 4 (2021): 1025–1031, https://doi.org/10.1038/s41893-021-00756-w.

[288] Ross Bennett-Cook, "It's Time to Limit How Often We Can Travel Abroad—'Carbon Passports' May Be the Answer," CNN, November 27, 2023, accessed July 12, 2025, https://edition.cnn.com/travel/carbon-passports-explainer.

[289] Ibid.

[290] Ibid.

[291] "How Banks Can Drive Customer Retention in Times of Uncertainty," *Doconomy*, April 8, 2025, accessed July 12, 2025, https://www.doconomy.com/resources/how-banks-can-drive-customer-retention.

[292] Ibid.

[293] "Innovative Climate Action—New Credit Card Limits Climate Impact of Users," United Nations Climate Change, April 30, 2019, accessed July 12, 2025, https://unfccc.int/news/innovative-climate-action-new-credit-card-limits-climate-impact-of-users.

[294] "How Banks Can Drive Customer Retention in Times of Uncertainty," *Doconomy*, April 8, 2025, accessed July 12, 2025, https://www.doconomy.com/resources/how-banks-can-drive-customer-retention.

[295] Ibid.

[296] Michael Posner, "How BlackRock Abandoned Social And Environmental Engagement," *Forbes*, September 12, 2024, accessed

July 14, 2025, https://www.forbes.com/sites/michaelposner/2024/09/04/how-blackrock-abandoned-social-and-environmental-engagement/.

[297] Andrew Pudzer, "The ESG Threat and the Rise of the Red States," Heritage Foundation, February 3, 2023, accessed July 8, 2025, https://www.heritage.org/progressivism/commentary/the-esg-threat-and-the-rise-the-red-states.

[298] Free Enterprise Project, National Center for Public Policy Research, https://nationalcenter.org/programs/free-enterprise-project/.

[299] Phil Galewitz, Julie Appleby, et al., "5 Ways Trump's Megabill Will Limit Health Care Access," NPR, July 3, 2025, accessed July 16, 2025, https://www.npr.org/sections/shots-health-news/2025/07/02/nx-s1-5453870/senate-republicans-tax-bill-medicaid-health-care.

[300] David Dayden, "Republicans Are Cutting Medicare: Not Only Medicaid, Medicare," *The American Prospect,* July 3, 2025, accessed July 16, 2025, https://prospect.org/politics/2025-07-03-republicans-cutting-medicare-not-only-medicaid/.

[301] Stone Washington, "Has ESG Gone Guerrilla Warfare?" Competitive Enterprise Institute, May 20, 2024, accessed July 16, 2025, https://cei.org/blog/has-esg-gone-guerrilla-warfare/.

[302] Ibid.

[303] French Hill, "Capital Markets Subcommittee Examines Market Influence by Proxy Advisory Firms," press release, House Committee on Financial Services, April 29, 2025, accessed July 16, 2025, https://financialservices.house.gov/news/documentsingle.aspx?DocumentID=409711.

[304] Michael Faulkender, "Fact Sheet: Why You Need to Understand the ESG Threat," America First Policy Institute, December 13, 2022, accessed July 14, 2025, https://www.americafirstpolicy.com/issues/fact-sheet-why-you-need-to-understand-the-esg-threat.

[305] "Climate Control: Exposing the Decarbonization Collusion in Environmental, Social, and Governance Investing," Interim Staff Report of the Committee on the Judiciary Committee, US House of

Representatives, July 11, 2024, accessed July 16, 2025, https://
judiciary.house.gov/sites/evo-subsites/republicans-judiciary.house.gov/
files/evo-media-document/2024-06-11%20Climate%20Control%20
-%20Exposing%20the%20Decarbonization%20Collusion%20
in%20Environmental%2C%20Social%2C%20and%20
Governance%20%28ESG%29%20.

306 Ibid.

307 Kevin Mooney, "Bloomberg Could Benefit from Climate Rules He
Helped Craft," *Daily Signal*, December 8, 2022, accessed July 16,
2025,https://www.dailysignal.com/2022/12/08/bloomberg-could-benefit-
from-climate-rules-he-helped-craft/.

308 Ibid.

309 Vince Bielski, "The Green U.S. Supply-Chain Rules Set to Unspool
and Rattle the Global Economy," *RealClear Investigations*, April 7,
2022, accessed July 16, 2025, https://www.realclearinvestigations.
com/articles/2022/04/07/the_green_supply-chain_rules_set_to_
unspool_and_rattle_the_economy_825567.html.

310 Interview with Tammy Nemeth, May 5, 2025.

311 Bloomberg Philanthropies, "UN Special Envoy Michael R.
Bloomberg Announces Effort to Ensure U.S. Honors Paris Agreement
Commitments," press release, January 23, 2025, accessed July 17,
2025, https://www.bloomberg.org/press/un-special-envoy-michael-r-
bloomberg-announces-effort-to-ensure-u-s-honors-paris-agreement-
commitments/.

312 Securities and Exchange Council, "SEC Votes to End Defense of
Climate Disclosure Rules," press release, March 27, 2025, accessed
July 17, 2025, https://www.sec.gov/newsroom/press-releases/2025-58.

313 Interview with J. P. Teti, Passyunk Avenue Bar and Restaurant,
Fitzrovia, London, June 6, 2025.

314 Ibid.

315 Ibid.

[316] "Red Goes Green: Phillies Fight Climate Change Through New Initiatives at the Ballpark," NBC 10 Philadelphia, April 2023, YouTube, https://www.youtube.com/watch?v=CZIIEbiAiUc.

[317] "Is the Sky Falling? Reconsidering the Endangerment Finding," Heritage Foundation, May 13, 2025, https://www.heritage.org/climate/event/the-sky-falling-reconsidering-the-endangerment-finding#:~:text=May%2013%2C%202025%20Is%20the,that%20fueled%20the%20Endangerment%20Finding.

[318] Ibid.

[319] Heritage Foundation, "Calculate the Temperature Changes for Alternative Carbon Dioxide-Reduction Policies," Heritage Climate Calculator, June 17, 2024, accessed June 28, 2025, https://calculators.heritage.org/climate/calculate-the-temperature-changes-for-alternative-carbon-dioxide-reduction-policies/.

[320] "Is the Sky Falling? Reconsidering the Endangerment Finding," Heritage Foundation, May 13, 2025, https://www.heritage.org/climate/event/the-sky-falling-reconsidering-the-endangerment-finding#:~:text=May%2013%2C%202025%20Is%20the,that%20fueled%20the%20Endangerment%20Finding.

[321] Jack McPherrin and Justin Haskins, "CSDDD: The European Union's Corporate Sustainability Due Diligence Directive Is a Direct Threat to U.S. Sovereignty, Free Markets, and Individual Liberty," Heartland Institute, March 31, 2025, accessed April 12, 2025, https://heartland.org/publications/csddd-the-european-unions-corporate-sustainability-due-diligence-directive-is-a-direct-threat-to-u-s-sovereignty-free-markets-and-individual-liberty/.

[322] Interview with Tami Nemeth, May 5, 2025.

[323] Ibid.

[324] Ibid.

[325] "The UK-ETU ETS Agreement: What It Is and How It Will Affect UK Businesses," Energy Advice Hub, May 28, 2025, accessed August 26, 2025, https://energyadvicehub.org/

the-uk-eu-ets-agreement-what-it-is-and-how-it-will-affect-uk-businesses/.

326 Ibid.

327 "Annual Conference of Financial Street Forum 2024 Concludes," The People's Government of Beijing Municipality, October 22, 2024, accessed July 27, 2025, https://wb.beijing.gov.cn/en/center_for_international_exchanges/headlines/202412/t20241224_3972367.html.

328 Transcript of Financial Street Forum.

329 Ibid.

330 Ibid.

331 Ibid.

332 Diana Furchtgott-Roth and Jared Meyer, *Disinherited: How Washington Is Betraying America's Young* (New York: Encounter Books, 2015).

333 CO_2 Coalition, CO_2 Learning Center, accessed August 15, 2025, https://co2learningcenter.com/.

334 John Berlau, "Gore Flunks Oscar Documentary Rules," Competitive Enterprise Institute, February 22, 2007, accessed August 15, 2025, https://cei.org/blog/gore-flunks-oscar-documentary-rules/.

335 Ibid.

336 Marlo Lewis, "Al Gore's Science Fiction: A Skeptic's Guide to *An Inconvenient Truth*," Competitive Enterprise Institute Working Paper, August 21, 2006, accessed August 15, 2025, https://cei.org/studies/al-gores-science-fiction-a-skeptics-guide-to-an-inconvenient-truth/.

337 Calvin Beisner interview, May 28, 2025.

338 CO_2 Learning Center, CO_2 Coalition, accessed August 15, 2025, https://co2learningcenter.com/.

339 Libreria Editrice Vaticana, *Catechism of the Catholic Church*. (First Image Books, a division of Bantam Doubleday Publishing Group. New York, New York. Published 1995. Pg. 624)

340 New Jersey Climate Change Education Resources, New Jersey Department of Education, https://www.nj.gov/education/climate/learning/gradeband/.

341 "AEA's Statement on EPA Draft Rule Withdrawing Endangerment Finding," American Energy Alliance, August 4, 2025, accessed August 21, 2025, https://www.americanenergyalliance.org/2025/07/aeas-statement-on-epa-draft-rule-withdrawing-endangerment-finding/.

342 "EPA Moves to Rescind the Obama-Era Endangerment Finding," Institute for Energy Research, August 4, 2025, accessed August 21, 2025,https://www.instituteforenergyresearch.org/regulation/epa-moves-to-rescind-the-obama-era-endangerment-finding/.

343 Ibid.

344 Interview with Linda Bonvie and Brook Folino, Beach Haven, Long Beach Island, May 2025.

345 Ibid.

346 Ibid.

347 Linda Bonvie, "What Will 357 Wind Turbines Operating off the New Jersey Coast Sound Like?" *Badditives*, October 16, 2024, https://lindabonvie.substack.com/p/what-will-357-wind-turbines-operating.

348 Congressman Jefferson Van Drew, "Congressman Van Drew Responds to Governor Murphy's Plan to Make His Extreme Energy Agenda Law," press release, August 7, 2025, accessed August 28, 2025, https://vandrew.house.gov/news/documentsingle.aspx?DocumentID=1888.

349 Save LBI, "The Benefits & Risks of Offshore Wind Projects: The Facts," June 2025, accessed July 8, 2025, https://www.savelbi.org/_files/ugd/a85a2b f1d6ad1a99984bb2bb3abcf6adfa78b2.pdf.

350 Ibid.

351 Ibid.

352 Ibid.

353 Scott Walter, "Testimony to Senate Judiciary Subcommittee on Federal Courts, Oversight, Agency Action, and Federal Rights,"

Capital Research Center, June 25, 2025, accessed August 28, 2025, https://capitalresearch.org/article/climate-lawfare-scott-walters-oral-testimony-to-the-senate-judiciary-subcommittee/.

[354] Peter Pinedo and Andrew Mark Miller, "'Web of Dark Money' Tied to Obama, Dems Fuels Green Opposition to Crucial Trump Energy Plan," Fox News, August 29, 2025, accessed August 30, 2025, https://www.foxnews.com/politics/web-dark-money-tied-obama-dems-fuels-green-opposition-crucial-trump-energy-plan.

[355] CO_2 Coalition, "Challenging the NSTA's Position Statement on Climate Change," March 18, 2023, accessed November 15, 2025, https://co2coalition.org/publications/challenging-the-nsta-position-on-climate-change/.

[356] Chris Melore, "Top MIT Scientist Blasts 'Climate Hysteria,' Says Global Warming Fears Are Driven by Money…Not Evidence," *Daily Mail*, November 16, 2025, accessed Nov. 16, 2025, https://www.dailymail.co.uk/sciencetech/article-15236133/Scientist-climate-change-hysteria-nonsense.html.

[357] Franklin Roosevelt Inaugural Address, March 4, 1933.

[358] Ronald Reagan announcing his presidential candidacy on November 13, 1979.

[359] Lea Kahn, "Because of Col. Hand's Ingenuity, We Were Able to Prevail. Mercer County Making Plans to Spotlight the Role in the American Revolutionary War for 250th Anniversary," *Lawrence Ledger*, January 10, 2025. https://centraljersey.media/featured/because-of-col-hands-ingenuity-we-were-able-to-prevail/

[360] Nick Baker, "Queers for Climate Justice Organizers Invited to Speak at San Francisco State; Conservatives Haven't Been Invited in Years," Young America's Foundation, February 6, 2024, accessed July 2, 2025,https://yaf.org/news/queers-for-climate-justice-organizers-invited-to-speak-at-san-francisco-state-conservatives-havent-been-invited-in-years/.

[361] Nick Baker, "University of Colorado Offers 'Climate Anxiety' Coping Tips," Young America's Foundation, January 11, 2024, accessed July

18, 2025, https://yaf.org/news/university-of-colorado-offers-climate-anxiety-coping-tips/.

362 Ibid.

363 Ibid.

364 Ibid.

365 Sophia Corso, "Berkeley Students Plan 'Rally to Ban Cars' in Name of 'Climate Justice,'" Young America's Foundation, July 19, 2023, accessed July 8, 2025, https://yaf.org/news/berkeley-students-plan-rally-to-ban-cars-in-name-of-climate-justice/.

366 Dan Eichenbaum, "On Losing Our Most Crucial Battle," *Dr. Dan's Freedom Forum Radio,* October 9, 2014, accessed August 4, 2025, https://drdansfreedomforum.com/coffman2/.

367 Senator Mike Lee, "Lee introduces DEFUND Act to Pull USA from UN," press release, February 20, 2025, accessed August 28, 2025, https://www.lee.senate.gov/2025/2/lee-introduces-defund-act-to-pull-usa-from-un#:~:text=WASHINGTON%20%E2%80%93%20Sen.,the%20United%20Nations%20(UN).

368 Ibid.

ABOUT THE AUTHOR

Kevin Mooney is an investigative reporter who works with several national publications including *Restoration News*, *The Daily Signal*, *The Daily Caller*, *National Review*, *The American Spectator*, and *The Washington Examiner*. He specializes in covering policies that touch on environmental, energy, and educational matters.

Kevin also has a joint Master's Degree in Government and Communications from Regent University in Virginia Beach, VA. He studied British and American Constitutional Law at Hertford College in the University of Oxford as part of his Master's program. He received his BA from Rider University in Lawrenceville, NJ.

www.ingramcontent.com/pod-product-compliance
Lightning Source LLC
Chambersburg PA
CBHW062158270326
41930CB00009B/1572